MW00757211

THERE WAS A GARDEN IN NUREMBERG

A NOVEL

NAVINA MICHAL CLEMERSON

ISBN 9789493231559 (ebook)

ISBN 9789493231542 (paperback)

ISBN 9789493276277 (hardcover)

Publisher: Amsterdam Publishers, The Netherlands

info@amsterdampublishers.com

There was a Garden in Nuremberg is part of the series New Jewish Fiction

Cover image: Nuremberg in ruins from National Archives and Records Administration (public domain) (part & reworked)

In loving memory of my mother, Ann Berlin Gerzon

ONE

Twelve-year old Max Mannheim didn't want his departure noticed. He was leaving home in a hurry, without his coat, despite the January weather. He stepped onto the porch holding a tin box, which he put down on the mat. He shut the heavy front door with both hands, anxious to keep his movements silent. His mother was overseeing his sister's homework in the dining room and he didn't have much time.

He picked up the tin and bolted down the garden path, through the wrought iron gate onto Pierckheimerstrasse, running full tilt along the wide pavement to the corner, where he turned left into the Bucherstrasse. The year was 1933, in the Bavarian city of Nuremberg.

The street was lined with shops and apartment buildings. It led to the old city, with its wide moat and medieval ramparts, but Max wasn't going that far. He stopped outside a tobacconist's, clutching the tin to his chest. He pushed the door open, and a little bell rang, announcing his entrance.

The bell's tinkle was lost in the overwhelming blast of a blaring radio broadcast – a man's voice, gabbling a political report. To Max's surprise, the narrow shop was crowded, men and women standing and listening, hardly moving. The damp smell of their winter coats overpowered the sweet spiciness of tobacco.

Max wriggled through the throng and deposited his box on the counter's glass surface. This was the moment he'd been anticipating for months. As an ardent collector, he'd wheedled cigarette vouchers from every possible source, from uncles, cousins and family friends, from the maids and from Frau Bauer, the laundry woman. At last he'd amassed the huge number of coupons required and could now exchange them for the enchantment of a complete set of glossy pictures on the topic of his choice: military uniforms.

The people in the shop were listening intently. The man on the radio was reporting from the president's office. Max knew that the president was about to nominate a new Chancellor of the Reich. It was all the adults could talk about. Max opened his tin; he had counted and recounted the fat bunch of vouchers innumerable times. The cigarette company's album had arrived in the post a week ago, and he could hardly wait to paste the pictures into the alluring blank spaces above the text.

The shopkeeper in his grey work coat noticed him at last and leant towards him. "Want to exchange those, my boy? Which series?"

"German Uniforms," said Max. The man couldn't hear him above the din, so Max repeated the words louder. "German Uniforms!"

At that exact moment, the presenter's voice rose in a crescendo. "Chancellor of the Reich – Adolf Hitler!"

A full-throated roar erupted in the shop. *Heil Hitler!* Arms were thrust out in fervent salutes, people roaring their delight; the shopkeeper was as fired up as the rest of them. "He'll rid us of this bunch of wankers! Who gives a damn for bloody Weimar!" The radio blared on. Jubilation reigned – yells, gesticulation, slaps on the back.

The *meerschaum* pipes and cigar boxes on the shelves trembled and shuddered with the commotion.

"Those communist assholes will shit themselves!", "A real leader at last!", "The bloody Jews can go to hell!"

Hitler – Chancellor of the Reich! The words jolted Max like physical blows. Stunned, he looked around and realised that except for him, every single person in the shop was ecstatic at the news. They were Nazis! The Nazis were in charge of the country!

He had to get out. Grabbing the vouchers and the box, he pushed and shoved his way through the delirious crowd, struggling to extricate himself, to reach open space, fresh air. They let him through, hardly noticing, exhilarated, intoxicated by their hero's success. Max reached the door and managed to pull it open. He burst out onto the street, and the door swung shut behind him. He could still hear the uproar reverberating inside. His knees felt weak.

Daylight was receding, the colours turning blue and grey. On the pavement, dirty patches of hard snow glittered in the light from the shop window. The tall apartment buildings, the bare trees along the street and the street itself had not changed from a few minutes earlier, except that everything now seemed imbued with menace. He had to get home. He took off, running as fast as he could.

"Hitler will never succeed!" His father's words coursed through Max's mind; his father had been wrong, completely, utterly wrong! Hitler had won, and Max knew that it was a catastrophe, a disaster! His thoughts churned and whirled. He wanted desperately to reach the safety of his own home.

He knew that except for the president, Hitler was now the most powerful man in the country. Max had listened to many political discussions at home. He knew that Germany's president was old, and that the local Nazi chief, Julius Streicher, was a fanatic antisemite as well as one of Hitler's favourite acolytes. Max had seen Streicher in person – once on the Hauptplatz and once near the local SA headquarters on the Spittlertorgraben; he'd recognised him from the newspaper photos: short, fat and bald, unprepossessing. Max had watched as he swaggered and joked among his men, slapping a riding whip against his polished boots.

A stitch in his side forced Max to slow down. He'd once heard an older cousin declare that Streicher was the most antisemitic asshole in Germany's most antisemitic city; his father said that Julius Streicher was half mad, his rabid hatred of Jews an irrational perversion. This was the man who would from now on hold the city and all those who lived in it in his power.

His uncle Georg Loewenthal and his father had particular reason to scrutinise Streicher's activities: over the years, they had sued him repeatedly on behalf of the Jewish community, for the calumny and defamation of Jews published in his weekly broadsheet, *Der Stürmer*. Max's father had explained to Max that no German law forbade the denigration of religious groups or ethnicity. That left only the much weaker accusation of "class hatred". They had won their case just once, when they'd managed to persuade a presiding judge to select a jury among people who were not Nuremberg residents, whose minds had not been tainted by Streicher's foulness. That one time, Streicher bore the consequence of his actions and was thrown into jail – for a mere two months. Free again, he barely faltered, resuming his slandering with gusto. The authorities jailed him frequently for their own reasons – for creating unrest in the city and for leading street brawls against the communists and the Social Democrats. But *Der Stürmer* never failed to appear, spreading lies about anyone who opposed the Nazis – the Jews in particular. No one seemed willing or able to stop it. Max aimed a kick at a lump of grimy ice by the side of the pavement. A gust of icy wind cut through him, and he shivered. Tucking the box under his arm, he hurried on. As he opened the gate to the garden, he heard his father's voice call out, "Max!"

His father strode towards him, an imposing figure in his smart black overcoat and hat, carrying his black briefcase.

"Have you heard?" asked Max.

His father was smiling at him. He couldn't know, surely?

"Heard what?"

"Hitler is the new chancellor." The words came out in a kind of croak. His throat had gone dry.

His father stood stock still, his mouth open, staring at him. Then he frowned and shook his head vigorously. "Where did you hear *that*? Who said that?" He clamped his hand tight onto Max's shoulder, peering down at him.

"On the radio, at the tobacconists."

"Come!" said Father. He marched down the path to the front door, still gripping Max's shoulder.

Max struggled to free himself. "You're hurting me!"

Inside the house, appetising smells of dinner wafted from the kitchen. His father walked through to the living room, calling, "Sonia, I'm home!" He turned on the radio, threw his hat and briefcase onto the low table and dropped into his armchair which creaked under the weight. He still wore his overcoat. Max's mother appeared. His father indicated the radio, which was humming, its little green light aglow. Without a word, she sat down in the chair opposite him, her back straight, hands folded in her lap. The newsreader's voice came on, distant at first and then stronger, reporting people's reactions to the president's decision. Max's sister Helena ran in and his mother shushed her before she could speak.

After a while, his father stood up and turned the radio off, interrupting the flow of words. He left the room and disappeared into his study. His mother picked up the hat and briefcase and went to the hall where she hung the hat in its usual place.

Carrying the briefcase, she knocked on the study door and entered. Max heard her say, "Walter, dinner is ready, *Liebling.*"

Max stood up, confused, staring at the empty hall. His box of vouchers lay on the sofa.

Helena asked, "What's wrong? What's happening?"

Max didn't answer, because he was watching his father who'd emerged from the study, his face grim. Father took off his coat, which his mother hung up as she always did. She followed him into the dining room. The maid had brought the food in. They sat down at their usual places.

Father didn't ask anyone about their day at school. He didn't look at them or comment on the meat in its rich brown gravy or on any other aspect of the meal. Mama didn't say anything either. She served Father first, as usual. Her expression was remote. Helena caught the mood and kept quiet.

After dinner, the phone rang and Father took the call in his study. Max heard it ring again later, and again and again. As far as he was concerned, from that time on, things were never the same.

TWO

The Nazis ascended to power. On that first Monday in February 1933, Max returned from school as usual. He kicked the ball aimlessly round the lawn, waiting for his friends to show up. Everyone always came to play football after school in the Mannheim's garden because their lawn was the largest in the neighbourhood. The grass would wear out at the goals, leaving bald patches of mud in winter, dry beaten earth in summer. His mother complained, but it couldn't be helped.

His friends were late. After a few circuits round the lawn, he realised that they were very late, later than they'd ever been. He ran in and asked his mother if anyone had phoned.

"No," she said. "Why don't you get yourself a drink."

An unusual suggestion from her – the drinks, lemonade or raspberry syrup, were strictly for half-time when people were thirsty. He wasn't thirsty, but he drank anyway; he had a strange feeling. Surely people would turn up soon, and there'd be a perfectly good explanation for their lateness, something he should have known about. All of them, so late... Kris usually appeared as soon as his homework was done, at the rusty little gate at the far end of the back garden. Max listened for its familiar two-time squeak – open and shut. It gave onto a private path which ran along the back of the gardens. Kris lived several doors down. They played together most evenings when the weather was good.

Half an hour later he had to confront the truth, to admit to himself that they would not come, that no one was coming. He felt an ache in his chest. He stood without moving in the middle of the lawn, wrestling with his confusion; no messages had been delivered, no phone calls. What was the meaning of this absence, this silence? They didn't want to play with him – but why? This had never happened before, not in all the years they'd played football. He'd always been popular at school, welcome wherever he went. He tried phoning Kris's house, but someone there said that Kris was out. Kris's mother was apparently out too. The voice was unfamiliar, with a local accent, probably a maid.

It was unbelievable. He was astounded. He went back to the garden, walked to and fro across the lawn not knowing what to do with his agitation, the threatening emptiness of time, time which until that day had been filled with friends and play. He struggled to understand. The image of a tap came to mind, a tap tightly turned off, the flow of water halted, not a drop allowed through. He shook his head to dispel it. What was he to do now?

His mother had come out of the house and stood watching him with a sorrowful air. He couldn't bear the sight of her distress, and he ran past her into the house, taking the stairs two at a time to his room, slamming the door shut, anxious to hide his upset. There were gentle knocks on the door, and his mother called his name.

"Leave me alone!" he yelled. He paced round the room, punching his fist into his hand until it hurt. He threw himself on the bed and buried his head in the pillow.

His mother was shaking him gently as he opened his eyes. "Darling, dinner time. Wash your face. Your father's expecting you."

He felt groggy. The room was shadowy. His mother had switched on the table lamp, and it was dark outside. "I've been asleep," he said, surprised.

He remembered what had happened that afternoon, and the painful feelings flooded back.

His mother put her arms around him, and he was glad she was there. "Your father wants to see you, in the study."

———

His father said, "Bad things are happening at the moment, Max, and not just to Jews. Please keep in mind that this regime will not last. It cannot last. In the long run, evil does not prevail, because it carries the seeds of its own destruction. Our task is to endure and not allow ourselves to lose hope. Better days will come. It is quite possible that Kris and his family are under great pressure. It may be dangerous for him to be in touch with you. We must try to understand and not hold this against them."

"How can the Nazis make them not answer their phone? Or prevent them from letting me know that Kris isn't coming? I can't imagine..."

His father interrupted him firmly. "Indeed. You cannot imagine. The Nazis spy on people; they tap phones and eavesdrop. Keep that in mind yourself when you're on the phone. You have to give people the benefit of the doubt and be patient with them. These are some of your oldest friends. It is not good to harbour resentment. Think what it would be like if the situation were reversed."

"I'd find a way. I know I would!"

"The Nazis are showing their true colours, behaving outrageously across the country. The majority of Germans will not tolerate this behaviour and will vote them out at the coming election, in less than a month. This madness will soon be over. The Nazis have the Social Democrats and the communists to contend with. They'll have a hard time forming a majority. Our Frau Bauer is a communist; you know what she's like. She would never tolerate this nonsense."

Frau Bauer came to the house once a week to do the washing. As small children, Max and Helena had spent hours with her while she washed and ironed, and told them fairy tales in Franconian dialect. As they grew older, they had talked about other things, including politics. His mother had wanted to stop these conversations, but his grandmother had told her not to worry: Frau Bauer was the salt of the earth, and you could trust her with your life. It was true that his father was concerned about the communists. He said they would ruin the country if they took charge. But Frau Bauer was somehow different.

The next day at school, Kris moved away to sit beside someone else. No one talked to Max. He was ignored, left on his own, isolated and friendless. He was again astounded at the extent of the change and its suddenness, and as the day wore on and the attitude persisted, increasingly perplexed at what was happening to him.

The Old Gymnasium had been founded four hundred years ago. Max loved his school, as his father and grandfather had before him. He liked the clean-smelling wide corridors, the marble staircases, the peaceful library and the classrooms with their plain wooden benches. Only those able to pass the entrance exam were admitted. Should a family be too poor to pay, the fees were waived. One's social status was irrelevant – the studies alone mattered. The syllabus went unchanged for many years, the masters priding themselves on completing it, year in, year out. Max enjoyed the competition with the other students; he loved studying, the way knowledge about the world unfolded before him, his curiosity both fed and stimulated. He'd been on good terms with practically everyone, until now.

He tried talking to Kris, but Kris shook his head without answering, looking away, uncomfortable. The teacher reprimanded Max and sent Hans, the other Jewish boy, to sit next to him. A bench for the Jews, a separation from the rest. Hans was clever, good at maths, but no athlete. Hopeless at football.

The teacher didn't acknowledge them for the rest of the lesson, even when Max raised his hand to answer a question. Max couldn't make sense of his behaviour. But in the afternoon, with a teacher he particularly liked, he held his arm up for a long time and put it down for a moment to rest, and the teacher shot him a look, almost a message of approval, as if he were saying, "Don't try so hard; I can't choose you." Max was dumbfounded and watched the teacher closely for the rest of the lesson, hoping he'd misunderstood, but the teacher didn't look his way again.

As the weeks went by, the change became established. During the breaks, Max and Hans walked up and down the courtyard together, apparently encased in a bubble of invisibility. In class, their work was corrected and returned as usual, but otherwise they were ignored. Max felt that he'd rather not be there. He wanted to run away, but where to? He told his parents, "They don't want me. I don't belong anymore." His parents said that nothing could be done, that it couldn't be helped. "You must stay at school if you want to go to university." No other prospect was conceivable: he loved learning; he loved words and writing.

Some of the changes occurring under the new regime involved words and their meaning, for instance, the word "German". A new government decree – his father said it was not a law – encouraged people to use the "German" greeting, by which they meant *Heil Hitler* with the Nazi salute, instead of the usual "*Guten Tag*" and "*Aufwiedersehen*". Signs appeared on shop windows, in the trams, on walls and billboards all over town, reminding people that this was what they should do, that this was the "German way" – a greeting

Max could not, would not, adopt under any circumstance. A ridiculous question arose in his mind: was he himself a German? He thought about the inscription engraved on the classical pediment above the grand stairway of the Reichstag in Berlin that read, "*Dem Deutsches Volke*" – "For the German People." He'd seen it himself when he'd visited Berlin with his father. Father had explained that democracy encompassed everyone in Germany without exception, even a schoolboy like him. He'd then lectured Max about the Weimar Republic's beautiful Constitution that yet another Jewish lawyer had drafted. His father had explained how it embodied "unprecedented ideals of freedom and equality". Max had been embarrassed by the awe in his father's voice; he'd fidgeted while his father explained how it enabled minorities to become citizens with equal rights, granting them the freedom to live wherever they wanted, to practice whatever profession they wished.

According to the Nazis, a Jew could not be German, despite the thousand-year history of Jews in Germany. Yet Max felt in his bones that he and all the Mannheims were German. The two most recent generations lay buried in Nuremberg's Jewish cemetery, and many previous generations lay nearby in Ansbach's Jewish cemetery. The family name appeared on many gravestones, the older ones so worn they were barely legible. Besides, when the family went on holidays to Switzerland, the passport he used was a German one.

Another change in meaning affected the word "Jew". Its facets were increasingly contradictory – good within the community, where one was proud, and bad outside – as in *Der Stürmer*. His father asserted that Streicher wrote lies – "lies, falsehood and calumny."

Except for the Jews themselves, no one seemed to object in the slightest. It was as if people *wanted* to read these lies, wanted to believe them. One of the stand-alone glass-fronted *Stürmer* boxes exhibiting the broadsheet stood outside the grocery, near the tram station. His parents had emphatically instructed him to look away, to avoid reading it, but like others he was drawn to study the page in the display, fascinated by the large caricature of Jews on the front page – ugly, fat Jews with big warty noses, greasy hair and nasty expressions. They didn't resemble anyone he knew. These Jews were always up to no good, stealing from honest, hard-working Germans, leering disgustingly at pretty young women. Across the top of the page of every issue, in large bold letters, the banner shouted its accusation "The Jews are our misfortune!" Father said that most people knew the statement was not true; so much evidence pointed to the contrary – consider Foreign Minister Rathenau who had served his country with distinction until his death. Or the many Nobel Prizes, or closer to home, their friend Dr Fritz Klein, an eminent surgeon who headed the orthopaedics clinic at the hospital and ran a regular free clinic for the poor.

Yet no one stopped Streicher. At times Max couldn't help wishing someone would kill him, like they'd murdered Rathenau, despite knowing "Thou shalt not murder"; he'd had to study the commandments with the rabbi in preparation for his bar mitzvah next year, when he'd turn thirteen years old.

At the Old Gymnasium, the traditional early morning routine had been transformed; the black-red-and-gold flag of the Weimar republic disappeared, replaced by the black-white-red imperial tricolour and the flag of the Nazi Party. They sang the Nazi anthem, with the entire assembly smartly executing the Nazi salute. He wasn't supposed to salute, not that he wanted to, but the abstaining from saluting made him and the other Jews stand out. He could tell th~ few of the teachers were uncomfortable, even reluctant, but t⊦ complied. The single exception was one of the older st⋅ Protestant, who resisted the salute, resisted saying *Hei*ˡ after day. Max could see the strain in his posture, the face.

How to avoid the salute and remain polite? ⸍ was unwise to appear indifferent, or trucule⹀.

wrong ways of behaving. Trouble seemed forever imminent. It was exhausting. Some people left Germany for good, but Father said they were giving in too easily, that this trouble would pass. One must endure. At this point, his mother nodded and sighed as she always did. Max found her sighs particularly irritating.

THREE

Standing at the window of her little sitting room, looking out at the garden, Sonia sipped the first black coffee of the day. Apart from the maid who had lit the fire and brought her the coffee, no one was up yet; the house was still. She had a fondness for this quiet little room. Walter teased her about it, calling it her boudoir, her "sulking place".

She could see the cherry tree on the lawn, still leafless, the bare lilac bushes behind it, and beyond them and the invisible vegetable garden, the dark branches of the two large chestnut trees raised as if in supplication, silhouetted against the pale dawn sky. The first months of the Nazi regime, she thought. How long would it persist? Who would oppose it? What would happen to them all?

She turned away from the window, towards her writing desk – time to start the day's work. No matter what Hitler might have in store for Germany and her Jews, nine people would be at dinner that evening; eleven if one included Max and Helena.

Her desk had been Walter's wedding present, a French cherry wood secretaire that combined elegance and practicality. Its pigeonholes contained various pieces of paper, bills, lists, scrawled reminders she would have to attend to soon – household and garden, the children's schools, various Jewish community committees, her book group, and subscriptions to the tennis club, Nuremberg's opera and its theatre. In the tiny drawers beneath the pigeonholes were cards, pencils, pens and paperclips; the one lockable drawer contained postage stamps and the key to each of the house's cupboards. The accounts book and household inventory were stored in a large drawer below, likewise lockable, with her correspondence file tucked away at the back.

To her regret, she had little connection with the law firm. Mannheim & Loewenthal had celebrated its centenary a few years before she'd married Walter, and there were no further calls for festivities, nothing she might help organise. The traditional end-of-year dinner – called the "Christmas dinner" despite both partners being Jewish – was booked a year in advance at one of the best restaurants in town. She only needed to dress up and accompany Walter, smiling her closed-lip smile.

Their wedding photo stood on a shelf in a silver Biedermeier frame inherited from her grandmother, beside an older photo of Fanny and herself when they were young girls, with their parents. Fanny appeared slender, already elegant, her smile open and generous. Sonia's figure was fuller, her smile more reserved, her lips hiding crooked teeth. She seemed remote, as if she were guarding a secret. People said that her blue eyes were her best feature, but of course the black-and-white photo didn't do them justice. She sighed.

A knock at the door. "Come in, Greta," she said, opening the big housekeeping book. Greta stood by her chair and they discussed who would eat at home that day – lunch for the maids, for Frau Bauer, the laundry woman, and the children. Max disliked meat and required cheese or eggs. Walter stayed in town at midday. She encouraged him to be careful about what he ate, to exercise to lose weight, without much success. He only walked to the office when the weather was good. She sighed again, wishing he were more disciplined, more like her father who had gone out riding at dawn every day, an assertion of

Prussian discipline. Walter said he'd had enough of that during the war – four long years.

The discussion with Greta moved on to the shopping required for the evening meal. They would have a traditional chicken soup with knoedl, followed by roast beef with potatoes and vegetables, and a classic apple tart for dessert, served with whipped cream and a Riesling. Nothing difficult.

Besides Oma and the children, Fanny and her Otto would be there, as well as Tante Gusti, Uncle Hugo and their younger son, Georg, with his wife, Senta. She was fond of Georg despite his Zionist views. He ate with a gratifying appetite and enjoyed his food. But her favourite was Georg's older brother, Robert, who was away at the Frankfurt Book Fair with his wife, Hilde. She sighed again: Walter rarely went anywhere interesting.

Robert was Walter's closest friend. The others were big men with appetites to match, but Robert was shorter, finer, with grey eyes twinkling behind gold-rimmed glasses. He had resisted his parents' ardent wishes and refused to study law. He preferred to manage the publishing house founded by a Loewenthal uncle.

This dinner would be a far cry from those Sonia had organised in the early years of her marriage, when she'd invited distinguished people, both Jews and non-Jews, artists, intellectuals, business people and some of Walter's livelier confreres from the legal world. It had been fun, the food and wine refined, the conversation spirited, spiked with wit. But one day Walter had stated that he didn't wish these dinners to continue.

Sonia had asked, "Darling, why ever not?"

"Not everyone who comes is a friend."

"But it's so much fun!"

Walter had given her a look that made her uncomfortable. "*Liebling*, it's too much. It's ostentatious."

"I don't agree! What do you mean?" She could feel herself flushing.

"All this fuss, dressing up, mixing with the rich and the so-called elite."

"So-called?"

"There's a difference between status and quality."

She stared at him. He was losing patience. He had hinted more than once that she was too easily impressed. She didn't care. She was young, much younger than he was and wanted to enjoy herself, so didn't really give in. She waited a little longer to invite people and put off telling him that it would be a formal occasion, hiding her anticipatory excitement.

He came into the boudoir that morning in his coat, holding his hat, ready to leave for the office.

"Sonia, flowers have been delivered?"

She quaked. This was it. "For the dinner this evening." She kept her voice steady.

"You told me that this was 'just a few people', 'quite intimate'."

"Twenty."

"Elise and Philippe and some others?"

"Yes."

"Making twenty, for whom you need a special delivery of flowers? Please let me see the guest list."

"You know everyone." She found it in the secretaire and handed it to him.

He looked at the list, turned to the door and closed it. He faced her, his expression stern.

"I've told you before, this has to stop. These parties are meaningless. Some people on this list are no friends of ours – the occasion is a sham."

"Elise and Philippe are our friends," she protested. "And you'd asked me to invite the Siegels."

Michael Siegel was the president of the Law Society. His parents were family friends, as their parents had been before them.

"Sonia, please! The Siegels are always welcome here!"

He checked his watch, saying, "These dinners are not to take place without my agreement."

Sonia opened her mouth to argue, but he'd left the room. Her hands trembled a little; confrontations upset her. She sighed, reread her guest list and decided to cheer herself up by checking on Greta and the maids.

The windows of the drawing room had been thrown open, letting in the crisp air; in the dining room, the mahogany table had been extended to its full length, a fine damask tablecloth spread over it. The hothouse flowers would be arranged nearer the time in low vases along the centre. The children had been banned from the kitchen and the pantry. The hired maids sang as they worked, polishing the silver. They liked these events too, enjoying the sense of occasion. She felt more cheerful.

That afternoon, she heard Walter come home earlier than usual, as agreed. He disappeared into the study without speaking to her. That was not what she had planned – she wanted him to change straight away, to give her time to check that he was properly dressed. She had laid out his formal dinner jacket and a starched white shirt. He sometimes made a fuss about wearing his war medals. The little chain with its four miniature insignia looked elegant on the jacket. The Iron Cross First and Second Class; the Bavarian Order of Military Merit with Crown and Swords, her favourite because of the pretty blue enamel and the royal crown – awarded to officers only; and the dull black oval of the wounded-in-action badge, embossed with the profile of a helmeted soldier, plain by comparison. She regretted that the full-size medals were only worn with the dress uniform.

She let a little time go by so as not to rush him and then knocked on the study door. As she came in, he turned from the window, silhouetted in a cloud of cigar smoke.

"It's time," she said.

He stubbed out the cigar and followed her upstairs.

They did not speak as they changed clothes.

He picked up the medals. "I shall not be wearing these," he said.

She quickly went over, put her hand over his and looked up at him. "Oh please, Walter, please. I specially mentioned them to Elise and to the other wives. They know you'll be wearing yours, and everyone else will be wearing theirs."

"Sonia, these medals are an outcome of destruction and suffering. They're mine not because I was brave, but because I survived, one of a lucky few. They're not baubles, to be brought out to show off." He turned away.

She took a deep breath and said, "Everyone is looking forward to this evening – why must you be difficult? Please, Walter, people will be uncomfortable if you don't wear yours after I told everyone you would. It might offend them." She was the better judge of social niceties. She watched him hesitate. Better to let him make up his own mind. She sat down, ostensibly to finish putting on her make-up, powdering her face. She practised her smile, watching him in the mirror.

He said to her back, "You're taking over my life."

"What do you mean?" She swung round on her stool.

"Sonia, I'll remind you that I'm thirty-five years old, a veteran army officer, a partner in a legal firm with a solid reputation in Bavaria. As a corporate lawyer I deal daily with clever successful people, among the leaders in industry and trade. They listen to my advice; they sometimes even follow it. Then I come home to my very young wife, who attempts to dictate what I should wear, what I should eat or not eat, who complains that my cigars smell, that my books and papers are messy! In my own house!"

"Walter, I'm only trying to be a good wife. I *am* a good wife!" I keep my side of the bargain, she thought. She at least was faithful, but she would not say that aloud. Her voice must not quaver. She cleared her throat, clenched her hands in her lap and said, "The children don't disturb you, your meals are on time, there are no problems with servants..." His mother had not always managed them well.

"Leave my mother out of this!"

"Walter, shush, the maids..."

"I don't care!" he bellowed. That was true, he didn't care what anyone thought of him.

She flinched as he took a step towards her.

"You think I'd hit you?" he shouted, exasperated.

She felt angry, suddenly weary. After all her hard work, he was going to spoil the party. Last time, he'd drunk too much and argued about politics. He'd been rude to the guests and unrepentant the next day. He didn't care. Tears came to her eyes. She noticed the clock and said, "Walter, the time!"

The doorbell rang as she went down the stairs. A tall vase with fresh roses stood on the hall table. She glanced at the young maid and said, "Your hair." The maid tucked the loose strand under her cap and went to open the door. Sonia stood with her hands clasped, ready to welcome her guests.

Elise and Philippe were the first to arrive, according to plan.

As the maid was taking their hats and coats, Sonia heard Walter's voice behind her. "Good evening." Elise looked past her and seemed surprised. Why? What was the matter?

Sonia turned towards Walter. Something was wrong: the medals were correctly arrayed across Walter's chest, on a pyjama top, a striped pyjama top! He looked like some sort of inmate, a prisoner. The stripes spelled it out loud and clear.

Dumbstruck, Sonia gazed at her husband. People were about to arrive, important people; were they to be greeted by a man in pyjamas? Had Walter lost his mind? She realised that he was laughing, laughing at her. She felt a sharp pang of anger and fled into his study, slamming the door. She stood with her back to the door, sobbing.

Why was he so difficult? Why couldn't he be pleasant, ordinary, even if he didn't love her? Why did he behave like a clown? She winced at the thought of the maid and the eager gossip in the kitchen.

She could hear Elise's voice and then Walter's, or was it Philippe's? They were old friends who loved and respected Walter. Philippe was a lawyer too and Elise had helped a newly married Sonia understand the social intricacies of the legal fraternity.

She forced herself to stop crying and listened, but she could only hear a murmur; after a moment there was a cautious knock, and Elise slipped in. "Darling, Walter is upstairs getting dressed."

She smiled at Sonia and put her arms around her. Sonia took a deep breath and wiped her eyes with the tips of her fingers so as not to smudge her make-up.

The doorbell rang. "Quick now!"

"You look lovely, darling, off you go."

Sonia swept out to the hall, smiling her best smile. At her nod, the maid went to open the door.

That had been in 1928, five years ago, the last time they'd entertained formally. The world they now moved in was entirely Jewish. Except for the Jews among them, none of those people had kept in touch.

FOUR

Walter and Sonia were married in 1919, after the war. Oma moved to live in a small villa nearby, leaving Sonia to run the household on Pierckheimerstrasse as she pleased. She indulged her urge to review the household's inventory in its entirety. With a sense of reconnoitring new territory, she counted and listed every item in the house, all the silver, the glass, the china, the linen, the dusty old bottles of fine wine in the cellar and every item of furniture and decor, such as paintings and other objets d'art. The house had sheltered three generations of Mannheims and was full of surprises. While sorting through the boxes piled up in the cavernous cellar, she came across two crates which contained a complete set of lovely Meissen porcelain, each item individually wrapped in tissue paper – its original packing, never used, from what she could tell. Thirty-six settings, enough for a Passover feast. She asked Oma about it, and Oma recalled that it might have been a gift from a maiden aunt, some decades earlier.

As the Mannheims already owned a lovely set for special occasions, Sonia decided that the Meissen would replace the china in daily use.

She had it brought up, washed and stored in the dining room cupboard. Walter was surprised but didn't oppose the change. Neither did Oma when she came for dinner. A year or so later, Sonia donated the old china to charity.

To catalogue the books, she followed Walter's recommendation and hired a deserving young man from the firm. Unfortunately, he had a tendency to read, which was a pity – she caught him at it several times. He'd flinch when she came in and quickly close the book. She couldn't check on him all the time; consequently, the cataloguing took more time than planned. It couldn't be helped. Turning to Walter was no use; he dismissed her appeal, saying that the boy had a brilliant mind and could use the money.

Some of these books had not been read by anyone within living memory – ancient rabbinical commentaries, Torah books with frayed bindings, a huge one in large Hebrew print and copperplate etchings which had the Mannheim-Loewenthal family tree inside the back cover, the earlier part in illegible Hebrew script with different spidery handwritings and ink colours. Walter's name hung from the lowest branch with the year of his birth, 1887, beside his younger brother, Leo, born 1895 – died 1915. Walter had added her name beside his own, and later on, the children's names under theirs. That Bible had been passed down through seven generations from the oldest known ancestor. One of them had been an important rabbi in nearby Ansbach. Every Jewish family she knew descended from at least one important rabbi. This one's miniature portrait was in Walter's study, a small grey face with pinched features. In comparison, Walter seemed florid and outsized.

In the drawer of a bookcase, she came across a book so small that it fitted in the palm of her hand. It was bound in soft olive-green suede, with a dull golden edge, a book of love poems; the name Leo Mannheim was written inside the cover in an unfamiliar hand. All she knew of Leo was that he was the beloved younger brother who had died in the war. Whom had he loved? Who had been his lover? His other books had been on the shelves in the room that was now Helena's. Until her birth, that room had been a shrine to Leo, Oma arriving weekly at the house to oversee the dusting and polishing, ensuring every item was returned to its exact place. Sonia stayed out of the way during the ritual.

Then came the financial crash of the 1930s and Oma lost most of her capital. She was obliged to give up her villa and return to live with them. She resided upstairs in her own apartment and employed her own cook. She invited the children to lunch on Sundays and spoiled them with extravagant desserts of chocolate mousse or strawberries and cream. Sonia disapproved, but Oma ignored her. For the rest, they got on well.

Throughout the first year, Sonia had kept watch on the garden, but nothing came up, nothing at all. It remained plain, joyless and unloved, like the garden of an orphanage, yielding neither surprises nor delights, except for the cherry tree, which flowered gracefully in the spring against a backdrop of lilac bushes. In summer, strident orange geranium blossomed in a couple of rectangular planters on the terrace – plebeian, beer garden plants, she thought. She resisted the uncharitable impulse to dispose of them altogether and had the gardener move the planters to the far edge of the terrace where they were out of sight from the living room windows.

Her own parents' garden had been well-established, subject to continuous attention. She'd grown up watchful of the seasons and their flowers. Her favourites were the roses in summer, many kinds, climbing and sprawling, single-flowered or exuberant and frothy.

That spring she'd found herself pregnant and basked in the family's approval and delight, relieved that she'd managed to conceive ahead of her sister Fanny, who had recently married one of Walter's cousins. In an atavistic act of faith, Sonia prayed for her child to be a boy, a healthy male who would perpetuate the dynasty, become the head of the family and the Mannheim partner at the law firm.

In the months preceding the birth, she worked on a plan for the garden. She drew sketches, which she showed to the surprised family and a dubious gardener. With Oma's calm approval, she carried out her ideas, directed the curbing of the lawn into a wide slow oval, round enough to be smooth and provide a sense of completeness, long enough to match the proportions of the grounds so that from the terrace the viewer's eye was drawn evenly from one side of the garden to the other. A gravelled path now curved round the front and away to the sides. Bushes crowding the cherry tree at the farthest border were trimmed. Shaping the lawn had been the first step.

In the autumn, she'd identified places where the earth was resistant, unworked, needing to be dug up, turned over, fertilised and mulched. She'd bought a variety of bulbs, carrying them round the garden in their little brown paper bags, deep in thought. She had the gardener fork the soil over and rake it out again before pushing each bulb in herself, with a little grunt, because the pregnancy hampered her movements. The bulbs flowered the following spring; by then the lawn was smooth, almost velvety. The garden had become a place of change and charm.

After she'd recovered from Max's birth, she designed a pergola over the terrace and oversaw its construction. The heavy old pine table was shifted beneath it. She added wicker armchairs padded with cushions for the older generation; benches would do for everyone else. The family ate on the terrace whenever the weather was warm. Within a short time, wisteria climbed over the pergola, covering it with a profusion of flowers in the warm months. As a baby, Helena slept in her pram under the canopy of delicate down-hanging clusters of the same tender mauve as the scarves and belts Oma wore with her perpetual black dresses. The gardener developed an unexpected passion for the roses. He became expert at pruning; from time to time, a friend might ask for his advice, to Sonia's secret satisfaction. She once overheard Walter say to Fritz Klein, "The garden is wholly Sonia's creation, you know."

When Walter took the family away on holidays, he learnt to include visits to rose gardens in his planning. With time, even he came to recognise the better-known cultivars.

When Max was born, friends and relatives congregated from all over the country to celebrate the traditional *brit milah* of the Mannheim son and heir. To her dismay, Sonia found herself shunted to one side, left out, while Oma paraded the baby – Oma, who until then had been so thoughtful and kind.

When the baby was a month old and thriving, Tante Gusti Loewenthal invited Sonia with Max to afternoon tea. Tante Gusti was an imposing woman, the doyenne of the Mannheim-Loewenthal clan. She was quick in her movements and sharp in her understanding. Outsiders sometimes joked that she would have made an excellent lawyer, an observation which did not appear to amuse her.

That afternoon, Tante Gusti and Sonia had a captivating talk about babies, Sonia's and other people's, while Tante Gusti cooed over Max. As they sat side by side on the sofa, taking turns to hold the baby, Gusti mentioned Leo. Leo had been handsome and clever, she said, but he had chosen a difficult path. He had been a pacifist.

"A pacifist!" said Sonia, taken aback. Pacifists were remote figures, deficient in some way, lacking in courage or in the obscure military virtue that enabled men to risk their lives in defence of their women and children back home.

"Not at all like Walter – Leo wrote poetry and read literature, he was in touch with the Quakers, he was interested in their ideas on preventing war and how to change the way nations deal with conflict, the sort of thing that the League of Nations is supposed to do. He was a thinker, a philosopher. All our other young men were raring to fight, but he didn't want to – on principle. The family pulled strings, and we managed to help him avoid active duty, thanks to Walter's already serving as an officer at the front. Leo went to work as an orderly in a military hospital, a very basic job, caring for the wounded and the sick."

"So how...?" asked Sonia.

"How did he die? It's a sad story," said Gusti as she looked away for a moment, her face grave. She reached for the baby. Cradling Max, she told Sonia how Leo had written to Walter, could Walter come, he was having trouble and needed help. The letter arrived late; by then the war was advanced and communication difficult, not to say impossible. Even if Walter had been able to leave immediately, he would not have arrived in time.

When the news came that his brother had killed himself, had taken a gun and aimed a shot at his temple, Walter was given two days leave from the front. A handwritten note from Leo said that he loved Oma and Walter, but he couldn't go on. There was no proper inquest at the time because of the war. They knew he had found the work upsetting; he'd written poems about it – the anguish of people who had no idea why the war was happening, what it was for, now maimed in body and spirit, meaningless suffering, unlikely to end except in death. Walter discovered that Leo's fellow orderlies had tormented him. Naive and isolated, he'd been overwhelmed.

"We feared Lina – Oma – wouldn't recover. Losing her husband so young, she struggled to bring up the two boys. We helped as much as we could, especially with Walter such a wild one." She paused then and said, "Leo's death was terrible for her. With the birth of your Max, she's blossoming; it's wonderful to see. He means everything to her – he looks very much like Leo as a baby. Do try to understand, my dear; please be patient with her."

Two years later, when Helena was born, Leo's room was at last dismantled and became the nursery. Oma removed all the cherished items; space was found for Leo's books in Walter's study. It seemed to Sonia that they were not the kind of books Walter liked to read, novels, philosophy and poetry. As far as she knew, Walter's awareness of poetry was limited to often-quoted, self-serving smatterings of Heine, "God will forgive me, it's his trade," and Schiller, "With stupidity, the gods themselves struggle in vain," plus a few odes he'd learnt at school. When he sang, the songs were vulgar drinking ones from his student or army days.

She would hear those songs whenever Walter returned from a meeting of war veterans. She'd wake up in the dark to men roaring vulgarities in the street. Beside her, Walter's pillow would still be smooth, untouched. As the men approached the house, the words became distinct enough to be understood. She would rise, slip a dressing gown over her nightgown and hurry down the stairs without turning on the light. She was anxious to separate Walter from the rest, to get him into the house and limit the disturbance, though the neighbours did not complain. Walter was an esteemed war hero. Besides, in one way or another, every family had to deal with the war's aftermath.

The next ten minutes were bound to be unpleasant. She would open the front door. In the moonlight, the men looked alike, the long grey coats open, white shirttails hanging out. After Benno Martin, Walter was the tallest, standing with his middle-aged paunch thrust forward, legs wide apart – he and Benno supporting each other, singing, if one could call it that.

Seeing her, Walter would stop, shouting to the others to shut up, gesticulating with his free arm. They usually failed to notice and continued bellowing, having forgotten why they were there. Walter would roar her name, and she'd step out onto the porch.

"Shush," she'd call. "I'm here."

He would roar back, "My wife, my little wifey, open the door to my house."

"Shush, shush, Walter, I'm here, everyone's asleep, you'll wake the neighbours, do make less noise. Please come in now." She had to prevent the rest of them from joining him, convince them to go home.

As soon as Walter reached the porch, she would say as loudly as she dared, "Late now – off you go, go home to your own beds!"

On one occasion, Benno Martin had leered at her and made to follow Walter. "Dr Martin, please go home; your wife will be waiting."

"My wife?" His jaw dropped. Probably thinking of his latest floozy.

She felt sorry for his wife.

"No more singing. Time to sleep! Take your men away!" She managed to make her voice carry without shouting. The trick was in the tone. She would have made a decent officer, she thought.

"My men, my men," mumbled Benno, turning towards the group.

With some effort, she convinced them to leave, though Walter seemed inclined to rejoin them.

"Walter, for heaven's sake, let them go! Come on now, home!" She coaxed and cajoled him into the hall until she could close the door. The others would move farther up the street. She could hear the bellowing start up again.

Greta would appear in her dressing gown and help Sonia remove Walter's coat as he sang to himself.

"Walter, not so loud. You'll wake the children; they've got school in a couple of hours!"

Emphatic nod, burps. He switched to singing in a breathy, beery whisper.

"Better," said Sonia. "Up the stairs!"

He looked doubtfully at the stairs.

"Come on, Greta." They each draped an arm over their shoulders.

"Thassa good girl," slurred Walter, trying to pat Greta's rump.

"Walter, stop it!"

One on either side, they got him to climb the stairs. He forgot to sing, focusing on his feet and the steps.

"Time for bed," said Sonia.

"Yesh, bedtime."

On the landing, they sidled past Max's door. As they passed, it opened a little and closed again quickly. Max hated these episodes. Loyal to his father, he never spoke about them.

They'd reach the bedroom and position Walter with his back to the bed. He'd let himself drop onto it like a great felled tree, the bed groaning under the sudden assault. He lay sprawled, the eiderdown puffed up around him in snowy mounds, instantly asleep, his mouth hanging open. He began to snore, rattling and trumpeting. Sonia hurried to close the door; Greta undid his bootlaces and pulled his boots off with mighty heaves. They covered him with a blanket, and Greta disappeared without a word to her little room off the kitchen. Sonia first checked the children – Max pretending to sleep – and then went down to the kitchen, where she warmed a cupful of milk. She drank in slow sips, willing herself to calm. On nights like these, she slept in the guest room.

In the morning, Walter would mix himself a concoction of raw egg and schnapps, which he would swallow in one gulp, throwing his head back with a grimace. He expressed no regret for the disturbance he'd caused. The first time it happened, she'd told him what she thought, but he'd cut her diatribe short – "Enough!" – and had left for the office without saying goodbye. Greta would never mention the night's disturbance, and the little maid apparently believed that men getting drunk out of their minds was normal and acceptable. Maybe it was so among German men, thought Sonia, but not among German Jews. She had never seen her father drunk. As a member of a fortunate, educated class, she believed Walter was duty-bound to provide an example of sobriety and restraint. Besides, he owed decent behaviour to her, to their children and to himself.

He would return from work bad-tempered and sallow-looking and go to bed after dinner. Oma knew about these episodes. She'd once said to Sonia in a quiet firm voice, different from her usual manner, "They had a tough war and were lucky to survive." Was she referring to Leo, who had not survived? Sonia wasn't sure.

Sonia knew her thoughts were unkind. She was fed up with the war, how great and terrible it had been, how awful the conditions, how courageous the men, how appalling the losses, how brutal the enemy, culminating in the cruel unfairness of the Versailles Treaty that marked its end. The war was past, finished, but its shadow still loomed over their lives. What was happening now was a consequence of what had happened then. They were powerless to influence events – the loss of family fortunes, hyperinflation ruining everyone, millions of marks for a simple cut of beef, though admittedly that was over now, her mother-in-law obliged to return to live with them, everywhere men out of work, war invalids, children and women reduced to begging, punitive demands for reparation from London and Paris. A kind of craziness was manifest, including violence in the streets, gangs of ruffians, fights between the Right and the Left – the communists and the Social Democrats – no security, no knowing what might happen next.

The celebrated Weimar democracy seemed misguided. It was failing as far as she could see. Walter and his friends remained enthusiastic about the whole enterprise with its grand, unrealistic ideals. What most people wanted, what she herself really wanted, was an ordinary family life – to be able to enjoy everyday things – the garden, pretty clothes, dinner in a nice restaurant with friends, a season at the opera.

Why did everything have to be so difficult, so complicated? And now on top of it all, there were the Nazis.

FIVE

In July 1933, when the first raid was carried out, Walter was away on business in Koenigsberg. On his return, distressed members of the community described how Streicher's men had hammered on front doors at daybreak, screaming orders to open up. They'd invaded homes, explained nothing, allowed no time. Yelling, swearing and jeering, they rounded up a total of three hundred Jewish men, kidnapped them, including the rabbis and members of the Central Association Committee, the congregational board and B'nai Brith members, herded them into lorries under brutal blows, the noise tremendous, mind-numbing, terrifying. Some of the men were in pyjamas, barefoot; many were elderly. The lorries took off, leaving wives, daughters, children and grandchildren standing in the streets, bereft, outraged, in tears.

The men were downloaded in town, marched through the streets and kept captive in a stadium on the outskirts of Nuremberg. Walter gathered that they'd been systematically brutalised and humiliated, though they were reluctant to describe the indignities they'd endured. At sundown, they were brought back, shocked and confused.

They wanted to forget, and besides, they'd been threatened with further harassment if the story got out. When he quizzed them, they sighed, looked away and said, "Thank God no one died." They were demoralised. Streicher's intention exactly, thought Walter.

The Nazis had not come to the house on Pierckheimerstrasse. Had the SA known Walter was away, or was there some other reason? Next door, Dr Fritz Klein was unscathed, having left for the hospital a few minutes before the Nazis arrived. Georg Loewenthal and his father, Hugo, were also left in peace, despite their many attempts to take Streicher to court. It didn't make sense.

A month or so later, Walter was walking to the office through the cobbled squares and narrow winding streets of the old city, following a meeting with representatives of the Orthodox congregation about delays in paying their dues, again. He was surprised to notice a *Stürmer* display box outside Heinz's pub. He was sure it hadn't been there when he'd last walked that way. He stopped to examine the main article in the tabloid. It slandered several people he knew, among them Max Uhlfelder and the Katzenbergers. The Katzenberger brothers ran a chain of expensive shoe shops throughout Bavaria, with headquarters in Nuremberg. Uhlfelder owned a luxury department store in Munich. As usual, the main item on the *Stürmer's* front page was grotesque – a revolting cartoon depicting Jews engaged in nefarious activities, abusing the helpless salesgirls who worked for them.

Heinz was a good man; he'd been a sergeant under Walter's command during the war in France, in the 8th Royal Bavarian Artillery Regiment. He was reliable, honest. He'd lost a hand just as the hostilities ceased, the wound marking the end of active service and the loss of his livelihood as a carpenter. Luckily, his father-in-law had been able to help, setting him up with the pub. He seemed to be doing well. The facade was neat and well kept, bright-red geraniums blooming in the flower boxes. Walter hadn't seen Heinz for some time.

He greeted Walter from behind the bar. "Kommandant!"

Walter accepted the offer of a beer and inquired after the family. After a pause, he said, "I see you've got a display outside your pub now, Heinz."

Heinz examined the bar's surface and wiped it with care. "The Nazis give me trouble. Neighbours two houses down." He stepped out from behind the bar and leant back against it, crossing his arms. The smooth rounded stump protruded from his shirtsleeve, healthy and repulsive at the same time. "I'd refused to sell their crappy rag, so in he comes with his SA mates; they order a round like normal citizens, and then the bastards pretend to start a fight, throwing my chairs around and my steins on the floor, breaking them, frightening away my regulars. A man can't keep his business going with that sort of circus. I tried selling the newspaper inside, but no, not good enough. The ugly sods kept checking up on me. They still do. Some jacked up so-and-so in a brown shirt, calling himself a goddamned *Scharführer*, Heil Hitlering all over the show. 'Put a hoarding out the front!' they shouted. Threw a couple more chairs over."

There was no point in calling the police. Streicher was now the king of the district, and the SA were the king's men. Heinz was a practical man. As there was no other way, he adapted to the situation. Walter could understand his point of view; it wasn't worth getting into strife with the Nazis, not about a mere newspaper, however scurrilous. Heinz deserved a quiet life as much as anyone else.

The door from the street opened, and a teenage schoolboy came in. Same blond hair as Heinz's, the same upturned nose, the same blue eyes. About Max's age.

"Chip off the old block," said Walter, smiling at the boy.

37

"This is Heinrich." Heinz swiped the school cap off his son's head. "Manners!"

The boy grinned at his father and greeted Walter.

"Off you go now. See what your mother wants!"

When the door to the kitchen had swung shut, Heinz sighed and said, "They noticed my boy, you know. They want him in the Hitler Youth. I told them he was needed here after school, to help out, which happens to be true."

The bullying was consistent with everything else they did. What surprised Walter was how successful they were. The paper's circulation was rising, display boxes appearing everywhere. Not just in Nuremberg, which after all was the paper's home town, but in other cities too. During a recent visit to Hamburg, he'd noticed the proliferation of boxes there, fewer than in Nuremberg, but too many for comfort. People couldn't help being affected by what they read. In the countryside, people rarely met any Jews; they had no experience against which to evaluate the stories they read. In the towns, Jewish artists might be popular, loved even, but Jewish financiers and business people were envied. The envy went hand in hand with malice, a corrosive lode from which their enemies extracted the worst slander.

Heinz seemed uncomfortable, so Walter took his leave. As the door shut behind him, he noticed one of those signs in the window, *Juden unerwünscht*, Jews unwelcome, half-hidden by the geraniums. He'd missed it on his way in. It shook him. He felt betrayed – though again, it was hard to blame Heinz.

A few weeks later, on a dank March afternoon, when daylight was slowly seeping away and the lights were coming on in the windows of the expensive stores and cafés on the Karolinenstrasse, Walter was working at the big oak desk which had been his father's, in the comfort of his office. The Mannheim & Loewenthal law practice occupied the second floor of a venerable old house at the top end of the street by the St Lawrence Church. Blue pencil in hand, he read through the typewritten text of a contract. A secretary in the outer office would type out the corrected version, clacking busily at one of the Underwood typewriters his father had imported from America.

There was a peremptory rap on the door, and Georg Loewenthal walked in. Walter looked up, surprised. They'd shared lunch a few hours ago; had they not covered all the matters at hand? He put the pencil down and waited while Georg shut the door with more than usual care. Georg was the Loewenthal partner at Mannheim & Loewenthal since Uncle Hugo had retired.

"Is something the matter?" asked Walter.

Georg leant back against the door, hands in his pockets. He was a tall ungainly man; his suit was creased, his tie crooked, as usual.

"I've just had a phone call from Munich, about Uhlfelder."

Uhlfelder was not a client, but they had discussed his arrest at length. The radio stations and national press were parroting the *Stürmer* accusations – that the department store's employees were exploited and sexually abused, and Uhlfelder's affluent lifestyle suspect, corrupt. The police had come for him at dawn, taking him first to the police prison then to the new concentration camp at Dachau. Getting him released would require a good lawyer.

Georg said, "Siegel went to the police headquarters on Uhlfelder's behalf, and a bunch of SA thugs beat him up." Siegel was one of the best lawyers in Munich.

"Siegel? *Our* Siegel?"

"Yes. At Munich Police HQ."

"At the *police HQ*?" He heard himself parroting Georg's words and shook his head in irritation.

Georg nodded and said, "Yes, the SA marched him through the centre of Munich with an outrageous notice hanging round his neck. They'd torn his clothes, made him look like a clown."

"Michael Siegel?" Walter was incredulous. "Yes," said Georg again.

"Where's he now?"

"At home."

"He's all right?"

"On the whole, yes. Shock, mainly. Apparently they broke his front teeth."

Walter looked out of the window at the bare trees in the dwindling light. He was aware of an irrational urge to deny what he was hearing. At the same time, he was not altogether surprised. He leaned forward, his elbows on the desk, clasping his hands. "Georg, I'm finding this hard to take in. Could you please repeat what you know, from the beginning?"

"When he arrived at Munich Police HQ to discuss the Uhlfelder case, Siegel was shown to a room where he was ambushed by a group of SA. They were waiting for him; there's no doubt it was planned. They beat him up, punched him in the face, removed his shoes and his hat, hung a giant notice round his neck and ridiculed him, took him on a forced march through the centre of Munich, barefoot and hatless, his clothes in disarray, shouting that he was a stinking Jew who didn't know his place, calling him all the names under the sun."

"How did he get away?"

"Not sure. He took a taxi. He's in bed, refuses to see anyone."

"But did no one intervene? Did no one try to prevent the SA from leaving the police station with him? Or later, in the street?"

"Think about it, Walter: in the street, people would have stopped and watched, but no one would lift a finger – who would dare confront a group of rowdy SA? They would turn on whoever interfered. Too risky. It could have ended worse, far worse. Besides, the man in the street doesn't know Siegel; they don't know who he is."

"But the police knew who Siegel was; they knew full well his standing in the courts, his status!"

"They seem to have allowed the SA the freedom to do whatever they pleased."

"It's unimaginable."

Georg sat down in one of the leather armchairs in front of the desk. He rubbed his forehead again, took out a handkerchief and mopped his forehead.

Walter walked to the window. He looked up at the darkening sky before turning back to Georg. "I'd have thought that there would be one man at least at Munich Police HQ, one honest man, who'd have found a way of warning Siegel. A hint would have been enough." Walter returned to his desk. He asked, "What are they planning to do now?"

"No idea. It happened only this morning. Maybe while we were happily eating our lunch. I imagine they'll want to leave the country. Most people would."

Walter sat down beside Georg. He buried his face in his hands.

After a moment, Georg said, "What do you think our Nuremberg police would do, in a similar situation?"

"You mean, what would Benno do?"

Benno Martin was deputy commander of Nuremberg's police force. He and Walter had both served as army officers during the war, and before that, they'd studied law together, forming a firm friendship despite the prevailing antisemitism. Walter hadn't seen or heard from him since the Nazis' assumption of power, but that might not mean anything. Months sometimes went by without their meeting.

There was a knock, and Walter's secretary put her head round the door.

"Thank you, Monica. I'll call you in a minute."

She opened her mouth to speak, but they said in unison, "Not now!" and her head disappeared.

Walter said slowly, trying to come to grips with what he'd heard, "Siegel believed he was safe."

"So did Uhlfelder, until they came for him."

Der Stürmer has been vilifying him for months," said Walter. "One might almost say it was predictable."

Georg was stubborn in his refusal to read *Der Stürmer*.

"The Katzenbergers were mentioned too. I'll ring them, tell them about Siegel. I want to know what they think."

"I'm sure they've heard about Uhlfelder," said Georg. After a pause, he said, "If a lawyer representing a client can be attacked in broad daylight..."

"...at police headquarters," added Walter.

"Yes, while carrying out duties which are his responsibility by law!"

"Anything may happen to anyone," said Walter.

For a moment, neither of them spoke.

Georg said, "It's mob rule, plus unwarranted hatred. Pure antisemitism." He leant back in his chair. "We've experienced SA action here already, haven't we. Fortunately, none of those three hundred ended up in Dachau."

Walter sighed. Then he said, "I forgot to mention it earlier, but it's rumoured that Streicher wants the SA amalgamated with the police."

Georg raised his eyebrows.

Walter said, "As far as I can tell, there's no sign of it happening."

"Where would that leave Benno?"

"In a tricky situation, I think. But so far it looks as if he's managed to circumvent the suggestion."

"His men would leave in droves."

"They might not dare to," said Walter, thinking of Heinz.

"They know Streicher; they know what he's like. They've thrown him in jail so many times over the years – they utterly despise him. As far as they're concerned, his SA are scum."

"True. However, that was the past. Today Streicher is the *Gauleiter* – our highest official, Hitler's choice. Altogether a different proposition."

Georg sighed and stood up. "Bad for us." He went to the door.

"And in the long run, bad for everyone, bad for the entire country," said Walter.

When the door closed behind him, Walter picked up the blue pencil. He looked at the contract, but it seemed irrelevant. He put the pencil down and leant back in his chair, hands clasped behind his head, staring at the darkness beyond the windows, waiting for the turmoil of his thoughts to calm down.

A week or so later, Bernhard Kolb phoned Walter, requesting his presence at the Jewish cemetery. Kolb was the board's executive director. His voice sounded strained. A body had been delivered from Dachau. He'd hesitated, coughed and added, "My nephew."

Walter didn't know Kolb well. They were both army veterans, and like him, Kolb had lost brothers in the war – four brothers. Four! At the inauguration of the Jewish community's memorial in honour of those they had lost in the war, Walter had seen Kolb's mother, a little bent woman swathed in black. Kolb stood beside her, her only remaining son. Standing next to his own mother, Walter had pondered the impact of four to his one – four unknown deaths in foreign battlefields, four telegrams, four times the mother bereft, tears unable to flow, food uneaten, no funeral, no grave, ghosts, nightmares, grief without end.

By the time he arrived at the cemetery and entered the *Beit Tehara*,[1] the doctor and Kolb had removed the young man's body from the coffin and placed it on the metal table. The eyes were closed, the face serene. His skin was smooth and unblemished, almost like a girl's, except for a light moustache above the full lips. He was very young. Probably never been with a woman, thought Walter. There was a black hole in the neck. Someone had washed the blood away. Walter shivered. The *Beit Tahara* seemed full of pain, suffering swirling around them. Members of the *Chevra Kadisha*[2] would soon arrive to prepare the body for burial – prayers, washing, wrapping.

Kolb's face was very pale, with dark rings under his eyes; an inner sinking had occurred, a yellowing under the skin. His moustache and hair seemed darker than usual, as if dyed. Some Jewish men had shaved off their moustaches since Hitler, but not Kolb.

The Gestapo had recently announced that Kolb was to be their liaison with the Jewish community. Walter had seen his own troubled feelings reflected in the faces of the board members round the table – overwhelming relief at not having been chosen, and pity for the man who found himself at such an impasse. The appointment was a curse, impossible to avoid.

Despite Kolb's connection to the powerful Gestapo, the SA had arrested his nephew, had taken the boy into so-called protective custody, on a shadowy pretext – some trumped-up accusation. At first, the family had been able to visit him at the prison, bringing him food and clothing. But after barely a week, he'd been transported to Dachau. The family had lobbied every agency connected to the law and the camp, however remote; Kolb had pleaded with the Gestapo and his SA contacts. The community had fought hard – Walter himself had tried to save this young man, exploring every avenue, both legal and illegal. The inexorable days had slipped by. Some people could not survive the conditions at the camp for long.

Walter had managed to get a message to Benno Martin asking for assistance, and Martin had responded with a brief note, saying he'd see. Walter knew that Benno's decision to engage with Streicher's administration on any issue depended on myriad considerations which neither Walter nor anyone else in the Jewish community could know of. The main factor would be the ebb and flow of power between the Nazis and the Police Commission.

Nothing was achieved. At the camp in Dachau, a summons to appear in front of Streicher amounted to a death sentence. The boy had been called, and Streicher had decreed. A week later, Kolb received the sealed coffin in his official capacity as executive director of the community's board.

Despite the risk, Kolb was determined to gather evidence of the murder, and he'd advised the doctor of the body's arrival. He'd broken the seals, opened the coffin and called Walter to witness the state of the corpse. The doctor came to examine the body. Keeping the autopsy report hidden and safe would be a further challenge. Kolb would have worked something out. Best not to know. May the day of reckoning come soon, thought Walter.

Death's shadow. Walter wiped his forehead. Images from the past appeared in his mind. A field in France, muddy snow, black, broken tree stumps, black crows scavenging off the corpses in no-man's land. Shooting the birds would trigger retaliation from the enemy trenches. They'd watch the crows, swear at them, throw whatever was at hand if they were near enough – stones, empty cartridges, tin cans, the occasional bottle, bits of wood. Rats also fed off the corpses, but one could hardly see them, even with field glasses.

This boy had been killed differently. There were deep gouges in his flesh – neck, arms, chest, belly, thighs. Walter watched the doctor examine him with meticulous care. Kolb stood at the head of the table, once leaning over to touch the face gently. A tremor ran through him, and he retreated to one of the metal folding chairs by the white-washed wall; he sat there with his face hidden in his hands.

The doctor moved quietly around the table, examining the body's wounds closely. He sniffed at them, touched them, peered through a magnifying glass. Walter helped him turn the body onto its side, first one then the other, to examine the back. The wounds looked strange, different. The camp authorities had issued a death certificate that gave the usual story. "Shot while attempting to escape." To Walter, the wounds did not appear to have been made by a bullet or by the cut and thrust of a bayonet. Here someone had dug into the body, big holes, almost pits, larger where the wound was in the flesh, away from the bones. The chest wounds were the messiest; there were lacerations where a knife had slipped on the ribs. Not much blood there either. He couldn't make sense of it. The coffin was a rough pine box. He examined the shattered seals and wondered what the consequences would be, if any. The Nazis were unlikely to find out, for who would tell them?

Finally, the doctor looked up. "He was shot at close range. He was facing them. Most of the burnt flesh was cut away afterwards – a clumsy job. There's some left in places. I'll write it up and get the report to you tomorrow." He looked at Kolb and touched his arm.

Kolb nodded.

"I'm sorry," said the doctor. "May his memory be a blessing." He went to the metal sink, turned on the taps and began the slow business of washing his hands and arms, soaping them to the elbows, rinsing them under the running water for a long time. Walter was reminded of field hospitals during the war.

He took his leave and stepped out of the *Beit Tahara* into the sunlight. After the chill and the horror, he was relieved to be in the open air, in the fresh breeze with the sun on his face. It was a beautiful day, as if winter were in abeyance. He followed the path among the gravestones to the main portal. The road to the city centre was almost empty. He would walk some of the way.

Here and there, on either side of the road, people were working in the market gardens and orchards. Walter felt remote from their activities, as if isolated under a bell jar. He paused to watch the green ripple of the shadow-flecked grass in the orchards. Birds twittered as if all was well.

The news of the murder would have spread by the time he reached the office. Multiple phone calls, more distress, more fear.

That evening, a packed crowd filled the house of mourning, overflowing into the street, enveloped in the murmured rhythm of shared prayer. Policemen had been posted nearby to prevent any antisemitic attacks. There was to be no trouble. Walter attended the *minyan* every night that week; Sonia accompanied him on the last evening. She was determined the children should be spared all knowledge of the events. She told them that she and Walter were attending a meeting. Fortunately the children displayed the normal indifference of children to their parents' activities, except for those affecting them directly.

SIX

Weeks went by and grass grew back over the lawn's bald patches. Max studied for his bar mitzvah, meeting the rabbi for an hour's drilling in Hebrew every week. He joined the Nuremberg Bar Kochba sports club and played football in the afternoons with other Jewish boys. The gardener vanished and his mother hired a Jewish man to look after the garden. She said he would do, though he wasn't a real gardener. He'd been fired from his job as a salesman, told that the company had no work for Jews. Another change came when Oma joined them for dinner in the evenings after her cook decided to return to her village. Oma's cook had been a part of her household since Oma was a young bride. Oma seemed unperturbed. She said she enjoyed spending more time with her beloved grandchildren.

The football was all right, but he sometimes had trouble falling asleep at night, thinking about the friends he'd lost and the fun they'd had. He longed for the time gone by when he'd woken to the sun streaming through the curtains, birds singing in the garden, the day full of promise, and on those rare occasions when he had no duties, on days when he was free to run around – no school, no homework, no relatives to visit, no synagogue, no obligations of any kind – he was free to swim at the pool or cycle in the forest with his friends. The joy of being Max Mannheim, of being alive in this wonderful world, had once filled him to the brim until he thought he might burst.

Nowadays he often felt angry, frustrated. He was only a schoolboy – he could only wait for the government to fall after the March elections, when the vast majority of Germans, those who didn't agree with Hitler, would boot him out.

When he couldn't sleep, he'd reach for his torch and read under the bed covers one of Karl May's stories about proud, honourable Indians in faraway America. He would read till late and have trouble waking up in the morning. He often felt like punching those who bullied him, except that he knew they'd welcome the excuse – they'd gang up on him and beat him up. He'd seen it happen to others. He and Hans read all the time, even during lessons. The teachers didn't seem to care.

His mother had booked a fortnight's holiday for the family on a farm in the Alps. It was just the four of them because the Loewenthals were away in the Thüringerwald. The farm was situated near a small lake in the foothills, far from the nearest village. They swam and walked every day. Helena was ecstatic because she was allowed to wear a pair of Max's old *Lederhosen* instead of a skirt. They avoided tourist haunts, walking the shepherds' tracks up to the high pastures. They would stop to admire the view, drink from the little streams tumbling down the mountainside and eat their lunch. Helena searched the undergrowth in vain for the tiny wild strawberries and the blueberries they loved. "It's not yet summer," said their mother.

In the evening after dinner, they played cards or read. Sometimes they sang traditional folk songs from the old handwritten songbook which belonged to his mother. Max and his father mapped out a long hike which would take them further and higher than Max had ever been in a single day. Helena was not coming because she was not a good climber. Their mother would stay behind with her.

Max's father woke him before dawn. The world outside seemed mysteriously still; a couple of birds called, one answering the other. The jagged silhouettes of the mountains were outlined against a sky streaked with silver light, mirrored in the iridescent lake. A lone cow mooed nearby, the mournful sound dying out among the hills.

The farmer had lent Max a tall alpenstock with a sharp metal spike, useful in the rocky reaches. His father had brought his own stick, old and polished with use. They each carried a canvas rucksack containing a jacket and food: dark, dense bread, sausage, cheese and some apples along with a small bar of chocolate. Max's Swiss army knife dangled from his belt. They filled their metal water bottles at the long stone trough in front of the farmhouse, where the icy water murmured and whispered, slipping out at the far end with a low gurgle. Max was excited to be awake at this early hour, at the thought of embarking on a trek in the mountains following the route he and his father had planned together and at having his father to himself for an entire day.

They walked through the pastures, past the cows which swung their heavy heads round to watch them go by, their bells clanging. By full daylight, they'd been walking almost an hour, and they paused for breakfast. They could see the lake below and the farm near it, the landscape as neat as a child's drawing – the pale path emerging from the pine forest, winding between meadows towards the farm. They could see the cows in the pastures, the glint of water in the trough, the chicken coop at the end of the long vegetable garden, the sharp pitch of the main house's roof, and the logs stacked against the wall up to the eaves in a neat pattern. A pleasant, peaceful view, thought Max.

They walked on for an hour or so, hardly talking, pausing occasionally to drink from their bottles. Above the pastures, the path was stonier. Their alpenstocks rang against the rocks. The trees were sparse and crooked, bent over by the prevailing wind.

Max's rucksack rubbed against the small of his back.

His father noticed his discomfort and rearranged the bag's contents for him. He pointed to a peak. "There! That's our goal."

"It's not that high." Max was disappointed.

"High enough," said his father.

A deer, a hind, bounded out of bushes near them and froze in surprise, her head held high, half turned away, one shiny dark eye assessing the danger. With a flick of her short tail, she fled, gone.

They stopped for lunch near a stream, sitting in the inadequate shade of a scrawny bush. Now they were in the upper reaches of the mountain, high up. Not far to go.

A steep slope of grey scree confronted them, a river of dry rocks, its downward flow immobilised, the path a barely visible trace meandering across it.

"It's unstable, so walk slowly and keep your alpenstock handy," said Father. "Try not to dislodge any stones."

Max made his way to the other side, step by careful step. He stopped there and watched his father walk over. The climb was steep, heat radiating up from the rocky path. Max could feel rivulets of sweat trickling down his forehead and neck. His father mopped his red face with a handkerchief.

The path had narrowed, winding up among massive boulders speckled with lichen. The only bright colours were the sky's cobalt blue and the scattered green of alpine plants. His father was gasping for breath. After a pause to rest and drink, they reached the top – the world opened up, wide and welcoming. Immense blue space above and mountains around them, grand and wonderful, peak upon peak, in jumbled rows, snow gleaming silver and white, to the far horizon.

Max felt as if the beauty was his, or rather, that he was a part of it, that he belonged in it. He wished he had wings to fly into the vastness. He took a deep breath and stretched out his arms.

Father smiled at him. "Beautiful, isn't it?"

The walk back to the farm was easy.

As Max trotted ahead, his rucksack bouncing lightly on his back, he said, "I wish Helena could have seen it too."

"When she's older," said his father.

At Helena's school, everyone was excited, happy with the Führer, delighted with their wonderful new leader. Helena knew that he wanted to harm Jews, but she had yet to discover why. She knew that he also encouraged bad behaviour towards people like Frau Bauer, who were communist.

Father said, "Fortunately, Führers come, and Führers go, while Germany and the German people remain forever!" It was only a month or so until the election, after which Hitler would disappear.

The older girls sometimes sang the Nazi song loudly in the corridors – with the dreadful line about "Jewish blood spurting under the knife" – as if they wanted to kill Jews! Helena had noticed the teachers' reluctance to stop them; they would protest weakly, too late, when the song was almost finished.

She sang the national anthem at the morning assembly, which went well except for the end, when everyone said *Heil Hitler* enthusiastically, raising their arms in the salute. It made the children and teachers seem united, strong and happy. She herself was not required to join in; rather, she was required not to join in. She worried in case she was swept along, as happened once when the words *Heil Hitler* popped out of her mouth while the class was greeting a teacher. She'd quickly said, "God forbid!" to make up for it, but in a low voice.

She and Lore were sent to the back of the class, to sit only with each other, no one else, on this bench which was now called "the Jews' bench". She'd told her parents; she could tell that they didn't like it, but they had no solution to offer.

Nobody talked to Helena and Lore any more. They tried to carry on as usual, but whatever they said or did seemed to fade away and disappear as if absorbed into cotton wool or sucked into a void, because no one looked at them or listened to what they said or reacted to them in any way. Helena had not minded school too much until then. Her favourite time had been playing games during the breaks, though she was not a good runner, because she soon became breathless. Nevertheless, people had wanted her on their team because she was strong and had a good eye for the ball. They also liked her; she knew that. She knew she'd been liked, once.

Her parents told her to keep her chin up, that this state of affairs would not last and things would soon be back to normal. "It's an aberration," said her mother, a new word for Helena.

The lessons were a different matter. When Helena had started school three years ago at the age of seven, she had discovered that children she'd thought less clever than herself learnt to read and write with surprising ease, whereas she often wrote her letters the wrong way round and had trouble recognising them on the printed page. The teacher told her to pay attention, to be more precise. She was taken aback because she was paying attention. She tried harder. She couldn't understand what was happening. The other children progressed. They seemed to find it simple, whereas she was one of the worst in the class. She felt humiliated. Her friend Lore was good at everything, but Helena didn't mind that so much because Lore had always found everything easy; she just was that way, and they'd been friends forever. Lore knew Helena wasn't stupid.

She remembered the thrill of her very first day. Besides the huge shiny cardboard cornet filled with sweets and chocolates from her mother and father, she'd been given a lovely new slate, glossy and black, full of promise. Horizontal red lines were painted on one side, to help one write straight. The frame was of pale varnished wood with a single hole drilled in it for the loop of string by which the slate hung on a hook at school, under her name. The slate pencil wrote on the slate in white, and the writing could be erased – her mother had given Helena a freshly laundered cloth for that purpose. On that first day, Helena discovered that once the slate had been used, no amount of washing and wiping could return it to its original rich blackness.

In those early days, she'd worked hard at her homework. She'd struggled with writing, sometimes wanting to shout or cry with frustration. The slate pencil was fragile and broke easily. It squeaked and scratched as she wrote. Her mother frowned and told her to take care. She very much wanted to be more careful, like Max or Lore, but she couldn't manage it. Once or twice she'd found satisfaction in doing her homework, particularly enjoying the writing of capital Ls because of the curlicues. Max helped her, making sure the letters went in the right direction. On that particular weekend, Tante Fanny and Uncle Otto had come to visit, with little Rudi who was learning to walk.

Helena had been asked to kindly take Rudi out to the garden. Rudi and the pushchair were carried down the terrace steps for her. She was instructed to be careful, not to rush, a recommendation she thought superfluous, as one couldn't push the pushchair fast over the gravel. Rudi sat facing her. His big blue eyes watched everything she did. She took him all over the garden and explained about the vegetable patch, the compost heap, the fruit trees, the washing lines, the gardener's shed and the laundry house. He chuckled and gurgled. She showed him her special hiding place among the lilac bushes. Then she remembered that ginger cake would be served with the coffee, and there would be lemonade for the children. They'd been gone long enough. The chair was harder to push now than when she started. She helped Rudi out and held his hand as they slowly climbed the three steps to the terrace. In the living room he let go and waddled over to Tante Fanny. Helena's mother fussed over him with what Helena thought was an excess of attention, exclaiming how well he walked.

Helena had noticed a damp patch on the seat of Rudi's woollen pants. She also noticed that the maid had not yet brought in the cake and the other refreshments. Tante Fanny settled Rudi on her knee as he sucked his thumb. She bobbed him up and down, her bright gaze on Helena.

"Thank you for taking him out, Helena. I'll change his nappy in a minute, and then he'll have a sleep. Tell me, darling, how do you like being a schoolgirl?"

Helena told Tante Fanny about her homework and the capital Ls.

"Helena, I'd love to see them."

Helena ran upstairs to fetch the slate. When she came back with it, Tante Fanny put Rudi down. She took the slate in both hands and looked at it. "Helena, this is wonderful, such beautiful L's, and so many of them! Look, Otto, our Helena is such a clever girl." She held out the slate to her husband. Uncle Otto was older than her father; he seemed almost old enough to be a grandfather. He made approving noises and then held the slate, at a loss.

Helena went over to him and took it back.

Her mother smiled at her across the room. "Helena works hard."

Her father said, "Show me, Helena."

Everyone was looking at her and smiling.

Father examined her work and put his arm around her as she leant against the arm of the chair. "Well done, Helena. Good girl!" He gave the slate back, and she went to sit beside Tante Fanny on the window seat, very happy.

"Max is studying *Erlkönig* at school," said her mother. "He learnt it in no time at all."

Father said, "Helena, please find your brother and tell him to come down; Tante Fanny and Uncle Otto would like to hear him recite *Erlkönig*."

She went upstairs to fetch Max who was reading in his room, away from the visitors.

"Father says to come and recite your stupid poem. Now." There was no question of disobeying their father's orders.

Max sighed. "Not my poem. Goethe's – Goethe, you moron!"

Holding his book in one hand, he ran across the landing and bounded down the stairs, jumping over the last three steps. Helena followed him but did not jump; three steps were more than she could manage. She was thinking about Goethe, and she remembered that moment well because of what happened afterwards.

As they burst into the room, the adults turned towards them. Rudi was standing close to his mother on the window seat, holding onto her. He turned too, lost his balance and sat down with a bump.

Tante Fanny laughed and helped him up again. Then her expression changed and she said, "Oh, Helena!" She picked up the slate which Rudi had sat on. His damp bottom had wiped out most of the L's, leaving a big round smudge. A great surge of anguish rose in Helena. She grabbed the slate and threw it on the floor as hard as she could. It cracked on impact. She stamped on it, yelling, "I hate you! I hate you!

I hate you!" Splinters escaped the frame, shards of slate scattering across the polished floor.

She ran into the garden, to the lilac bushes, where she crawled and hid, burying her head in her arms.

After some time, she stopped crying. She got up and brushed the twigs and dead leaves off her skirt. She'd missed the ginger cake. She was hungry and a little cold. She knew her mother would tell her off for her bad temper and punish her, like the *Struwelpeter* in the story book. If she didn't finish the homework by Monday morning, she'd be punished at school too.

The sun was going down. The shadows were longer and darker, and the colours in the garden were seeping away.

That had happened in the first year, and by now she had learnt her letters and numbers. But school remained a challenging place for her, more so than for her brother or for Lore or most of the other children.

It was April 1933. Sonia and Oma sat without speaking in the living room's deepening gloom – almost seven in the evening, past dinner time and no Walter, no phone call. Max came in and turned on the light, and they blinked up at him. Sonia thought how much he'd grown.

"When's dinner? Why are you sitting in the dark like a pair of owls?" he asked.

"Your father should be home any moment. We'll call you."

That afternoon, Greta had reported that SA men and other Nazi supporters were roaming the streets looking for trouble, shouting slogans, beating up anyone they suspected of sympathising with the communists or the Social Democrats.

The intimidation had worsened as the Nazis increased their ascendance over their political opponents through a dubious emergency decree, accusing the communists of the Reichstag arson, though no one seemed to know if they were truly to blame, and jailing them in their thousands, with what Walter had described as the complicity of the law courts. The leaders of the Social Democrats were nowhere to be seen. It was rumoured they had fled the country. Any opposition to the Nazis came under violent attack. Nevertheless, the Nazis had failed to gain an absolute majority at the election and were now in a coalition government.

Over coffee, Sonia had discussed the political situation with Elise that morning, in the kind of frustrating conversation which occurred so often these days, a re-examination of what everyone knew and a reiteration of tired opinions, including the fact that nobody seemed able to predict what might happen next. The leaders of the Jewish community were careful to avoid voicing despondency so as not to undermine the community's fragile morale. Though she would not admit to it publicly, Sonia was convinced that their situation could only deteriorate further, with Hitler aiming for a complete takeover. Besides the Nazis, there were only insignificant parties; what kind of elections would there be in the future?

Waiting for Walter, she tried to contain her rising anxiety, reminding herself that a man of his size and vigour was an unlikely target for harassment. They heard the front door open. She tried not to rush as she stepped into the hall. Walter took off his hat; she helped him out of his coat and looked up into his face to read his expression.

Oma stood close by, listening.

He said quickly, "Not now!" as Max arrived, followed by Helena.

"You're so late, Father, what happened?" Helena asked.

"A meeting."

Max ignored his father's answer. "People at school said that a new law forbids Jews to work in the civil service. That won't affect you, will it?"

That's the cat out of the bag, thought Sonia. No need for pretence. She scrutinised Walter's face as he answered, "No, that law won't affect me. But many families will suffer, and we shall have to help wherever we can. You remember how hard it is for families when a father is deprived of work, don't you?"

Unemployment had been widespread when Max was little. At the local primary school, many pupils went ill-clothed and hungry. Sonia had done her best to help. She would have preferred her son to attend a good private school with children of their milieu, but Walter had insisted, wanting Max to meet children of ordinary hard-working families, "the backbone of the nation". Max had brought home stories of desperate fist-fights in the playground, communists versus Nazis. The children's lives had been contaminated by politics from early on, and it seemed likely that the future would be no different.

She hung up Walter's coat. "Come, children, time for dinner."

Helena turned to her father and asked, "Why won't those fathers be able to work?"

"Because of the Nazis' new law."

"But you'll be allowed to work, won't you?"

"War veterans will be allowed to work. President Hindenburg said so."

"Anyway, you're a partner, aren't you, not an employee," said Max.

"Indeed, a partner in a firm, not an employee of the state or the municipality. It's important to remember that this law applies to all the opponents of the Nazi regime. Not just to Jews." He went to wash his hands.

They filed into the dining room and took their usual places. Walter sat down in the big carver at the head of the table as Sonia brought the food in from the kitchen. Greta was out tonight.

"*Der Stürmer* says that the Jews are the cause of Germany's troubles. That's why they don't like us," said Helena.

"Helena, you're not to read that newspaper. You mustn't even glance at it."

"I can't help it, Mama. The words are at the top and so big; they shout it out: 'The Jews are our misfortune!'"

"Shush, darling. It's bad enough that they print it. Don't repeat it." Helena was right, she thought, impossible to avoid seeing those words; difficult not to be influenced by them.

Walter laid his napkin on the table. "Come here, *mein Schätzlein.*"

He took Helena onto his lap, where she settled in comfort. She was too old to sit on her father's knee, thought Sonia.

Walter said, "Helena, we've done nothing wrong."

She looked up at her father. "But everyone says so..."

"You must believe me. These are lies, lies spread by Streicher and the Nazis. No one we know – not me, your mother or Oma, or Tante Fanny and Uncle Otto, or Tante Gusti and Uncle Hugo, or Uncle Fritz and Tante Frieda, or any other Jewish grown-up you know has harmed Germany. On the contrary, Uncle Fritz helps people get better every day, you know that. *Der Stürmer* is a nasty newspaper which prints lies. You mustn't read it."

"I wasn't thinking that any of our friends would harm Germany."

"Helena, there are very few Jews in Germany, less than one per cent..."

"One person out of every hundred," said Max.

Sonia smiled at him. Helena found percentages difficult.

"...and while some Jews may indeed be criminals, they are very rare. Most Jews are respected businessmen, doctors, lawyers, rabbis and teachers."

"And scientists, like Einstein. Everyone likes him," said Max.

"And painters and musicians," added Sonia.

"Yes. Since the war ended, times have been hard, and the people are poor and resent our success. This won't last. The German people are honest. They know that we belong here and have been loyal subjects for a long time, for hundreds of years. We fought hard in the last war; a great many Jews died for Germany, as you know."

Oma nodded. "You can be proud of being Jewish, though the Nazis would like it otherwise."

Helena slipped off her father's lap and returned to her seat. She began to eat the food on her plate.

"Why is *Der Stürmer* allowed to publish lies?" asked Max.

Sonia and Walter exchanged a glance, and Walter said, "Streicher is being held accountable in court, Max. We confront him whenever we can. Remember what Fritz Josephthal did to Streicher?"

Der Stürmer had featured a denigrating, contemptuous obituary of Fritz Josephthal's father, a respected lawyer who had been the much-loved chairman of the Nuremberg Jewish community for many years. On the day the obituary appeared, Fritz Josephthal – himself a well-known lawyer – waited outside the primary school where Streicher taught. He held a riding crop in his hand, and when Streicher emerged carrying his own whip, Fritz challenged him and struck him with it.

"Whipped him like a dog!" said the delighted Jews, invariably concluding the story by saying, "He's never dared attack a Josephthal since, not in print nor otherwise."

Speaking with his mouth full, Max said in dialect, "Frau Bauer says that Streicher looks like a pig and behaves like a pig, only happy when he's knee-deep in mud."

"Speak proper German please, Max. Not with your mouth full," said Sonia.

"An astute political commentator," said Walter, smiling.

Helena piped up, saying, "Gustav once told me that's not true." Gustav was the gardener who had left.

The conversation stopped. She hesitated. "Gustav said," and quoting him in dialect, "'Pigs are no different from people; they like living in a nice green meadow just as we would.'" When they all laughed, she turned to her mother in surprise and Sonia stroked her hand.

Oma said, "Frau Bauer may be uneducated, but she's far from stupid. If all communists were like her, the world would be a paradise."

Sonia knew that Frau Bauer had been engaged as a washerwoman during the war and that she'd been at the house when the dreaded telegram arrived from the War Office, announcing a death. But whose death? Which son? Oma stood in the hall weeping, clutching the envelope, unable to open it. Frau Bauer was somehow alerted. "Shall I read it for you?" she asked and Oma gave her the envelope. She opened it and read out the name, reaching for Oma, holding her. Tante Gusti was sent for; Frau Bauer had stayed with Oma until she arrived with the doctor.

Max addressed his father, asking, "Since he's been made Gauleiter of Franconia, Streicher thinks he's beyond the law, doesn't he?"

Sonia refrained from smiling. He must have heard his father use that expression.

"Yes, Max, it seems so. But Nazi contempt for the due process of the law will make the people turn against them, people like Frau Bauer, the communists, and the Social Democrats. In due course, dissatisfaction with this regime will grow, and because we live in a democracy, the government will fall, and the Nazis will be dismissed. The Streichers of the present regime are bound to disappear. Patience – we must be patient. The tide will turn. Germany is a civilised country, a great country."

The thought occurred to Sonia that much patience might be required, for a good long time. Still, Walter was wiser and better informed than she was. She nodded in agreement.

"Maybe someone'll shoot him," muttered Max. "Like they did Rathenau."

His father had often told him that Rathenau had been a great statesman, a Jew they could be proud of, who had made significant contributions to the country. A Nazi ban on the annual commemoration of Rathenau's service to the nation had recently been reported in the newspapers.

"Max! Enough!" said Sonia.

Walter added in a quiet tone, "In due course, Streicher will get his just deserts; you can be sure of that."

Later that evening when the children were in bed, Walter said, "Leo Katzenberger is determined to sue Streicher for libel."

The Katzenbergers' luxurious lifestyle had been caricatured in *Der Stürmer*. There was a small grain of truth in it, thought Sonia. Their house on Praterstrasse was beautiful, both inside and out. So was their shop on Karolinenstrasse, and the shoes they sold – on par with the best shops in Berlin. The Katzenbergers had taste.

"He was livid," said Walter. "He said that the article could cause serious harm to their reputation, in Bavaria and in the rest of the country."

"This is a bad time for Jews to attract attention," said Oma, putting down her book.

"Katzenberger's attracting attention in other ways too," said Walter. "There's a young woman... Not the usual sort; she owns her own photo studio."

"Jewish?" asked Oma.

Walter shook his head.

Sonia watched her husband and wondered about him and women, the usual sort and the others.

Sonia had been out walking in the park with the children and her friend Ursula, and Ursula mentioned that her husband had bumped into Walter in Leipzig. She felt a stabbing pain in her chest, which she'd blamed on indigestion, though in reality it was the feeling of betrayal, of being unloved, because Walter wasn't supposed to be in Leipzig, but in Dresden. Rose now lived in Leipzig; that was common knowledge.

In the beginning, when she'd been married for a year and was expecting Max, she'd met Elise in a coffee shop on Karolinenstrasse, not far from Walter's office; she'd seen Walter walk by in the company of a woman, a woman older than herself. Something about the way they were together affected her; she had that pain in her chest – her heart? – and for a moment she'd thought she might faint. Elise noticed her unease, and Sonia had blamed it on the pregnancy.

Nuremberg's Jewish community was large, but in due course she'd met everyone in their milieu, including the woman she'd seen with

Walter, Rose Dessauer. Sonia arranged to have afternoon coffee with Tante Gusti and asked the question outright – had Walter ever been in love with Rose Dessauer? Tante Gusti had fidgeted and sighed and then seemed to make up her mind and said, "My dear, he was in love with her when they were young, in their twenties. They're the same age and more or less grew up together – the Dessauers are distant cousins. Everyone thought they would get married. But she married someone else during the war, while he was away. He was very hurt, and it took him some time to recover. We were all very happy when he fell in love with you." She smiled at Sonia. But a mean little voice in Sonia's mind said, "Does he love you? Really love you?"

She'd cried on and off for several months and wondered how she could bear it until she came to realise that she was his wife, after all, and he seemed happy with her in most ways that mattered. It occurred to her that maybe she should try to put thoughts of other women out of her mind because there was really nothing she could do about them. Easier said than done, because he occasionally came home very late and he'd say – and it was probably true at least some of the time – that he'd been out drinking with some army friends – sometimes the Jewish veterans and sometimes Benno and the others.

She wondered whether there were women at these gatherings. Some men had mistresses as a matter of course. She had no way of knowing. She tried to distract herself by giving her mind something to do, like sorting out the accounts or planning the family holidays. Her thoughts kept returning to this issue of Walter's faithfulness or lack of it. After a while, she concluded that the problem was Walter's fondness for excess. He liked eating and drinking, he liked sex, he liked to laugh and tell stories and to travel and meet new people; he also liked his work – he had a large appetite for life.

He wasn't a handsome man like his friend Benno Martin. His nose was too big, his eyes too small. He was much older than she was. Nevertheless, she found him attractive, and she noticed that other women did so too. Newly married, she had watched anxiously as they turned to him like flowers to the sun. Friends who were brainy, those who were practical, or sporty, even some who didn't much like men – they would look at him with a fond expression, which she half grew to expect. He didn't seem to do anything to make it happen; if he came home when they were visiting, the change happened as he walked in. They sat up straight and preened, tried to sparkle, to be witty. With maids, waitresses and Helena's teachers, it was the same. He liked people in general and women in particular, especially if they were clever. He would respond, and before she knew how it happened, she felt left out, a spectator. She'd wondered whether she was being oversensitive, until she'd found out about Rose.

It was so complicated. Walter wasn't cruel or unkind. She knew he had no wish to hurt her. She ached because she didn't know what he really felt about her. He was kind to most people as far as she could tell. He and she were different. He was a professional man, whereas she was good at practical everyday things, like cooking and managing the household. He didn't notice much, didn't appreciate that the servants were devoted to her. Greta, who'd been with the family for a long time, seemed to know how she felt and would at times be particularly kind to her, as if their roles were reversed and she was the mistress rather than Sonia.

When she'd been married for several years and had gained confidence, she challenged Walter outright about Rose. He told her that they were old friends. "There's nothing to worry about, my dear." He'd been very nice to her for a while and bought her a gold ring with a lovely emerald. She'd been delighted with the gift until the thought occurred to her that it was a guilt offering. She hadn't worn it since.

SEVEN

A few months later, on a hot summer afternoon, Fanny arrived at Pierckheimerstrasse. She was wearing a summer dress and a wide-brimmed sun hat. Sonia greeted her sister at the door, kissing her.

"How is Rudi?" she asked.

"Spending the afternoon with Otto's niece, whom he loves. She has kindly agreed to take him off my hands for a couple of hours. How are the children?" asked Fanny, removing her hat.

"Helena has gone to swim at the river with Lore and some other friends."

"The river?"

"We're *unerwünscht* at the pool."

"There too? I hadn't realised. Where's Max?"

"In his room, grounded. He was rude to me, and his father overheard," said Sonia.

"Shall I visit him later?"

"He'd love to see you."

They walked through the living room onto the terrace.

"How's Otto?" asked Sonia.

"Trouble with his heart again; he's taking it easy. No more than usual. He mustn't overdo it."

Sonia's private opinion was that Otto did not have enough to do. He'd always seemed older than his age, and he'd taken the loss of his job as a salesman for a toy manufacturer as if it were a gift, having inherited enough capital to enable his family to live in comfort. He spent his time reading, eating, with an occasional walk in the afternoon.

In the pool of shade beneath the cherry tree, Elise reclined in a striped deckchair, fanning herself with her hat. A white cloth covered a low table laid with cups and plates. Elise waved a greeting as they crossed the lawn.

Fanny removed her hat and looked around with a sigh of pleasure. "This garden is always beautiful!"

Settling into her chair, Sonia said, "No shouting boys; no football on the lawn, peace and quiet."

Elise and Fanny knew about the abrupt spurning, the isolation which had become the rule.

"How is Max these days?" asked Elise.

"He's grieving, I think. It was a terrible shock, particularly where Kris is concerned. Mind you, I could never warm to Kris's mother."

Greta appeared with a laden tray, and the conversation ceased until she left.

Sonia poured coffee and served the chocolate cake.

Elise said, "Last time I visited, Max was also grounded – something to do with an apple tart?"

"Yes, he'd polished off an entire apple tart. I was expecting visitors; you can imagine how cross I was."

"Boys are always hungry."

Black cherries were piled on a platter, their fine stalks barely visible against the dark shiny flesh. Fanny chose one and ate it, placing the stone on the rim of her plate.

Greta reappeared; Sonia was wanted at the front door.

"Excuse me," said Sonia. She walked briskly over the lawn and disappeared into the house.

A small splash erupted in Fanny's cup of coffee, making Fanny start.

"What was that?" asked Elise.

Fanny peered into her cup. Something small and round bobbed in her coffee – she spooned it out. "A cherry stone!" she said. She placed it tidily on her plate and looked up. A pair of large soles was visible among the foliage. Above them, Max's smiling face peered down at her.

"Max! What are you doing there?"

"Eating cherries."

"Come right down, you naughty boy."

"I don't want to."

Fanny lay back in her deckchair, looking up. "You can't stay there all afternoon. Max, your father will punish you again if he hears you escaped. Do be sensible."

Elise said, "Come down now. You can get back to your room without your mother noticing."

"She's in the hall; she'd see me," said Max.

"Hide behind the sofa in the living room until your mother returns. You can go upstairs when the coast is clear. Here, have my chocolate cake. I'll come and see you later."

"You won't tell?"

"No, we won't. Hurry, your poor mother will be back any minute."

He swung himself down quickly and crouched beside her. His brown hair was tousled, his eyes bright. "That apple tart story is from ages ago. I ate it with Kris and the others; we were hungry."

Fanny held out her plate. "Go now!"

He grabbed the slice of cake – "Thanks!" – and dashed to the house.

———

Helena caught the flu and her mother obliged her to stay in bed for two days. At first she ached all over and was happy to sleep, noticing the strangeness of not wanting to get up, her bed the only place she wanted to be. Greta helped her mother apply a hot poultice to Helena's back. They told her it was linseed, a kind of thick paste wrapped in a linen tea-towel, very hot, almost burning, with a metallic kind of smell, but in fact it felt lovely once her skin accepted the heat, which seeped right through to her bones. Her mother gave her camomile tea with honey to lower her temperature and she fell asleep almost immediately and was feeling much better today. She wanted to get up, but her mother wouldn't hear of it. Already she felt confined, the day interminable.

"Can we look at your jewels in the ivory box this morning?" she'd asked.

"Yes, I've a little time before Frau Koslovski arrives."

Frau Koslovski was the seamstress who made all Mama's clothes and Helena's. Helena sat up and arranged the white eiderdown, almost knocking over the glass of apple juice on her bed-side table. She sat her teddy bear beside her. Her father had bought Bärchen for her when she was a baby.

Her mother plumped up the pillows behind her, including the little oval one with the embroidery of the apple-tree and the snake in the Garden of Eden, which fitted nicely behind her head. Helena smoothed out the eiderdown, stretching her arms as far as she could reach, making the surface as flat as a table; her mother spread a white linen towel onto it. "He's in the way, isn't he?" she said, reaching out to remove Bärchen.

"I want him here," protested Helena. Her mother thought she was too old to have a teddy-bear, but Helena refused to be without him. She could hear her mother's quick steps on the floorboards as she crossed the landing to her bedroom to fetch the ivory jewellery box. It had come from China a long time ago. Her mother had noticed it in a Berlin antique shop and couldn't forget it, so in the end her father had bought it for her. It was covered in an intricate relief of tiny people in procession among miniature palm trees. It had a small silver keyhole with a small silver key. Inside, the two trays were lined with dark blue velvet picked out in gold.

They emptied out the compartments with care, one item after the other, and laid them on the towel. Helena was fond of this game which her mother played with her from time to time. The best part was her mother telling stories about who had given what to whom, and why and when. As she answered Helena's questions her mother moved around the room, tidying.

"The big ring?"

"The one with the limpid green square stone in the plain gold setting? From your father."

"Limpid?"

"Clear. You can see all the way through."

"It's lovely, why don't you wear it?"

"Yes, it's nice. I do wear it sometimes, but it's a little heavy, not comfortable."

"The big gold brooch with the pearls. Father gave you this when I was born."

"That's right."

"What did you get when Max was born, then?"

"A necklace."

"Which necklace?"

"It's not here; it's at the bank."

"The bank?"

"It's safer there. It's in a box with important papers and some other old jewellery, in their vault."

"Is it not safe here?"

"Helena, do stop asking so many questions, it's tiresome."

An oval brooch with the profile of a lady on it, black on white, was a source of frustration. Her mother said it was the portrait of one of Helena's great-grandmothers, but the profile looked too young to be anyone's grandmother. Besides, Helena preferred proper portraits where you could see the person's face and the colour of their hair and their eyes looking out of the picture at you, and you could look back at them as if they were right there in the room, and feel what kind of person they were. Paintings like the ancestor miniatures in her father's study.

Helena was fond of a long necklace of interlocked silver leaves her mother had received from her parents for her twenty-first birthday and which would be Helena's when she was twenty-one and grown-up, or when she got engaged, whichever came first. Helena loved to hear her mother say that: "When you are twenty-one or when you get engaged, whichever comes first." She couldn't wait.

A few weeks later, Sonia stood in the kitchen, lost in thought, waiting for the kettle to boil. It was late, almost midnight. An infusion of chamomile would help her sleep.

The kitchen was quiet except for the clock's tick-tock. The lamp above the wooden table cast a pool of light on its scrubbed surface. She suddenly came to without knowing why – had there been a noise? Then it came again, a light knock on the door to the garden. She was on her own with the children and Oma; Walter was due back soon. She opened the cutlery drawer and took out a carving knife that she held pointing down, hidden in the folds of her skirt. She unlocked the door quickly and opened it. The person in the garden shrank back into the darkness. A young woman, cringing.

"Who are you? What do you want?" Sonia's voice sounded harsh to her own ears.

The girl sat at the end of the table, eyes cast down. Her face was very pale, her straight fair hair tied back in a long ponytail. She was pregnant, her hands crossed over her swollen belly. The steam from her cup of tea curled upwards, disappearing into the dark above the lamplight. Sonia and Walter sat on either side of the table. The kitchen clock ticked, the only sound.

Sonia spoke in dialect, "I was surprised when your mother didn't come this week. I thought maybe she was ill." Frau Bauer was usually reliable.

In a flash, the girl said, "Mother's never ill!"

73

"They came for her yesterday?" asked Walter.

"Yesterday evening." She gulped. She was trying not to cry.

Walter said, "My child, tell me what happened."

"We don't know where she is... She has practically nothing with her, no warm clothes. The SA came, a bunch of them. They made a terrible noise, hammering on the door, swearing and shouting." A tear rolled down her cheek.

"It was late, we were getting ready for bed, my mother was already in her nightdress. I managed to give her a shawl before... My brother tried to hold on to her, but they beat him with a truncheon; they pulled her out of his arms. We got him to hospital – head injuries. He's unconscious. They're not sure he'll survive. No one will tell us where she is."

"The police?"

"They say they don't know anything. I'm scared of going to the SA like this," she said, indicating her belly with her chin.

"Anyone else you've asked?"

"The others from her group are gone, the comrades, I mean. People say they've run away to Moscow. I don't believe it. I think they've been taken."

"I'll see," said Walter. "I'll make enquiries."

They gave her some money; she said they had enough food. Her husband was employed by the railways. He was at work that night and didn't know she'd gone to the Mannheims for help. He wouldn't have allowed it. She seemed like a wraith, almost absent, except for her belly. Sonia reminded her to drink the tea and she complied.

Walter would see what could be done; they agreed that Sonia would bring her news when there was some. Sonia would walk her to the tram stop. Walter said, "If I came with you, and we were stopped, you could be in worse trouble."

She nodded, understanding the risk.

Sonia left with the girl through the garden. Not far to go.

When she returned, Walter was in his study. In the kitchen, Sonia poured her cold tea into the sink and set the kettle to boil. She waited leaning against the sideboard, her arms crossed. She prepared a fresh infusion. Carrying her cup, she went to Walter's study, and settled in one of the armchairs. Walter stopped reading and leant back, his hands folded across his waistcoat.

Sonia blew on her tea and took a sip. "Their neighbourhood is no more than a village. They're all related to each other. How do the Nazis manage to entice people to such treachery, to get them to betray one of their own, a *Landsman*?"

"Frau Bauer must have assumed she was safe, that she could trust people not to talk. Like us in our community, I suppose. Except that no Jew can become a Nazi, so we're safe from that particular treachery."

"You'll have to ask Benno where she is," said Sonia firmly.

"Ask Benno about a washer-woman? A communist washer-woman?"

"She's been with us for almost twenty years; she's been a loyal servant. More than that. She's a friend and a good woman." A tear trickled down her face.

Walter said wryly, "He'll not be pleased."

EIGHT

Deputy Commissioner of Police Dr Benno Franz Theodor Martin woke to his wife's gentle snores just before the alarm rang. He reached for the clock, silenced it, thrust aside the warm eiderdown and swung his legs out of the high bed. He could hear a bird calling in the garden, clear and purposeful. Leaning out the window, he peered up at the sky – cloudless, an auspicious start.

For several chilly minutes, he executed vigorous exercises in front of the open window, then padded to the bathroom where he washed and shaved, edging the razor around the curved scar under his left cheekbone. He selected his best uniform from the wardrobe and dressed quickly. His polished boots stood outside the bedroom door. An enticing aroma of coffee wafted up from below. He pulled the boots on, grunting with the final tug – he should really exercise more. After a final examination in the mirror, pulling at the sleeves of his jacket, checking the Van Epp insignia on his sleeve and the Iron Crosses, his hair combed, his tie straightened, he left the room, closing the door with care so as not to disturb his wife.

In the breakfast room a single setting had been laid on the starched white tablecloth. He unfolded his napkin and reached for a crisp *Brötchen* in the silver basket. There was butter, cheese, the usual platter of cold meats, and homemade blueberry jam in a crystal bowl. The maid in her black dress and white apron bobbed a greeting and poured his coffee without a word.

He unfolded the *Völkischer Beobachter* as he ate, scanned it – another article in praise of *Gau* Leader Streicher, accompanied by a photo with Hitler dating from the early days of the Nazi Party, when it was still a ragtag political movement. In those days he'd arrested Streicher more than once, kept him in the cells for the night to prevent him from inciting further trouble. His father had preached, "Always be civil, always." Animosity is unhelpful. He'd found it useful advice. One never knew when a contact might prove useful. Streicher was a perfect example; who'd have predicted the Nazis would come to rule the roost?

He turned the pages of the newspaper – propaganda and more propaganda – how do they expect to maintain their readership? Not that he would cancel his subscription. One needed to know the party's slant on events. Besides, word of the cancellation might get out and cause unhelpful speculation. He picked up the *Frankfurter Zeitung*[1], a newspaper that took itself seriously. He glanced at his watch – still time enough for him to read the paper's analysis of the state of the nation's finances.

He made the most of the quiet moment, knowing change was imminent. All the elements were in place. Events might unfold differently from the way he'd planned them; life could be messy. In a way, this was like wartime because only the starting point was knowable. Nothing ventured, nothing gained – he enjoyed a gamble. Until now he'd succeeded more often than not. He was almost sure Streicher would prevail.

After breakfast, he climbed the stairs two at a time to take leave of his wife. She was sitting up in bed with a breakfast tray on her lap, her hair tousled, her cheeks pink. He handed her the newspapers. "Nothing interesting."

She smiled at him, and he bent to kiss her. He'd married late because of the war. Their one son was coming along nicely, reminded him of himself at the same age.

"I hope your meeting goes well," she said.

The maid was waiting in the hall, holding his leather belt and his hat with the Bavarian police emblem. The police headquarters were a fifteen minutes walk away, and church bells were ringing; it was seven o'clock. Hitler would arrive from Munich in three hours' time. Hitler was not an early riser. Dr Martin kept a good pace as he walked through the silent streets. He passed a neighbour and acknowledged him with a nod. The man was a Jew, but no one was likely to witness the greeting this early in the day.

At the office, this first quiet hour was his most productive. He would finish preparing for the big meeting and review the action plan for the forthcoming rally, the first since Hitler's ascent to power. They'd decided to name it "The Victory Rally".

His secretary placed the files of the '27 and '29 rallies on his desk. Then she brought him a cup of good coffee. She had it made specially for him because he didn't like the cafeteria's brew.

"Von Malsen?" he asked.

"Not in yet."

No sign on her face of what she thought, either of his question or of Von Malsen's absence. She was renowned for her inscrutability. He liked that. He also liked her trustworthiness and that she understood the workings of power in the city – better than Von Malsen any day. A gem, though not the prettiest bird in the tree. He didn't find redheads attractive; besides, she was ageing fast, a war widow needing the work. He took her out to lunch once a year around Christmas, somewhere expensive, to thank her and give her some fun. They got on well. He reflected on his luck: he got along with almost everyone. He was sometimes surprised that people liked him as much as they seemed to – from his wife to the court judges, from the mail-room clerks to the Jews. His popularity helped him achieve what really mattered, which at the moment was the establishment of a collegial understanding between his people and the Gau administration, despite Von Malsen's exasperating propensity for mucking things up.

He was probably out on his morning ride. Dr Martin had to admit that he was an impressive sight, a superb rider on a superb beast from the Von Malsen stud farm. In his elegant black uniform, he appeared the embodiment of the SS warrior caste. Dr Martin scowled. Beneath his polished appearance, Von Malsen was a complete fool, ignorant of policing and politics, incapable of realising the depths of his own incompetence, an incompetence which most if not all the members of Nuremberg's police corps had come to recognise. His record was abysmal. The appointment was a widely acknowledged travesty – in reality, the man in charge at Nuremberg's Police Commission was none other than Dr Martin himself.

Had he been the new deputy commissioner, Dr Martin would have scrutinised the latest reports, reviewed them with the responsible section heads, inspected every police station, from the smallest suburban post to the headquarters on the Jakobsplatz, as well as the arsenal and the prison. He'd have checked the readiness and fitness of the men and increased the intensity of their training – he'd have learnt everything there was to know about the local force and shown them who was boss, whereas Von Malsen was content to attend the routine morning meetings, during which he rarely failed to display what Dr Martin described (to his wife and one or two trustworthy friends) as "fathomless stupidity". Von Malsen would produce a little notebook from his breast pocket in which he wrote down facts he presumably deemed important, though Dr Martin had failed to observe any significant action following the note-taking. At lunchtime, Von Malsen would disappear with his horse-loving cronies to one or another of Nuremberg's better restaurants, returning in mid-afternoon to doze at his desk. Among the police rank and file, Von Malsen's nickname was "The Dud".

When Von Malsen first arrived, Dr Martin had briefed him with care and emphasised how important it was to maintain a good rapport with Streicher and the upper echelons of the Gau. He'd explained how nothing could be achieved in Nuremberg without Streicher's consent, however deranged Streicher might appear. But Von Malsen seemed unable to grasp the implications of the local set-up. Though he and Streicher manifested an equal devotion to the Nazi Party, he had condescended to Streicher with the contempt of an aristocrat for a yokel: arrogance and snobbery layered over the stupidity. In private, Von Malsen's remarks about the Gau were marked by disdain and derision.

In Nuremberg, everyone knew about Streicher's legendary rise to the rank of officer during the war, his energy and courage in battle overcoming – in Dr Martin's view – the double disadvantage of mediocre intelligence and a lack of education. He was a hero of the people: Iron Cross First and Second Class, a genuine leader of men. They flocked to his weekly speeches where he ranted and he raved. They lapped up his outrageous rhetoric, revelled in his obscene antisemitism. Recruits flocked to his SA cohorts. Von Malsen, on the other hand, lacked charisma entirely. However he was a member of the elite SS officers' corps, an absolute requirement for the post of Commissioner of Police.

In Himmler's defence, the pool of available SS officers was limited. Candidates applying to join the SS were required to have a solid war record and prove incontrovertible Aryan descent since the year 1750.

Dr Martin squared his shoulders. Should he choose to apply, he would pass muster on both counts.

Of course, one would also have to join the Nazi Party. Some of his friends had taken the plunge, and Dr Martin felt the prickle of temptation. He knew that most of his men would follow if he joined. There was a scattering of Nazi sympathisers among them, whom he kept a close eye on. With a sigh, Dr Martin curbed a recurrent desire to contemplate what he might have achieved had he been born an aristocrat. It was rumoured that against all evidence to the contrary, Himmler believed that aristocrats were born to lead.

Streicher had recently hinted that he'd like his SA to merge with the police. Dr Martin could understand the craving for the legitimacy of the police's professional mantle. Unfortunately, it was out of the question. The SA was a gang of untrained thugs; his men would only tolerate them occasionally, when necessary.

Knowing that the situation might evolve, he'd taken great care that Streicher should remain unaware of his repugnance. He'd kept Von Malsen's derogatory comments about the Gau administration to himself; discussions with his superior were confidential. But about ten days ago, in response to a direct question from Streicher, he'd admitted that Von Malsen appeared to nurture "a certain enmity" towards Gau staff. He'd spoken with suitable reluctance. Streicher already knew everything he'd told him, but even so – the fire had been fanned.

A week later, Von Malsen barged into his office, strode over to his desk, shoving a sheet of paper under his nose. "Read this! The flaming impudence!"

As Dr Martin read the letter, Von Malsen paced up and down, pausing by the window to glance down at the bustling Jakobsplatz before returning to stand in front of Dr Martin's desk, rocking on his heels, his thumbs tucked in his belt.

Dr Martin examined the letter: it was typed on the familiar Gau letterhead. He noted that it did not emanate from Streicher himself but from one of his aides. It referred to Nuremberg's Theatre, a favourite gathering place for Nuremberg's wealthier citizens and for Gau worthies such as Streicher and his entourage, including on occasion Dr Martin himself. The theatre was one of the least painful ways of spending time with Streicher; even Streicher had to shut up during performances.

The author of the letter drew Von Malsen's attention to a rule which existed to protect the actresses from the attentions of their fervid public, limiting visitor access to the theatre's wings. The letter did not mention – but everyone knew – that members of the theatre's inner circle (such as Dr Martin and Streicher) ignored this rule and visited the actresses whenever they pleased. The writer went on to suggest that Freiherr Von Malsen-Ponickau "should control his interest in what is happening in the wings and refrain from questionable visits to the Nuremberg Theatre."

Streicher would know exactly what was in that letter, no doubt about it, thought Dr Martin. He'd probably dictated it himself.

"The impertinence!" hissed Von Malsen.

The inevitable had happened. It was paramount to avoid a rift with the all-important Gau; he would distance himself from Von Malsen. It was time to take sides.

In a quiet corner of the pub a week or so later, at the end of a day's work, Dr Martin sat at ease in the company of Julius Streicher. The waitress brought them Steins brimming with froth. He took an appreciative first gulp and wiped the foam off his upper lip. Streicher drank deeply. Then he said, "Do you know what he's done now?" and launched into a tirade against Von Malsen. Dr Martin had heard these diatribes many times. After listening for some minutes, he chose to gently remind Streicher of his, Streicher's, unquestionable prominence as a founding member of the Nazi Party, as leader of the Franconia Gau, and a decorated war veteran with indubitable heroic acts to his record.

"It is known that the Führer trusts you absolutely. Besides which, you are without doubt the most eminent personality in Franconia. How can a newcomer like Von Malsen-Ponickau compare?"

In the friendly exchange that followed, Dr Martin mentioned the forthcoming meeting with the Führer. It was easy to let slip that Von Malsen had taken the lead and had decreed that he alone would attend as the sole representative of the police.

"What?" exclaimed Streicher, sitting bolt upright. "That idiot's coming without you? He's never run a rally – what does he know? My word, he's bypassing you, isn't he? Leaving you to scratch your arse at headquarters! Punishing you for taking my side! You're ten times, a hundred times the man he is! You're the one who should be cracking the whip, not that imbecile!"

Dr Martin shrugged. He said nothing, though he was in complete agreement with Streicher. He was by far the man best qualified to run this rally. In fact, he was the man most qualified to run the entire Nuremberg police force – by dint of training, experience and temperament – an opinion he knew was shared by the upper echelons at national headquarters, including Himmler himself.

Streicher held up a hand. "Not another word! I can sort this out, I, Julius Streicher!" He thumped his chest. "It's the least I can do!" His tone was triumphant.

"Sort this out?"

"I want you there!" trumpeted Streicher.

Dr Martin glanced around, reminding Streicher that someone might overhear him.

Streicher lowered his voice and leaned forward, "I'm inviting you as my expert, to advise me! That hound dog can't do a damned thing about it! What d'you think? Hey?"

Dr Martin swirled the beer in his tankard and was silent for a moment. Then he looked up. "Very good of you, Streicher! I'll be there on the day."

All he had to do was show up today for the meeting at the Grand Hotel.

––––––

And so it happened that he joined Streicher's retinue and entered the conference room around ten o'clock that morning, to a chorus of *Heil Hitler,* clicking heels and thrust-out arms. The large room had been thoroughly Nazified. A giant scarlet flag draped the far wall from ceiling to floor, its black swastika relentlessly echoed on armbands, badges, fanions, on the miniature red flags in decorative clusters along the centre of the polished conference table, and on the notepaper and pencils aligned in front of every chair.

Von Malsen was standing at the foot of the flag among a group of city council officials. Dr Martin watched him out of the corner of his eye, waiting for him to notice his presence, which did not take long. As Von Malsen drew near, he decided to sit at the table and chat with an old acquaintance.

Von Malsen tapped his shoulder to get his attention.

"Come!" he said, as if addressing a dog.

Dr Martin took leave of his friend and rose without haste, drawing himself up to his full height, towering over Von Malsen. He was aware of Streicher's watchful gaze as they left the room

Von Malsen made sure the door was shut before addressing Dr Martin. He snapped, "My orders were for you to remain at headquarters!"

The door opened again, and one of Streicher's people came into the corridor, nodding to them in casual acknowledgement before lighting a cigarette. Dr Martin repressed a smile. In a calm voice he said, "Gauleiter Streicher requested my presence today."

Constrained by the presence of a witness, Von Malsen could only glare furiously and exclaim, "Well!"

Saluting smartly, Dr Martin returned to the conference room, leaving him on his own. A short time later Hitler arrived, triggering another full round of salutes, and the meeting began. It ran smoothly enough; there were no surprises. After a pleasant lunch – the hotel staff bursting with pride to be serving their Führer – they drove in convoy to the rally grounds for Hitler to inspect the recently completed grandstand. Dr Martin was naturally invited to join Streicher in his car and took the opportunity to report briefly on his encounter with Von Malsen. Streicher fumed, "I'll get that bastard; wait and see!"

Crowds of cheering citizens lined the streets, craning to see the Führer and their favourite local politician, Streicher. When the procession reached the rally grounds, Streicher alighted and waved to his enthusiastic followers, followed by Dr Martin.

Von Malsen stood some distance away, glaring. He roared at Dr Martin, "Polizeioberkommissar Martin! Return to headquarters! Immediately!" The watching public fell silent, aware that something unusual was taking place.

Dr Martin gave no sign of having heard the order. He made not the slightest gesture in Von Malsen's direction, though he was aware that Von Malsen was approaching. When he was near, Dr Martin addressed him in a mild tone. "Gauleiter Streicher personally requested my presence here today. Please discuss your objections with him."

He turned to Streicher and said, "Von Malsen is ordering me to leave."

The scene was set. This was Streicher's call. Streicher strode towards Von Malsen, exuding menace, shoulders rolling like a backstreet fighter. The back of his thick neck turned red.

Dr Martin was aware of the Führer standing nearby, his back to the scene.

Streicher roared at Von Malsen. "You're a swine, d'you hear!" He brandished his riding crop in his gloved hand. "You dare to challenge me! On my home turf! Do that again, and I'll whip you!" Streicher slashed the riding crop against his boot.

Von Malsen flinched.

The watching crowd held its collective breath.

Bull-like, Streicher thrust his bald head forward. "Should I express the wish to speak to Dr Martin, you have no business countermanding that order! As far as I am concerned, the one and only head of the Police Commission is Dr Martin! Never you!" Taking a breath, he roared again, spittle flying. "You've no business here, you son of a bitch!"

In a quieter tone, he continued, "Why don't you take off? Go away now. Go back to wherever you came from! Go mind your damned estate!"

They were standing face to face, Von Malsen pale, shrinking, Streicher in his element. The crowd was enthralled. The Führer must have heard the shouting, but betrayed no interest, gave no sign of having noticed. Now! thought Dr Martin; this was Von Malsen's moment, when he might confront Streicher directly, man to man. What would he do?

Von Malsen reached into his pocket and pulled out his notebook and a pencil. He wrote feverishly.

Streicher's expression turned to disgust, and he roared again, "You're nothing but a dirty hound, d'you hear? What's more, you're a coward, a coward! Write that down in your little book, Freiherr Von Malsen-Ponickau; write down that today Gauleiter Julius Streicher called you," and he spat out his final words of contempt, "a filthy degenerate dog!"

He turned his back on Von Malsen and rejoined Dr Martin.

By the time they'd caught up with the Führer's group, Von Malsen had disappeared.

NINE

"Who's to be Himmler's next deputy in Nuremberg?" asked Sonia as Walter walked into the bedroom. She was already in her nightgown, brushing her hair in long regular strokes.

"Von Obernitz, the top guy at the SA Franconia group."

Sonia stopped brushing and looked at him in the mirror. "What's he like?"

"No police experience. Barbarian. Reputation for arrogance, cruelty and stupidity."

Sonia put down her brush and got up from her stool as Walter removed his jacket. He gave it to her, sat down and bent over to untie his shoelaces. She draped the jacket over a coat hanger and hung it in the cupboard. "Not an improvement then. How will he get along with Streicher, do you think?"

"They know each other well, work hand in glove from what I've heard. Mind you, Streicher's never easy. There's always a possibility they'll fall out. Even Benno has trouble with him sometimes." Walter stood up to unbuckle his belt.

Sonia took the trousers. "I thought Streicher liked Benno."

"Everyone likes Benno. Hitler likes him too," said Walter irritably, pulling on his pyjamas. He went to brush his teeth.

When he returned, Sonia was sitting in front of her dressing table, rubbing cream into her hands in a slow repetitive motion. She said, "Even though Streicher is a difficult customer, people say he's infatuated with Benno."

"Infatuated? Who says that?"

"Someone I once knew whose husband worked at the city council. He attended meetings with both Streicher and Benno. He said that Streicher fawned over Benno. He said it was embarrassing."

"They're mates, no doubt about it. But from there to fawning..."

"I'd have thought Streicher would be jealous of Benno, his looks, his popularity – there's a story about a blanket?" Sonia said.

"That story's rubbish – typical Streicher propaganda."

"Well?" said Sonia.

Walter hated gossip, but he gave in. "About ten years ago, when the Nazis and the communists brawled in the streets and Streicher was in and out of prison like the proverbial cuckoo from a cuckoo clock, Benno happened to be on duty when Streicher was arrested. Streicher complained of the cold in his cell and Benno brought him another blanket."

"That's it?"

"That's it."

"Ridiculous, going on as if Benno had saved his life."

"Well, others would probably not have bothered. They'd have let him shiver and freeze through the night. But Streicher's reaction is typical of the man – either raising people up to the gods or treating them like vermin. Nothing in between, always in deadly earnest. Some might say, getting it wrong every time."

"An act of ordinary consideration."

"Benno understands people better than most. Streicher was frequently in prison; he'd often have experienced rough treatment and probably expected more of the same."

"Like the SA's appalling behaviour when they've got someone in their clutches."

Walter nodded. "They're worse, but yes, Benno's show of humanity towards Streicher when he was down would go a long way with him."

Sonia finished putting night-cream on her face and climbed into the high bed. She leaned back against the pillows and absent-mindedly smoothed down the white eiderdown. "He could have told someone else to bring Streicher the blanket."

"What do you mean?"

"Benno didn't have to do it himself. He could have handed the task to a subordinate."

"True." Walter settled in bed beside her. "There may not have been anyone else around."

"Benno was hedging his bets. The Nazis were gaining popular support, and he probably thought there was no harm in being friendly."

"He's a good chap, Sonia."

"You always say that."

"Because it's true. Besides, there are three hundred years of public service in the Martin family – dedication to duty, commitment to justice, that sort of thing; his brothers, his father, the lot of them."

"Isn't he in line to become police president since he's joined the party?" She was on thin ice now; Walter hated any mention of Benno's betrayal.

"Being a party member is not enough; he'd have to join the SS as well."

"But otherwise?"

"Otherwise, he's the best man for the job, no doubt about it. He's the one in charge at the Jakobsplatz, has been for some years. Himmler counts on him to keep things in order, no matter who appears to be the boss."

After a moment, Sonia said, "Streicher must believe Benno is truly sympathetic to the cause, or he wouldn't like him so much."

"Benno's a born diplomat. Who knows what he's led the Nazis to think. He's probably convinced them he's more use to them outside the SS than inside."

"And is he?" Sonia stared Walter down.

"Who knows. Good night, Sonia."

He turned his back on her and switched off his bedside lamp.

On the anniversary of Leo's death, Walter and Oma never failed to visit Leo's grave. In the enclosed Jewish cemetery, Leo's black obelisk stood among the tallest. Their father's grave was at the other end of the burial ground, where the gravestones were modest and lay flat on the ground.

We've lost the habit of humility, thought Walter as he placed the ritual pebble on the grave. He turned to the graves of the other war dead, most of whom he'd known. The columns stood crowded together, a small grove of death, mounds of pebbles at their feet. His mother visited the grave every week. The other mothers probably did too.

The anniversary visit had been preceded by lunch with his mother, just the two of them. On the mantelpiece, a memorial candle flickered in front of Leo's framed photograph, Leo looking younger than his twenty-three years, sitting up straight and tidy. The uniform suited him, though the quizzical gleam in his eye seemed at odds with it.

Walter laid down his knife and fork, wiped his mouth with his napkin and said, "Mother, it may be unwise to attend the service on Shabbat." Bands of SA roamed the streets around the synagogue on Saturdays.

"Unwise?" she asked, with a touch of irony.

"Not safe. That's the gist of it. Simply not safe. Even if I'm around."

"*Kvatsch!*" said his mother firmly.

Walter sighed. Oma pursed her mouth and said, "You're worried because Arlene Blum was pushed around by some louts on the Hauptplatz." Earlier that month, the Hauptplatz had undergone an official renaming to Adolf Hitler Platz. Calling it by its old name could get people into trouble.

She gathered the plates and cutlery. "Let me tell you, I don't propose to wear a badge with a shiny Mogen Dovid in the middle – 'Come and get me!'"

Walter had seen the brooch in question. It was discreet, the Star of David hardly noticeable. Arlene was a distant cousin, younger and less confident than Oma. Walter had visited her after the incident. She'd been afraid of the group from the moment she'd noticed it – ordinary young men, not SA, standing outside a pub, drinking. They'd probably seen she was frightened and had yelled drunken insults and obscenities that shocked her, if she understood them at all.

In her hurry to get away, she'd stumbled and fallen. They'd jeered as a passer-by, someone she vaguely knew, helped her up and took her home. She was unhurt but upset. Walter hadn't asked her what had been shouted; she'd said over and over she couldn't possibly repeat it. In the retelling, much was made of the brooch. Walter thought it possible, even likely, that the hecklers hadn't noticed it. Arlene was recognisably Jewish. So was his mother, come to think of it.

"You're being unfair to Arlene," said Walter.

"Asking for trouble," she said and placed the dishes on the trolley.

"She may move in with her sister."

"Afraid to be on her own. Walter, you're not suggesting I stay away from shul on Leo's yahrzeit, are you?"

Walter would be called to the Torah during the service, in memory of his brother. In two months' time, he'd be called again, for his father.

He'd been sixteen when his father died of a heart attack. Every day for a year, she'd woken him before dawn; in the half-light he'd made his way to the big synagogue where he joined the cluster of men facing the ark to recite morning prayers and the Kaddish. Once a week, Leo had come too. The cadence of the Hebrew words had grown on Walter. He found them grave, even beautiful. The gathering every morning with the same men, men who had known his father, the praying together, seemed to serve a purpose, to provide a bulwark against the tremendous sense of loss. Nowadays, he didn't tend towards religion, not believing in anything since the war, when God had been notable for His absence. After Leo died, he'd recited the prayer every morning anyway as a way of keeping him close. He attended the services on the anniversaries of the deaths of his brother and his father for his own sake as much as for his mother's. With the deteriorating political situation, he attended services more often anyway, like many others. People met in the synagogue and exchanged news which was otherwise hard to come by. Jewish broadsheets were censored and the main newspapers did not report what the Nazis were doing to the Jews.

He told his mother, "I would rather you stayed home; I'd be grateful if you did so until quiet returns."

"Walter, I don't give in to bullies. Besides, I'll surely be safe if you wait for me." They would walk home; she wouldn't take the tram or a taxi, not on Shabbat. "It's not just me, Mother. The board has discussed this. We're very concerned. We're calling for volunteers. We'll have two men on guard outside – veterans, of course."

"Two won't make much difference."

"We discussed it with the Orthodox, and they've concluded like we did that too many guards might seem a provocation." It was impossible to know where an objection might come from or on what grounds, but should the Jews act in any way which attracted attention, someone somewhere would protest and create a wave of indignation resulting in new measures against them which would further embitter their lives.

On the sideboard, the coffee pot simmered on its little china heater. She poured them each a cup.

"Have you decided to accept the nomination to the board of the Central Association? Since the Chamber of Commerce has decided to manage without you?"

She was changing the subject. He knew better than to pursue the argument. He placed two lumps of sugar in his cup and stirred. The letter from Nuremberg's Chamber of Commerce had arrived a few days ago, the polite terminology barely masking the insult. They hadn't the guts to tell him to his face that they wanted him gone. He'd grown up with some of the men who now shunned him and had served with them during the war. Others were colleagues he'd worked with for twenty years or more. *Unerwünscht,* "undesirable".

The antipathy had lain deep, dormant; it seeped out like a noxious gas, invisible, persistent, penetrating everywhere.

His mother had been proud of his association with the Chamber, and of his father's before him. She minded as much as he did. He stared into the coffee as he said, "Indeed. I am available to work on behalf of the Central Association."

The Central Association of German Citizens of Jewish Faith represented Jews who considered their German identity at least as significant as their Jewishness. Their indisputable loyalty to Germany had been demonstrated during the war, when they'd risked their life to defend the Fatherland. They had fought as Germans, not as Jews, as Germans devoted to Germany, like every other German. Many had died. He'd survived and been decorated for his contribution. He loved his country – how dare anyone doubt it! He stirred fiercely, watching the coffee swirl.

For years antisemites had sung "Out with the Jews!" in Germany's backstreet pubs. One shrugged and carried on. But with the brutal expulsion from all professional bodies, cultural societies and sports clubs, the situation was unimaginably different. That song could be heard everywhere now, triumphant.

He raised his head. "Fritz Klein says that many younger doctors may be obliged to leave the Medical Association. He's still safe because of his army record."

He added, "Rosenstrauss has been obliged to abandon his beloved theatre..."

"Gusti told me the Jewish dancers at the Rot Weiss club had to leave," said his mother.

The Nazis had only been in power for only a short time, but the isolation was spreading fast, like a plague.

Walter said, "A difficult time, but it won't last. Too extreme. The wheel of fortune will turn, what is below will rise again. This government will fall, and we'll return to what we were, to normality."

His mother did not answer. They finished their coffee in silence and he helped her into her black coat, handed her the umbrella she liked to use instead of a stick. She set her black hat on her head and they left the house. A gentle rain was falling.

"Mistrust the Jew," said the decorative painting on the wall, "as sly as a fox." Large and colourful, it spread across the house's entire facade. When Walter first qualified as a lawyer, he'd searched the books for a law which would get the slur removed. Most Jewish lawyers in Nuremberg had done so at one time or another, to no avail.

Walter's regular route through the old city bypassed the fresco. The narrow streets were deserted, his footsteps the only sound. He was tired; the day had been marked by difficult decisions concerning the future of Mannheim & Loewenthal. He would have to tell Sonia about them when he got home. Then the board's meeting had run late. As he passed the Sebaldus Church, the bells rang the quarter hour. He hoped Sonia would still be up when he got home.

He thought about the work ahead. Three more rural congregations had applied to join Nuremberg's community, following the drastic deterioration in their circumstances. An initial attack on the cemetery – gravestones overturned and defaced – had been met with studied indifference by local police. The harassment had escalated: swastikas scrawled on the synagogue, people insulted in the street, children hounded on their way to school. Threatening groups interrupted the religious services, shouted invective. The final straw was a physical attack, someone seriously hurt, which triggered an exodus of Jews from the village, from homes where they had lived for generations, for the relative safety of a large city such as Hamburg or

Berlin where they might live under the protective cover of anonymity.

The few remaining Jews in these villages could no longer afford to maintain the synagogue, further their children's Jewish education or carry out wedding and funerary rituals. And so they approached Nuremberg's wealthy community and requested to come under its financial and rabbinical wings. To refuse was not an option– they could not be abandoned. Someone from the board would have to negotiate conditions with them. In his experience, the villagers tended to overestimate the community's resources; compromises would have to be worked out with people who were fragile, vulnerable. He had implemented this process a few times already and the thought of repeating it was depressing.

He'd reached the wooden bridge over the moat; beyond lay his own neighbourhood, with straight wide streets lined with tall fin-de-siècle apartment buildings. Many Jewish families lived there. For how long, he wondered. Less established than their elders, less rooted in tradition, the younger generation were leaving. Some followed the Zionists and wanted to establish a Jewish state in Palestine, giving up everything for a fantasy, a mirage. He turned from Bucherstrasse into Pierckheimerstrasse. The houses here stood in their own grounds, trees shielding them from view. A late tram rattled down the road's central strip.

He could see no one, but he felt alarmed for some reason. He walked faster; with his height, his girth and his army training, he'd put up a good fight if someone attacked him, unless there were several assailants.

They'd discussed a recent incident at the meeting – a group of louts had pawed and pushed a woman on her way to a meeting at the Community Centre. She'd fallen and broken an ankle. The Nuremberg police had not responded adequately, and the ladies demanded action. He'd been asked by the board yet again to get a word to his "friend, Dr Martin". Two other board members lived on the same street as Martin and could count on him to station a couple of policemen outside their homes during the rallies; he himself could always call on Martin should his house come under threat. But for the police to protect an identifiable Jewish institution such as the Jewish Community Centre would be a different matter altogether, given current public opinion.

One could but try. He felt deeply tired; more so than during the war, when he'd been younger and an officer in the Reichswehr, when he'd gained respect for his ability and his endurance. His religion, his race had been irrelevant. He'd belonged, almost unconditionally. Almost fifteen years had passed since then.

He arrived at the house and opened the gate. Behind the wrought-iron fence and the hedge, the front garden was narrow: a strip of lawn and a few flowering bushes. Something sweet-scented was blooming. He paused and looked up at the house in the moonlight. It was large, but not ostentatious; solid, strong, his redoubt, protecting his family and himself. At Sonia's behest, it had recently been painted a light colour, almost white.

The first row of windows was high above the heads of passers-by, their panes reflecting the moonlight, light edging the borders of the drawn curtains: Sonia was still up. Above the second row of windows was a narrow architectural frieze, something vaguely Greek. From where he stood, he could see the steep slope of the roof and the row of attic windows.

It had once happened in France during the war that the bombing paused while he was asleep, and the sudden silence woke him from a dream. He'd been walking down this path, opening the front door, entering peace and stability as he stepped over the threshold into the hall, which turned into a still mountain lake in which he swam towards the rising sun. He'd woken refreshed, confident of his future. It had been like a prediction; someone more mystically inclined might say like a blessing. He felt as if nothing truly bad could happen to them between these four solid walls. It was the only property they had left. The recent economic woes had impoverished the family. Fortunes had evaporated – the Mannheims suffering less than many, though his mother had been obliged to leave her villa. He didn't mind that she lived with them – on the contrary. For Sonia, of course, it was different.

A light had been left on for him in the enclosed porch. One of Sonia's less-likeable plants flourished there, a profusion of strong dark leaves crouching in the corner, like a belligerent guardian spirit. He opened the heavy door. He smelled the roses before he saw them, a lush arrangement of blossoms. Music drifted from the living room, something orchestral. He hung up his hat. Sonia was reading with the radio on. She smiled up at him. "I didn't hear you come in." He sat down in his armchair, and she closed her book. When the symphony ended, she switched off the radio.

"All well?" he asked.

She nodded. "Good meeting?"

"As expected. Children asleep?"

"Max may be reading under the bed covers. I've already stopped him twice." She looked at him and said, "What's troubling you, Walter?"

Walter said, "Georg and I decided today to advise our commercial clients that retaining us as their legal representatives may disadvantage them."

She didn't seem surprised.

He said, "It's a formality." For a moment he couldn't speak. He stared at the pattern in the carpet. When the emotion had passed, he said, "As you know, a few of our clients have already moved elsewhere; others will soon leave. Some may genuinely regret the step they have to take, but they'll go anyway."

"We can live more modestly."

"That would do no harm. No need to worry. I wanted you to know – a sign of the times."

Clients were increasingly uneasy about any connection to a Jewish firm, particularly one as well-known as theirs. No more lunches in the best restaurants, where their bookings were refused. Jewish-owned restaurants would host them, Jews their only clientele.

He sought to reassure her, saying, "Still plenty of work."

Some Jewish law firms had been obliged to curtail their activities for lack of staff, a few even closing down; it was rumoured the government had been dismayed to discover how many Jews had served on the front line and were therefore able to continue working thanks to the president's loyalty to his Jewish army veterans. Their numbers contradicted the antisemitic propaganda which claimed that Jewish soldiers had schemed to obtain safe assignments, away from the front line. He reminded himself again that the Nazis peddled lies intentionally, for their effect, and that there was no sense in arguing the case with them. The Nazi story bore no connection to reality. Those who invented the lies knew that, but it was difficult to keep in mind that as a group they preferred those lies to the truth.

A few new Jewish clients had approached Mannheim & Loewenthal, and he was grateful for the business. His out-of-work colleagues were facing ruin. The non-Jewish lawyers had failed to protest at the treatment of their confreres. There had been no rallying round in the face of oppression and injustice. After all, they stood to make a healthy gain from companies suddenly unable to employ Jewish lawyers. Nowadays they often dealt in cases they could not charge for, defending Jewish men arrested without reason, their desperate wives appearing at his rooms, often with a child in tow, imploring for help.

"Walter," said Sonia, leaning towards him, her blue eyes earnest, "we have to leave Germany. We must."

They had covered this ground before, more than once.

He leaned back. "Sonia, you know why I decided against leaving."

She ticked off the points on her fingers. "You think that Hitler won't last, you believe that it is your duty to stay and provide leadership to the community, and you don't think we could live anywhere else because German law is all you know. Besides which, you believe that you're too old to start afresh. We would lose absolutely everything; we'd be poverty-stricken, strangers in a strange land."

"Nothing has changed, has it?"

"Walter, they've told the entire world what they want to do, and they're carrying out their plans!"

"Not to war veterans, not to their families." He was tired of these futile discussions.

"Not yet. But if – when – the president dies, Hitler will be free to do exactly as he wishes."

He could see she was troubled. "Has something upset you?"

"Something upsetting is happening all the time!" She clutched the armrests, her fingertips white.

He realised she was trying to keep calm.

"Betty's husband was beaten by thugs on his way home; her son was attacked at school. They're leaving for Czechoslovakia. Many others are too. So should we."

More stories of suffering and disaster, more friends emigrating. Why did she have to bring this up?

"You'll miss Betty."

"Don't patronise me!" Her voice was sharp. "That's not why I want to go! I mentioned it as an example of events happening all around us, all the time. You believe that your contacts and influence will keep us safe. But the slander affects everyone; it's insidious, invisible. What appeared solid and reliable suddenly collapses into a pile of dust, like furniture infested with woodworm. Besides, they're afraid and won't take risks for us. Why should they?"

"Always the pessimist; you mustn't give up hope." He found himself reduced to repeating what his mother said. His weariness was immense. He could see that Sonia was not about to relent.

"Walter, please be sensible. If something should happen to you, God forbid, there would be no one to protect the children, your mother or me, and it would be impossible for us to get out. I am not a respected lawyer with widespread connections."

"The danger's not as great as you think; trust me. Do you think I'd keep you and the children here if I didn't believe that?"

"The breach between Jew and non-Jew is widening all the time. Can't you see? Our non-Jewish friends are abandoning us. They *have* to abandon us, or else." She wiped tears away with an angry gesture.

"My reading group met this morning. I didn't go last time, because I felt that my presence would be a problem. Then Mechtild rang and insisted I come, that it was unthinkable after all the years." Her voice trailed away. She took a breath. "You know that group, there's Gisella, whom I went to school with, and Mechtild, who was my bridesmaid. Teresa's son was born almost the same day as Max. I've known them and the others for years. We're close friends; we talk about everything. But when I arrived at the coffee shop, our usual table was empty. Not one felt able to come, not one. Someone must have spied on Mechtild, heard us on the phone, reported her or threatened her. It's not that they don't want to stay friends. They're afraid. All these senseless things going on, no law, no order, the Nazis given free rein to follow their worst impulses."

"You're upset," said Walter. He stood up. "You need to calm down."

"Of course I'm upset. How could I not be! Everything about our situation is upsetting, particularly for our children. Max will not be able to study; his education is compromised. They have no future here. They're exposed every day to Nazi propaganda, to hateful talk from German children."

"Our children are German children too! Don't allow yourself to be influenced by propaganda. Good night!"

After he'd left the room, Sonia remained hunched in the chair for a long time, her elbow on her knee, her chin in her hand.

TEN

Helena wore her white Shabbat dress and black patent leather shoes. It was late on Saturday morning and the house was hers alone until Father, Max and Oma returned from the service at the synagogue. Max was obliged to attend because he was preparing for his bar mitzvah. Her mother wasn't up yet; she would get up later, for a family lunch at Tante Gusti's.

A runner extended down the corridor from the hall to the living room. Sizing up the gap between the runner and the rug, Helena sprinted and leapt as far as she could onto the rug. She had vowed to jump the gap every single day of her life to avoid becoming like Oma who walked with a cane. Her mother said that for a woman of sixty-eight, Oma was quite fit, but she seemed very slow to Helena.

She skipped across the living room, through the French doors onto the terrace, down the stone steps and wandered over the lawn to the cherry tree with its welcoming low branch. Her mother had said that girls of eleven did not climb trees, but Helena found the urge irresistible. She reached up to the branch and lodged her foot on the familiar knot in the trunk, swinging herself up and sideways until she sat astride, legs dangling. She leant against the trunk and breathed in the musty smell of its bark. From her vantage point, she could see the whole garden and the back of the house, where a curtain fluttered at the open window to her room.

She wanted to climb higher, to reach thicker foliage where she might perch like a bird, concealed and protected, but seeing everything; grasping the trunk, she raised herself and stood on the big branch, reaching for the one above. The smooth soles of her patent leather shoes slid on the bark and she struggled to keep her balance, fell forward and collided with the tree-trunk which dealt an unfriendly blow to her chest, catching the dress. She felt the tug, heard the material rip. She caught hold of a branch, suspended by one arm, her feet scrabbling about for purchase.

<hr />

As soon as Helena appeared in the kitchen, Greta put her teacup down. Neither of them said anything. They went up to Helena's room, where Greta helped Helena change out of the torn dress into its twin, flawless and otherwise identical.

All Helena's clothes were sewn in duplicate by Frau Koslovski, her mother's Polish seamstress, because Helena was unable to remain tidy for any length of time. Eating, she spilled food or drink down her front; playing, her clothes became grubby or stained. Helena writhed under her mother's fierce displeasure, her mother who was always perfectly groomed. For Helena that goal was unachievable. Any blemished garment was to be exchanged for the identical flawless one as soon as anything went wrong, *immediately,* said her mother in tones of disapproval.

As a girl, she was supposed to be clean and pretty and wear delicate feminine clothes, whereas Helena wished she could wear *Lederhosen* more often. Short trousers were convenient for running about and the leather was impervious to harm.

With Greta's help, Helena did her best to conceal her mishaps from her mother and her friends, but she wasn't very successful. Her mother noticed anyway. She was a disappointing daughter, whereas Max was good at everything he did.

One summer morning, Helena overheard her father and mother talking about a bloodbath in Berlin.

"What bloodbath?" she asked, thinking of Bluebeard and his wives.

Her parents exchanged a glance and said that some Nazis had killed other Nazis and that she was not to ask any more questions or discuss it any further with anyone. They wouldn't say why the killings had happened. There was unrest in the streets and Helena was not to leave the house, not even to go to school. Max was to stay home too.

Helena was bored. Lore couldn't come to play, nor could she go to Lore's. She went to the kitchen and asked for a cup of milk. Greta was out and the maid was full of stories about the Berlin bloodbath, about the Brown Shirts beating people up, ganging up on the communists or the Social Democrats or on ordinary people if they did not shout *Heil Hitler* loudly enough. She didn't mention that they threatened Jews, but Helena knew that already. Father and other men from the community were guarding the synagogue at night to prevent Nazis from breaking in to steal things: some of the ritual ornaments were silver, old and valuable.

On the morning of Max's bar mitzvah, the rain stopped after breakfast. Greta helped Helena into her new ruffled petticoat, then the pink frilly dress, neat white ankle socks and her black patent leather shoes. She pinned Helena's hair back with a pink ribbon. Helena was made to stand still while Greta put finishing touches to the big bow at the back, after which Helena twirled and twirled. She ran to her mother's room to preen in front of the big mirror, but her mother wanted to get ready. "Very nice, Helena. Now please go and wait downstairs." Her mother would be wearing the special golden necklace that was usually kept in the bank's vault.

Helena wasn't good at waiting. She stood in the hall for a minute or so and then ran out into the garden.

<hr />

Helena made it back to the house and into the hall just as her mother came down the stairs, looking elegant in a soft green dress, the gold necklace and a hat. The taxi driver was standing outside the open front door, cap under arm.

"Helena!" Her mother pointed at Helena's feet.

Helena looked down: mud was spattered over her socks and shoes.

Her mother slapped her. "I told you to wait in the hall! Upstairs, quick, change! Greta!"

A grim Greta wiped Helena's shoes and helped her make a swift change into clean socks. Helena raced down the stairs to the hall, her cheek still stinging from the slap. Her mother was sitting in the taxi. Through its open door, Helena could see her elegant foot tapping an impatient cadence. She flew down the path, past the waiting driver, scrambled into the car and landed panting on the seat beside her mother. The driver slammed the door shut. As the car moved off, Helena glanced at her mother. Her face wore the tight-lipped expression Helena dreaded.

Her father, Oma and Max had left earlier, on foot. Max wore a real suit, with long trousers and a tie. People said that he was tall for a thirteen-year-old, but to Helena he looked like a child pretending to be grown-up. Her father said that after the bar mitzvah Max would be considered a man like any other in the Jewish congregation, able to lead services in the synagogue, which seemed amazing to Helena until her father added "in theory", which meant the whole thing was really a sham.

During the preceding months, she had observed Max as he studied the prayers and rituals. He'd struggled to learn his portion of Torah in Hebrew, though it was written in German letters. He was supposed to know it by heart, like a kind of magic incantation, thought Helena, which he chanted in a sing-song without knowing exactly what the words meant. He'd attended lessons with the rabbi and practiced daily for the last six months. By now he remembered the words well, but he worried because his voice was changing, swerving unpredictably into a deeper or higher register, out of control.

Helena had tried reading the portion herself and found it to be a strange jumble of letters, German characters making up the sound of Hebrew words. Father said he'd learnt to read Hebrew that way too. Helena reflected on this: she thought that it was stupid to memorise something one didn't understand. The rabbi could read Hebrew letters and understood the language. Helena had listened to Max reading the German translation: it was hard to follow, the wording old-fashioned and the story complicated, involving a scary God who threatened and cursed. Max said that unfortunately, people couldn't choose the portion they read. The rabbi figured that out for people and it depended when they were born. Father said that the rest of the Bible wasn't as fierce.

Some people learnt Hebrew because they wanted to speak it, like Uncle Georg. She'd asked him why he studied Hebrew, and he'd said that it would be useful: Jews from different countries, with different cultures and different languages had this one beautiful language in common, that of their ancestors; Hebrew and the Torah were their inheritance. When Helena asked her mother to explain, she'd said that Georg was planning to live in Palestine and wanted other people to immigrate too.

"Is Hebrew what they speak in Palestine?" she'd asked.

"A few do," said her mother. "People mostly speak Arabic and Turkish, probably some French and some English. Your Uncle Georg believes that if enough Jews were to immigrate to Palestine, they could create a Jewish state there and speak only Hebrew. A state of their own, in the heat and the dust, among scorpions, snakes and flies; it's a desert, a land fit for nomads and camels." Palestine didn't sound like a good idea even if her beloved Uncle Georg were to live there.

Helena felt lucky to be spared the bother of learning Hebrew. Her mother didn't send her to Sunday school because she didn't like religion, saying it was *kvatsch*, plain superstition. Helena knew she was referring to the *Ostjuden*, Polish and Russians Jews who lived in the poorer quarters and attended the Orthodox synagogue on the Essenweinstrasse. Some of the men wore their hair in sidelocks and beards, dressed in strange ways and spoke Yiddish. The one Polish Jew she knew herself was Frau Koslovski who didn't seem strange at all; everything about her was bright and sweet.

Other people kept kosher homes. The Mannheims didn't, though Oma never ate pork. She also had a mezuza on her doorpost. Max had explained that it contained a short verse of the *Shema*, the one prayer Helena knew and understood, about there being one God; there were no mezuzas elsewhere, not even by the front door. They celebrated both Chanukkah and Christmas, with an actual Christmas tree – it was fun, and her mother said that they were modern people, after all. But despite being modern, Father had insisted on Max's bar mitzvah. Tradition was to be observed.

On an ordinary Shabbat, the women's section on the balcony would be almost empty except for a few grandmothers and war widows. In the large space below, the rabbi and some elderly men ran the service, muttering unintelligible words at great speed over the Torah scroll and the prayer book, with sudden ragged outbursts of communal chanting. Today the balcony and the hall below would be crowded in honour of Max's bar mitzvah, almost like the High Holidays, when the entire community packed the massive synagogue.

Helena and her mother entered via the women's entrance, a door in the side of the building. They climbed up the narrow stairs ("So narrow!" she heard the women complaining) and sat on the wooden benches, cosily squeezed in between Tante Gusti and Tante Fanny. Oma, Tante Frieda and Alicia, Lore and her mother, and both Lore's grandmothers sat close by. Helena and Lore chatted in low voices while watching the men in the great blue and gold hall below. With only the prayer book to read, sitting still for such a long time was boring, though the music helped. Her heart beat fast as she waited for Max's name to be called for him to read from the Torah. Her mother was nervous too. Helena could tell by the way she smoothed down the skirt of the green dress and fingered her necklace.

Light streamed in from the central cupola and through the tall side windows. The colours of the great circular stained-glass windows glowed at either end of the synagogue, one above the ark where the Torah scrolls were kept, the other over the imposing main entrance, the men's entrance. The Kantor's voice rose, filling the space, harmonising with the choir and the organ. Helena loved the music.

She leant forward to watch Father and Max below. Father gave her a little wave from his seat next to the Loewenthals. Uncle Fritz sat nearby in his usual place. Max was up on the *bimah* where everyone could see him, standing beside the rabbi, reading from the prayer book in an uneven voice. He would read from the Torah scroll later, near the middle of the service. That would be the highlight.

This was the most people she had seen gathered in one place – hundreds of them; fathers and bearded grandfathers, sons and grandsons, all wearing kippahs or hats – black today, white on Yom Kippur – and long fringed cream-coloured, blue or black-striped prayer shawls folded back over their shoulders, billowing out behind them when they moved so that they looked larger than their usual selves, more powerful, whole tribes rising to their feet and sitting again in waves, like a sea; the sound of their voices also rising and falling in the prayers and chants. She felt small and secure, proud to belong. There was a close connection between the synagogue and great-grandpa Max, who'd been Bavaria's first Jewish judge. His name was engraved in gold on a polished board in the foyer. Max was named after him.

Their forefathers, hers and Max's, had all been bnei mitzvah, all the way back to Abraham. Helena was reminded of the tall mirrors inside the doors to her parents' wardrobe, each mirror reflecting Helena back to the mirror opposite, so that each showed a column of Helenas standing one behind the other, increasingly indistinct. Max said that the reflections went on to infinity. Helena had peered into the mirrors, first one, and then the other. She thought about the infinity of ancestors, Abraham far out of sight or was it Adam, in the beginning. She had examined the miniatures of more recent ancestors which hung in a double column, husband and wife side by side, in small black oval frames in Father's study. She could recognise Oma as the wife of the youngest couple, looking a little peculiar, much younger than she was now. Beside her was Opa, who'd died before she or Max were born. He looked nice enough, though younger than Father, which seemed odd. The couple above were Opa's father Max, the judge, and his wife and then above them one more couple, rather frail-looking, the great-great-grandpa and his wife. He'd been an important rabbi somewhere, not in Nuremberg. Father was important here, a synagogue trustee and a member of the board.

After the Torah reading and the Hebrew prayers, the service ended and they went down to the foyer where members of the congregation crowded around Max, her parents and Oma to congratulate and compliment them. Her father and mother were beaming, bright-eyed, happy and relieved that the ordeal was over. Helena watched Max. He was elated, enjoying the attention. She felt left out, drab and uninteresting despite her new dress.

At the hotel, the concierge greeted her parents by name. A few guests had already arrived, among them Tante Elise who looked different today. Her mother had once said about Tante Elise that she preferred books to clothes. Today she wore a beautiful dress, and her hair was sleek and tidy.

"Tante Elise, you look beautiful today!" said Helena.

Tante Elise laughed as if Helena had said something funny and kissed her. "Thank you, darling!" She smelled good too. "Max, congratulations! You read very well! Helena, please excuse me, I must talk to your mother for just a moment."

Gabriele, Elise's daughter, was standing nearby. She had come with her fiancé to the reception. Gabriele was twenty years old, an adult. "My fiancé," she said again and again as she introduced him to new people. They were getting married soon and planned to emigrate, though they didn't know where to yet.

Helena had seen the fiancé once or twice before. She caught herself staring, noticing that Gabriele wore lipstick. She had not seen her wear lipstick before. How old did one have to be to wear lipstick? She wondered how people knew whom they should marry. She'd heard that married people kissed in a special way – she wasn't sure what that was. Lore had told her that some people kissed even before they were engaged, and that she planned to start kissing as soon as she could. Helena was both shocked and thrilled.

Watching the young couple, Helena realised that her own mother wasn't young anymore. Her father was much older than her mother – thirteen years older. He was nearly fifty, almost an old man. Might he die soon? It was a frightening thought.

To pass the time until Lore's arrival, Helena explored the hotel's reception rooms. They were as dressed up and elegant as the guests, with bunches of flowers in large vases on pedestals and servants in smart uniforms. A waiter bowed, "Would the Fräulein like a grenadine or a menthe cordial?"

Father appeared beside her and said, "Thank you, but not yet, Helena." She knew Father was concerned in case she spilled something on her new dress. The waiter gave Helena a big smile, and she smiled too, a little taken aback. Her mother would have said that the waiter was being familiar. She'd been told not to eat or drink anything until they sat down to lunch. The other dress was hanging in a room upstairs. Her mother had brought it in a large bag and had given it to Tante Elise's maid Käthe who had come to help. "If you have an accident, you're to find Käthe and she'll help you change immediately. There's another pair of socks and a ribbon for your hair." Nothing was left to chance.

A string quartet was playing in a corner of the reception room. People were arriving whom Helena didn't know. Everyone seemed to be fussing. The waiter passed near her again, carrying a tray full of glasses. He winked at her. She noticed with distaste the thin moustache delineating his upper lip and turned away. At a loss, she wandered out to the garden, keeping to the paths to preserve her socks from dirt. She knew there was a large greenhouse in the grounds, which she had visited with her parents a few months earlier to admire the orchids blooming in the tropical atmosphere. They were beautiful and delicate, pink, purple and white.

The door to the greenhouse closed behind her, muting the sounds from the party. The air was warm and heavy. Between massed plants a tiled central alley led to a circular space with a bench under an exotic tree. She remembered someone saying it was a banana tree, but there were no bananas on it. Fruit grew here in winter, even peaches. She wondered if she could find the peach tree.

She sat for a moment on the bench under the banana tree. She heard someone come in and wondered who it might be. She was a little frightened of being in the wrong place, but she reassured herself that she hadn't touched or broken anything.

It was the waiter. "Hello," he said, smiling at her.

"Hello."

"Time for a breather. This is lovely, isn't it."

"Yes," said Helena, ill at ease.

He sat down near her, rather too close.

She felt like moving away but didn't want to seem rude.

"What's your name?" he asked.

"Helena." She didn't really want to talk to him.

He took her hand and she looked at him in surprise. She wanted to pull her hand away but didn't dare. She let her hand lie in his as if it did not belong to her.

"Do you know that you're a very pretty girl?" he said. "I noticed you the moment you came in." He was talking in a wrong way. He reached out to touch her hair and she ducked instinctively. He laughed and put his arm around her shoulders. Then he put his hand on her arm.

"What lovely skin you have," he said. "Smooth and ripe, like a peach."

She sat stiffly in his embrace. She was aware of his lips and his mouth as he spoke to her caressingly. She didn't want to look at them, but she was mesmerised.

"Let me look at you, this is a pretty dress, isn't it." He moved his hand to her leg and she froze. She started to struggle when he tried to kiss her, on her cheek and then on her mouth, but he was stronger than she was and his hands went all over her body, under her petticoat and between her legs and she was sobbing now and pushing him away, but it was no use. He forced her down onto the bench. His chest was smothering her face, his shirt buttons rubbing painfully. He kept thrusting at her. She felt as if she were a thing to him, a nothing and he went on moving on her, rubbing his body against her until he groaned and stopped and there was quiet except for his panting. He stood up and she could breathe again. She realised she was still sobbing. He tidied his clothes quickly and combed his hair. As he slipped the comb into his back pocket, he looked directly at her with hard, unfriendly eyes and said, "Tell anyone and I'll come and get you."

When the door had closed soundlessly behind him, she sat up slowly and stayed sitting without moving, trying to make the horrible feeling disappear so that she could be the old Helena once more. Eventually, she looked down at her dress which was crumpled and somehow sticky. She would have to find Käthe before her mother or father saw her.

ELEVEN

A light breeze caressed the wisteria fronds on the terrace and rustled the sheets of newspaper strewn around Walter's wicker chair. There was an empty coffee cup on the table beside him. Walter smoked his cigar, recalling the bar mitzvah with pleasure; the boy had done well, very well. He pondered the state of the world and conceded to himself that at this very instant he felt content, despite the difficult political situation. "Content" was the right word. Concerned about the future, certainly, but nevertheless, content.

Sonia appeared, carrying a bunch of red and pink flowers in a grey earthenware vase. Walter watched her deft movements as she arranged the blooms on the table. She stood back, her head to one side, stepped forward again and shifted the vase slightly to the centre. She looked trim and attractive, younger than her forty years.

"Pretty," he said.

"Peonies, from the garden." She smiled at him and went away.

Music floated out through the open windows, a violin solo, a recording she often listened to. He wasn't that fond of it himself: too melancholy.

He heard the familiar squeak of the gate at the end of the garden and watched the lilac bushes. Fritz Klein appeared and Walter stood to greet him. A surprise visit – something must have happened. It had been several weeks since they'd had a private conversation.

Crossing the lawn, Fritz brandished a newspaper. Walter recognised the *Völkischer Beobachter*. He'd looked at it the day before, as he usually did, without reading anything in detail, just wanting to know what the Nazis were up to. Nothing major – surely he'd have noticed?

"A drink, Fritz?" Walter gestured towards the wicker armchair next to his own.

"No thank you, Walter," said Fritz, settling into the chair. "Yesterday's," he said, holding up the newspaper. "Did you see the photos of the parade?"

"I glanced through."

Fritz opened the newspaper, folded back several pages and handed it to Walter, pointing to a photo. "Last week's parade in Munich. I'm sorry, you're not going to like what you see."

The photo showed Streicher, surrounded by a group of smiling officers. They were watching the parade from a dais. At the back, tallest among them, there was Benno Martin, handsome and at ease, wearing the black uniform of an SS Untersturmführer.

Walter stared at the image. That gleam above the cap's visor would be the silver death's head. He folded the newspaper and returned it to Fritz. He began walking up and down the terrace, his hands clasped behind his back, trying to dispel his agitation. He said, "That's disappointing, very disappointing!" He felt wounded, betrayed, but all he could find to say were the same words, "Very disappointing." He shook his head.

Fritz looked out at the garden.

Walter said, "I was warned, you know, and more than once, by Sonia and others. I haven't spoken to him for over a year."

Fritz crossed one long leg over the other. "Nevertheless, it's a shock."

Yes, that was it. Walter nodded. "During the war..."

Fritz knew Walter had served in the same Bavarian regiment as Martin. Fritz himself had been elsewhere, sawing off shattered arms and legs. "Ah yes, the war. Come, sit down, Walter."

"He was a good fellow. We had some great times," said Walter.

They sat in silence for a while.

Sonia appeared and offered Fritz a cup of coffee. After he'd politely refused, Walter showed her the photo. She patted Walter's arm, but said nothing. She went back into the house, leaving the two men by themselves.

Fritz asked, "What kind of a Nazi do you think he'll make?"

"Not the usual type."

"No."

"Even-tempered, fair," said Walter. "Gifted. A leader."

"Is that the key, d'you think?"

"Wanting to lead?"

Fritz nodded.

"The chief of police must be an SS even if he has to take a demotion in the process."

"I wondered about the Von Malsen debacle, the ten months with that brute Von Obernitz – that must have worn him down."

"That's no excuse! No excuse! His damned ambition, his bloody career! Allying himself with... with evil! Evil! Martin, with these thugs, these dregs! He knows exactly what they're like!"

"He must believe they're here to stay," said Fritz. After a pause he added, "In almost a year and a half the regime has managed to dispose of most of its opponents. It's likely to remain in place for the foreseeable future."

They sat side by side. Fritz reached into his jacket pocket and took out his old silver cigarette case. He offered the open case to Walter, who shook his head, indicating his cigar. Fritz searched through his pockets for the lighter, the unlit cigarette dangling from his mouth, a procedure Walter had witnessed many times.

The cigarette finally lit, cigarette case and lighter stowed away, Fritz removed a strand of tobacco from his lower lip and inhaled deeply. Walter watched the blue cigarette smoke rise and float away on the breeze.

"Frieda and I went to the cinema last night," Fritz paused and inhaled again. "The news report covered a ceremony with the president. He didn't seem well."

"They say he's becoming senile."

"That too," said Fritz, nodding. "His gait was uneven, dragging to one side, his speech a little slurred, though he didn't speak much – which was probably deliberate. I thought he might have suffered a stroke."

Walter stared at his friend, who added, "Hardly surprising. He's elderly, overweight, bearing a heavy responsibility under challenging circumstances."

"As long as he's still alive..."

Fritz grimaced. "He needs rest and quiet, plenty of both. He's not getting either." He shrugged.

Walter shifted in his chair. "If he dies..."

Fritz nodded. "Hitler's poised to take over, that's for sure."

Walter stared at the garden. "Restrictions are on the rise as it is."

Fritz raised his eyebrows and asked, "Anything new?"

"In Breslau, Jewish lawyers are now prohibited from appearing in court."

"I didn't know."

"They don't publicise what they're doing. A few decent people might object. They're careful what they print since the boycott last April."

"What do you mean?" asked Fritz.

"Some Nuremberg citizens were upset that Streicher's SA men refused them access to shops owned by Jews. Not many of them, but enough for the Nazis to consider the action less than a success."

"I don't recall the slightest protest," said Fritz.

"Far too little, from our point of view, but apparently more than expected. Self-interest, mainly."

"Feeling bitter, Walter?"

"My experiences leave me no illusions."

"The arrests?"

Walter nodded and said, "Our phone rings at all hours, both here and at the office: usually the wife, beside herself. The father or the son, sometimes both, have been arrested on trumped-up charges of tax evasion, exploitation of personnel, illegal business practices, the list goes on. The accusations keep coming, waves of muck, often from people who were trusted, in some cases treated like members of the family. Now they need to prove their loyalty to the regime. Mostly lies: a resentful employee trying to settle a score, or a jealous rival. It can happen to anyone."

"And then?"

"The law is still the law and we mostly succeed in getting the charges dropped. But as you've no doubt heard, the process is agonisingly slow; innocent people are locked up in so-called 'protective custody' – "against the wrath of the *Volk*" – for weeks or months, treated with the utmost contempt, beaten, abused, until the process has run its course. The man in jail is usually the breadwinner, so the families suffer financially as well as emotionally. Sometimes we can pressure or bribe a prison guard to ease conditions. But little can be done on the whole, because let's face it, they're executing their plan."

Fritz nodded. "And your commercial clients?"

"Abandoning the sinking ship, including a couple who'd been with us from my grandfather's time."

"Abandonment, separation, division – the Nazi curse," said Fritz.

Walter said, "That man brings out the worst in people. He's divisive even within his own party. A climate of denunciations and arbitrary punishments."

"They deserve it," said Fritz, adding, "Curious situations arise at the hospital. On the surface, everything remains the same, bar the ubiquitous swastika – people come in sick and we manage to heal some of them, God willing, and tend to the others. You should see the nurses when they cluster round the radio for that man's evening broadcast. They're like infatuated teenagers, hanging onto his every word. At the end, when their murderous song comes on, they stand up as one body and give the Nazi salute – to the radio." He shook his head. "They wear little enamel swastikas. I asked one whom I trust why she wore hers and she took that quick, guilty look over her shoulder, as if to make sure no one could hear us. She whispered that she was afraid *not* to wear it. She felt safe enough telling *me* that." He shook his head again.

"And how do they behave towards you?" asked Walter.

"The nurses are polite and respectful: Herr Doktor here, Herr Doktor there, but they're not so nice to the Jewish nurses. The great mystery is how they manage to reconcile antisemitic propaganda with their daily experience of us, of our behaviour towards them and towards our patients."

"As head of department, how long do you think you have?"

"I'll be forced out sooner or later. Probably sooner."

"Who'll replace you?"

"Plenty of candidates."

He drew on his cigarette and said, "On a lighter note, I've been banned from the Bridge Association."

"Really?"

As a young man, Fritz had spent six months in England and had founded the Nuremberg Bridge club on his return.

"I'm running out of indignation."

Walter said, "Some days I feel as if nothing could shock me anymore. And then something like this... Finding that someone one liked and trusted has gone over, shamelessly..." He gestured towards the newspaper.

"Frieda has been obliged to leave her choir, or more exactly, her choir left her. Our lives are continually shrinking."

Walter nodded. "The tennis club..."

"That too."

"Sonia was more upset than Max. I took Mother to watch a tournament in the Kronenbergs' garden last Sunday," said Walter. "Most of the tennis set were there, your Alicia too. The youth seem to have taken the expulsion in their stride."

"Alicia reported that Sonia distinguished herself," said Fritz.

Walter said, "She plays well. So does Max. He's athletic, good at games. I never had that level of coordination."

Fritz said, "He reminds me of Leo. Handsome chap."

Walter nodded, aware of Fritz's gaze.

Fritz cleared his throat and said, "There's something else I wanted to tell you: Frieda insists on sending Alicia away. Out of the country."

Walter turned to him, his eyebrows raised.

Fritz said, "You know how she worries; she's practically stopped eating. I've had to give in."

"Where to?"

"England, a boarding school." Fritz sighed. "Alicia's a sensible child; she'll manage. Her English will improve and she'll come home for the holidays, situation permitting."

"A big step," said Walter.

Alicia was a year or so older than Max; girls were more mature than boys at that age.

"An old school friend of Frieda's lives in England. She'll keep an eye on Alicia."

"Another separation."

"Temporary only; we'll bring her back in due course. Unless we leave Germany ourselves."

"You're considering it, seriously?"

"Yes. I won't wait to be pushed. I know it's only a question of time."

After a pause, Walter said, "I don't want to leave, and I don't want Sonia to leave either, or the children."

"You seem to believe that they're safe as long as they're close to you, no matter how destructive the situation in Nuremberg. And now, with Martin gone over to the other side?"

Walter nodded. "I don't want to leave."

"Is that rational?" asked Fritz.

Walter stubbed out his cigar and said, "I know damned well it isn't. I can't explain it. I want to remain here, with my family."

"But might you consider sending them away if the situation gets worse, or send at least one of them – if you could find a good place? Send Helena to Alicia's school?"

"Helena is difficult at the moment – temper tantrums, bed-wetting. Truly, we don't know what gets into her at times. Leaving home might make matters worse, let alone leaving Germany. Sonia tried to convince me yet again that we should go, the other day. But I believe we should stay. Those leaving are among our most able: people like you whom other countries are keen to have. Someone needs to stay for those Jews who cannot get out, whom no country wants. Besides, there's the fact that we're German citizens. We should resist Nazi attempts to disown us. It's our right to live here – in the house my grandfather built."

"I see," said Fritz.

Walter looked at his friend. "You don't agree."

"One day, a better option may be to count your losses and get out. For good."

"Easier for a doctor than a lawyer," said Walter.

"No matter your profession," said Fritz. "There's always Palestine."

"You sound like a Berlin Jew," said Walter. "Like Rabbi Baeck: 'The thousand-year history of Jewish life in Germany is at an end!'"

"A wise man," said Fritz. "His daughter's already in England."

Walter shook his head. "He wants us all to leave. It sounds brave, but in fact he's given up the battle, the battle for Jewish life in Germany. And who knows if England is actually safer, in the long run."

"Rabbi Baeck has said that he won't leave as long as a single Jew remains in Germany. They keep arresting him."

Walter nodded. "And letting him go again, because of international pressure."

Fritz said, "His renown protects him for the moment. He's in constant negotiations with the Nazis. He understands the situation better than anyone. He's a realist."

"But who will have us? Six hundred thousand German Jews; that was the estimate two years ago."

"I would choose Palestine. That's if the British let us in."

"The urge to create a national homeland weakens us, weakens our determination to keep what we have, what is ours," said Walter. "You may yearn for a return to Jerusalem, but I feel no affinity for the Middle East; I cannot imagine settling there or anywhere else. We shouldn't give up our rights here so easily. Less than ninety years have passed since we got citizenship! The present hateful madness must be challenged, for our sake and for our children's sake."

Max was practicing throwing his knife at a tree like a circus juggler and Helena was watching him. Mama disapproved of the knife, a present from a great-uncle who had no children, so Max had taken himself to the far end of the garden where he couldn't be seen from the house. He had learnt to let the knife fly blade first and he wanted to perfect his technique. He refused to let Helena touch the knife; Mama had given strict instructions to that effect. Helena thought how lucky he was to be a boy; so much more was allowed him.

"Move back, Helena!" he said after he retrieved the knife from the tree. "Right back!"

A branch on the ground marked his throwing position. She grimaced at him, sticking out her tongue and crossing her eyes.

He positioned himself with care, took a deep breath and threw. The knife flew in a slow arc, turning with elegance in the air, embedding itself in the trunk with a satisfying thud. He walked over and pulled it out again. She longed to have a go. She watched him stand still and breathe in before throwing again. As soon as the knife left his hand, she dashed forward, taking him by surprise, reaching the tree first. She pulled out the knife.

"Give me that knife, fatty!" Max strode towards her, his arm stretched out.

She hid the knife behind her back. "I'm not fat!"

"You are! You don't run well either!"

Tears came to her eyes.

"Let me have a go, Max!" she begged.

Max stopped and crossed his arms.

They stared at each other. She thought, it's no good, he won't let me, he's immovable.

He threatened. "I'll kidnap Bärchen and drown him in the toilet."

He had kidnapped her teddy bear before. She couldn't tell anyone about it because they would both be punished, she for telling tales and he for stealing Bärchen. She didn't believe he would harm Bärchen, but he was better at hiding things than she was at finding them.

"I'm getting him now," said Max and turned towards the house. They both knew he'd won.

In a fury, she threw the knife after him, imitating his throwing style, holding the blade and releasing it rapidly. To her horror, the knife flew perfectly, turning slowly in a graceful curve, righting itself till it pointed at his back, blade first. She wanted to warn him, to call out, but it was happening too fast. He was walking away. The blade shimmered in the sun, describing a downwards arc. Helena was unable to move. She stood frozen, her mouth open, her hand outstretched.

The knife struck above the familiar brown sandal. Max cried out, turning in surprise, looking at his leg. Then he gave a groan and sat down suddenly. She was to remember this moment all the years of her life, her fear and terror at the thought she had harmed him. He reached towards the handle of the knife which was now appallingly connected to his leg. He pulled at it, groaned again and the blood-stained blade emerged. A red patch appeared above his sock which spread rapidly. She ran to him. "Max! Max!" She crouched next to him and he looked up at her. He seemed stunned; she'd never seen a person turn white. "I'm sorry! I'm sorry!" she said, beginning to cry.

He said between clenched teeth that it didn't hurt much, and he didn't seem angry with her, but he stayed where he was, his hand gripping his calf. Bright blood seeped through his clenched fingers and seemed to stain everything, his sock, his hands, his face, his shirt, her hands as she tried to stop the flow and then her dress. She ran to the house which seemed terribly far away, calling frantically, "Mama, Mama!"

Their mother appeared suddenly at the living room door. "It's Max, he's hurt!" sobbed Helena, pointing. Mama ran very fast towards the back of the garden, tearing through the lilac bushes. She reached Max who looked up at her and said, "It was the knife".

She said, "Show me," and then to Helena, "Tell Gretchen to get Doctor Klein".

Helena ran.

After the doctor left, the turmoil ceased. Max sat on the couch in the living room with his bandaged foot up on a stool. He'd been given something to drink for shock and his eyes were shiny. Helena was sent to her room and told to stay there. Mama said that a suitable punishment would be found when Father came home. Helena thought she might have to stay in her room forever this time, on bread and water. She felt she deserved it.

They had not been able to lie. Max couldn't have stuck the knife in his leg himself. Mama had smacked Helena and Helena had not minded. The knife was confiscated.

"About time too," said Mama. "A stupid gift for a child if ever there was one."

TWELVE

A week or so later, Frau Koslovski emerged from the drapers' shop on Karolinenstrasse and hurried homewards, clasping her handbag to her chest. Daylight was disappearing fast even though it was only mid-afternoon; a summer storm seemed imminent, roiling clouds gathering over the steep roofs. A gust of wind bustled people along the street, women clutching their scarves, men their hats, struggling to retain their dignity. Two schoolboys huddling in a doorway watched and laughed. As she passed the antiquarian's shop, Frau Koslovski paused in front of the window, one hand holding her headscarf tight under her chin. Despite the wind's insistent buffeting, she examined the display; then she entered the shop.

"That antiquarian knows his business?" asked Herr Koslovski.

A few raindrops hit the windowpanes. It was getting dark and the kitchen was warm and cosy.

"Absolutely," said Frau Koslovski, removing her scarf and shaking out her dark curls. "He believes that someone in the community will pay for it."

"Did he mention where the Torah mantle came from?"

"From one of the village synagogues. There's hardly anyone left to watch over them."

"But a Jew would never sell..."

"Difficult times. They may have needed the money to pay for something else, something more important."

"Did he say that a Jew had sold it?"

"I didn't ask. It may be stolen – it doesn't matter. We should get it back. I made him take the parochet out of the shop window. He's promised to put it aside for a week."

He nodded, but she felt that he wasn't listening properly. He said, "When everyone leaves, what do you think happens to all the things in the synagogue?"

"What do you mean?"

"Everything that's in the synagogue – like this Torah mantle, and the prayer books, the Torah scrolls themselves, the bits and pieces of silver, menorahs, that sort of thing?" He shifted restlessly in his chair; she could see he was upset. He was a religious man; these things mattered to him.

"I suppose they give them to another congregation still able to function fully, like ours."

"But no one here would want used prayer books."

"I guess not; both our congregations have enough prayer books and besides, these would be old, maybe damaged or dirty."

"Only a Jew would ever want a siddur." He was leaning forward in his chair, his hands clasped between his knees, his head down. She couldn't see his face, only the black kippah.

"And a person really only needs one." She'd inherited hers from a great-aunt.

"There would be many copies to dispose of. I suppose they'll bury what they can't take along."

"Bury?"

"Yes, when our holy books are damaged beyond repair, the rabbi makes sure they're buried."

"How so?"

He looked up at her and said, "A Torah scroll is never thrown out, you Philistine, it's wrapped and disposed of in a dignified fashion, with ritual, usually in a coffin with a body. We do the same for our prayer books, for anything that carries God's holy name. Our Holy Scripture is not, God forbid, rubbish to be dumped."

She turned her back on him, tied her apron-strings and began to cook, peeling and chopping onions. Raindrops pelted hard against the windowpanes.

She busied herself at the stove, frying the onions, adding the mince she'd seasoned and fashioned into patties. He was quiet, reading the newspaper. Then she said, "I wouldn't mind being buried with a Torah scroll for company."

She added, "They didn't do that to this Torah mantle. Bury it, I mean."

"It would depend if God's name was embroidered on it."

"I can't remember." She didn't read Hebrew very well.

"Or maybe they unpicked that bit, took His name out?"

"No one's unpicked a single thing - that mantle is perfect! It's a work of art, old and beautiful."

She knew about embroidery. She'd helped embroider a cover for a Torah scroll once, silk on silk. A white one for the Days of Awe. Silver on white – a task for young eyes, an honour too. Her mother had been proud.

"Will you talk to the rabbi?"

"Yes, tomorrow. Some people may have the money."

"The chairman?"

He nodded. "We'll give some ourselves, start the ball rolling."

Over dinner, he said, "You realise we're dancing to their tune."

She shrugged. "We need to get it back."

"Certain people within the community may be willing to help retrieve this treasure," said the rabbi, who had taken the trouble to see it for himself.

"The chairman?" asked Herr Koslovski.

"Maybe, but we can't count on it. Many village synagogues are being closed down now."

"The ladies at the coffee morning?"

"I fear that the sum required is more than they can hope to raise."

A few months earlier the board of the Liberal congregation had held a vigorous discussion about a pair of seventeenth-century silver Torah finials.

"We must act fast, before the shopkeeper melts them down, God forbid."

"Nonsense, the value of the finials is far higher than the worth of the silver; the beauty of the work will keep it safe."

"The value depends on what people are willing to pay."

"They'll end up in our safe, in storage. An utter waste of money."

"Might the Orthodox have a use for them?"

"If the Orthodox want them, let them fork out the cash."

"That isn't a helpful..."

"They've trouble enough coughing up their dues."

The chairman had spoken: "We may have to pay *and* let the items go elsewhere. We are running a *Gemeinde*, not a museum. I also want to mention," he paused and looked round the table, "that by and large we have different priorities. I would ask board members to kindly keep that in mind."

The money had been found, but the following time someone wanted to rescue Jewish patrimony, the chairman advised against it. Community members were increasingly needing financial support to get by and the expense could not be justified. They could all see that.

———

Whenever she visited Robert and Hilde's house, Sonia would sit on the deep long sofa facing the hearth, the best position from which to contemplate the painting of a wild blue horse hanging over the mantelpiece. The brushstrokes were broad and confident, the colour vivid, the animal energetic, alive, indubitably a horse despite its unnatural colour. The painting spoke to Sonia of exuberant freedom. Her mood would lighten and she'd feel optimistic for a while.

A week earlier, Sonia and Hilde had queued at length to visit the *Degenerate Art* exhibition. The works had been confiscated by the regime from museums all over the country, paintings and sculptures embodying the latest trends in modern art. The exhibition was to be a swan song for these works; to the authorities' great surprise, viewing the *Degenerate Art* exhibition became an imperative for every art-lover in Germany, people crowding into the ill-lit rooms to admire the works, aware that they were likely to disappear for ever.

"It was marvellous!" said Hilde, describing the experience to Walter and Robert. She put a cup of coffee on the low table in front of Sonia. "We were lucky to get in," she added, as she brought the men their coffee. "Hardly anyone went to Great German Art." *Degenerate Art* had been set up as the foil to *The Great German Art Exhibition*, which showed works selected according to the Führer's own guidelines.

Walter said, "A Nazi miscalculation."

Robert sipped his coffee. "They'll probably sell those modern paintings overseas. They need the foreign currency."

Hilde said, "Oh Robert, do tell Walter and Sonia about our visitors this morning – another miscalculation!" She laughed.

Robert nodded, but did not smile. "A posse of soldiers arrived on our doorstep."

Walter raised his eyebrows and asked, "The army?"

Hilde interrupted, "They were after his sword, his officer's sword."

Sonia sat up, alarmed. Walter owned a sword too; it was stored in their basement, with his dress uniform and his spiked helmet, his *Pickelhaube*.

"A sergeant and two men. We do not rate the visit of an officer. I imagine they were instructed to be 'polite yet firm'" – Robert's eyes were twinkling now – "And so the good sergeant addressed us formally, a little pompously, explaining that we might perhaps have heard that recent legislation forbids Jews from serving in the army. Therefore, he told us, they'd come to retrieve the sword." His lips tightened. "*My* sword."

Hilde put her hand on his arm. Despite the lightness of his tone, he was like Walter, thought Sonia, who polished the metal pieces of his uniform every month or so – the belt's buckle, the handle of the sword, the helmet's spike and its coat of arms, the lions prancing either side of the escutcheon over the beloved Bavarian motto: *In steadfast loyalty*. Walter would work at the task with a devotion Sonia found disturbing. She wasn't sure what aspect she disliked more, the devotion itself or the fact that cleaning jobs were usually a servant's responsibility. During the war his batman had polished the equipment. She listened to Hilde: "...Robert went to fetch the sword without further ado. They were delighted, so pleased he was being 'reasonable'. He took it out of its scabbard and they reached for it. And then, quick as a flash, he bent the blade over his knee, the way you'd break a piece of kindling. He offered them the sword, now bent, a crooked shadow of its former self." She laughed. "You should have seen their faces."

Sonia noticed that Robert had recovered his composure and was smiling.

"What did they do?" she asked.

"They took it and they left. The sword is ruined." He shrugged. "Nothing more will come of it, Sonia my dear." His voice was kind, reassuring. "As a form of harassment, knocking on people's doors for a single piece of equipment is labour-intensive and unlikely to produce much benefit; some Nazi probably thought this up. I doubt it will be carried through. The army is not the SA."

As she walked home with a silent Walter that evening, the words 'In steadfast loyalty' reverberated in Sonia's mind. Thinking back, she realised that it had been several months since she'd seen him polishing his military kit.

THIRTEEN

At the Old Gymnasium that morning, Dr Jaeger's voice was expressionless as he dictated the topic of the weekly essay to the class. "Describe the Reich Rally Grounds." He was a tall man with thick brown hair and a lugubrious face. As he spoke, he wrote the words rapidly, almost violently on the blackboard, stabbing it with the stick of chalk, breaking it halfway through.

Essay writing was Max's forte, German literature and composition his favourite subjects, though over the last couple of years he'd lost much of his enthusiasm for study. It was 1936, three years since Hitler had come to power, and Nazi norms pervaded every aspect of school life, adopted by teachers and pupils without reluctance, as far as Max could tell. The lone Protestant boy had finished his schooling. He'd surrendered before he left, though his salute lacked conviction and he mumbled the words. On the day this boy gave in, Max had felt that all hope was lost, the old beloved ways defeated forever. One or two teachers – such as Dr Jaeger – did not hide their unhappiness with the new curriculum, its emphasis on physical fitness at the expense of classics and science, and the new biology and history books promoting ideas of race and *Lebensraum*. The teachers didn't care what he and Hans did at the back of the class: they were left to their own devices, abandoned. When Hans was the only student to solve a maths problem or when Max scored a goal, there was no praise. Hans had made life a little more bearable by constructing a minute radio in a tin box which they listened to covertly.

The topic of this essay was unusual. One would have to visit the tribune on the Zeppelin Field, a structure built to reflect the party's domination. Max could imagine the sycophantic outpouring of praise from the rest of the class. He thought about the topic again and decided he would take it up as a challenge; better than doing nothing. He'd not visited the park since the Nazis began holding their rallies there. The old zoo had been dismantled, the animals dispersed.

Max had listened to descriptions of the previous rally on Hans's little radio: the men in formation on the parade ground, the forest of fluttering flags, and the watching crowd, women folk and those either too young or too old to march, cheering for all they were worth. The Luitpold Arena provided a large space, but it was not large enough; the Nazis had appropriated the adjoining Zeppelin Field, so called because a Zeppelin had landed there a long time ago. A Zeppelin had once floated over their house, like a huge silvery divinity. Everyone, including his mother and the maids, had rushed into the garden to see it. They'd cheered and waved to the people in the little pod under the gigantic belly. Those had been happy days.

The tribune had been finished to great acclaim, but he'd not seen it himself. He'd been packed off with Helena during the rally to the provincial safety of relatives in Bamberg. He knew from the newspapers and radio that Nuremberg attained a state of hysterical revelry: the houses swathed in Nazi flags, swastikas everywhere, the oom pah pah music of military bands as the populace amassed along the streets to cheer the parading Storm Troopers, several hundred thousand of them swamping the city. He'd read about the preparations, discussed the logistics with Hans: it was an enormous undertaking – more than half a million visitors to be fed, lodged and entertained, each of them yearning for a Nazified Germany without any Jews.

He'd heard the other boys discuss last year's rally in tones of awe and fervour – the size of the tribune, the vast crowds, the Storm Troopers marching in, a wide river of men which flowed on and on for hours. When night fell, floodlights lining the periphery lit up, one hundred and fifty beams of light soaring straight up into the limitless black sky, the effect breath-taking, like the columns of an unimaginably high cathedral. He'd seen a photo, had studied it. He wished he could have witnessed the show himself. He'd seen local SA units on parade and once heard a man in the watching crowd say approvingly, "See how they all look the same!" It was true: they seemed identical in their brown uniforms, their eyes invisible under their helmets' low brim, like multiples of a single individual, moving to the rhythm of the beating drum, marching, marching. He'd considered the word 'uniform' and it reminded him of his unfinished project from years ago: the pictures of German military uniforms through the ages. He'd unearthed the box with the cigarette vouchers and the empty album from the bottom of his cupboard and thrown the lot out with a sense of good riddance.

For a cyclist, the Luitpold Park was not far from the Gymnasium, but as he reached the Dutzendteich Lake, he felt a surge of anxiety. He was in enemy territory now. He could see across the lake a construction site crawling with men at work, ant-like on an enormous semi-circular structure. He cycled past a notice board which shouted: "FOR THE GLORY OF THE REICH AND THE GERMAN PEOPLE!" It included a map. He stopped for a closer look; it explained that the building was to be a huge Congress Hall, "with seats for 55,000 people". The thought of so many Nazis was terrifying.

The Zeppelin Field was straight ahead. A dusty lorry drove past, gears grinding. Afraid of being called to account, he stood on the pedals and rode as fast as he could, though he knew that with his

Gymnasium school cap and his school bag he looked like any ordinary schoolboy. He was an ordinary schoolboy, he reminded himself. A schoolboy with an essay to write.

Entering the Zeppelin Field, he found himself by the tribune, dwarfed by it; to see it in its entirety, he rode to the centre of the field. Three sides were lined by plain concrete stands, for ordinary citizens. In front of him rose the monumental tribune, extending across the field's full width, with the giant three-tiered podium at its centre adorned with an enormous metal swastika. Two wings of graded tiers extended on either side. They could seat 5,000 people, according to the newspapers. At the far edge of each wing was an oblong tower adorned with a smaller swastika. A covered colonnade ran along the top, from one side of the structure to the other. The focal point of the structure was the podium for the orator, below the triumphant swastika. From where Max stood, that man would barely be visible.

They'd been told at school that the architect had followed the plan of a famous Greek altar, enlarging it multiple times. Max had seen the original in a Berlin museum and he recognised the design: in this Nazi version, it was overpowering, the embodiment of the hateful machine dedicated to destroying him, his family, and everything he loved. He reminded himself of what his father said: "Evil contains the seed of its own destruction."

He took out his writing pad. The task would take time; best to work methodically. He sketched an outline of the edifice, then rode closer to the stand. He ran from the middle to one end of the stand – about a hundred and fifty meters, he reckoned. He stood for a moment to catch his breath and then walked briskly back along it, pacing himself, until he reached the exact middle, the speaker's stand towering above him. He wrote down the number of steps he'd taken. He evaluated the height of the stands, the width of the walls, the length of the parapets, the number of flagpoles. He wrote down the stone, the concrete, the brick, the swastikas. He positioned himself again opposite the stand, evaluated its dimensions, counting the gradations, taking notes, precise and business-like. The task done, he rode away, glad to turn his back on the inhuman structure. He felt satisfied, almost happy.

His mother asked where he'd been. When he told her, she remonstrated with him; he didn't argue. After dinner, he wrote the report, a first draft. As much as possible, he left the Nazi Party out of the description. The following days he worked at it again, seeking precision, keeping the style spare, the words exact. He mentioned the other altar, the Greek one. When he handed the essay to Dr Jaeger, he felt at peace. It wasn't very long, but it was good. Good enough, anyway.

When essays were returned at the Gymnasium the tradition was for teachers to rank them in order of declining excellence, and to read out the names of the students in that order. The best essay was read out to the class. To Max's delight and amazement, he came second. Dr Jaeger's face was imperturbable. A beefy boy called Schmitt was first. He read his florid composition, faithfully regurgitating the Nazi slogans – "the thousand-year Reich", "the German people count on total victory", "the Führer challenging his people, the people responding to their Führer".

"Kindly return your essays to me," said Dr Jaeger. "The headmaster has asked to read them."

"I came second," said Max to his father that evening. "Schmitt came first, with propaganda."

"Not bad," said his father. "Not bad of old Jaeger. I suppose it was too much to ask that he put you first; you'd have had to read it aloud to the class, wouldn't you."

His father knew the Gymnasium's traditions well. Some of the present-day staff had been pupils in his day, returning from university to teach at their beloved school. A couple of the senior teachers like Papa Rast had even taught his father themselves, thirty-five years earlier. Papa Rast taught classics, which included the rise of democracy in Athens. His views were obvious to the boys; it was rumoured that he'd not last much longer. He was due to retire anyway.

A few days later, towards the end of a lesson, Dr Jaeger cleared his throat and said, "Before we finish, I've an announcement to make." He paused for the class to quieten down.

"As you know, Dr Staehlin, our respected headmaster, kindly took the time to read your essays on the subject of the Reich Rally Grounds. He has considered them on their merit and he corrected my earlier judgement." Dr Jaeger paused again and glanced around the class, briefly catching Max's eye. Max hunched his shoulders.

"Dr Staehlin has decided that the order of the first two papers is to be reversed. Mannheim's essay is first, Schmitt's second."

Max stared at his teacher, transfixed.

The silence in the class was absolute.

"Mannheim, read out your essay please."

Max stood up on shaking legs, made his way to the front of the class and took the sheet of paper from Dr Jaeger, willing his hands not to shake. He stood as tall as he could and took a deep breath. Something welled up in his chest and he stared at the page, concentrating on the words. At first, he had trouble finding his voice. He dared not look up from the page as he read. The students sat completely immobile. It was like reading into an abyss.

When he finished, the silence continued. No one moved. He felt suddenly out of breath, as if he'd run a great distance. His heart hammered in his chest.

"Thank you, Mannheim," said Dr Jaeger.

Max went back to his seat, glad to sit down.

Hans was wide-eyed.

"That's all for today," said Dr Jaeger, and the bell rang; Max realised that the whole business had been precisely timed. Dr Jaeger left the room, the boys standing up as usual in a clatter of steel-capped boots, arms raised to an indistinct *Heil Hitler*. From the back, Max and Hans watched them leave the room. Schmitt was pushing his way through the throng, trying to reach the teacher, his face swollen with rage; there was trouble ahead. Max was still amazed and shocked at what had happened: Staehlin had said that his essay was the best! Staehlin had stuck his neck out for him! He shook his head and swallowed hard.

Hans said, "Old Staehlin has guts!" and shook Max's hand. "Well done!" Hans hadn't bothered writing the essay; writing was not his forte and a failure on his record scarcely mattered. Under the present regime, neither he nor Max would be allowed to study at a German university.

That evening at dinner, his father announced that Max was to study English with a private teacher.

"But I'm doing fine in English."

"Indeed, you are," said Father, "but your mother and I want you to speak with fluency, like an Englishman. Early learning will enable you to speak like a native. Your mother has arranged lessons for you with an English lady, a Miss Winteringham; she comes highly recommended."

"What about me? When am I going to have special lessons?" asked Helena.

"Your turn will come, darling," said Sonia.

In his surprise, Max almost forgot to mention what had happened at school. He told his parents and they listened and remained silent after he finished speaking. Max and Helena exchanged surprised glances; why didn't they say anything? Had Max upset them, erred in some way?

His father sat with his hands flat on the table, looking intently at the tablecloth. Then he got up suddenly, almost knocking his chair over. His back turned, he blew his nose. His mother sighed deeply, in her usual manner.

His father cleared his throat and said loudly, "This calls for a celebration!" He poured out brandies from the drinks cabinet for himself and for their mother, plus a tot for Max and an even smaller one for Helena.

They raised their glasses and Father said, with deep feeling, "To Dr Staehlin's good health and long life!"

Miss Winteringham lived in a little flat in St Leonhard, a short trip by tram, via the Plaerrer Interchange. Max stood in her cluttered living room, clutching his leather satchel, afraid he might knock something over. She was willowy, her nose long and fine, her skin pale. Some of her soft brown hair escaped her loose bun. She spoke in English, offering him tea, which she poured into a delicate cup different in shape and colour from those he was used to. "Lemon or milk?" Her voice was low and her manner quiet. She explained the strange English habit of pouring a little milk into the cup before the tea. She gave him an English magazine called *The Economist* and asked him to read whatever interested him during the week. He was to look up

144

new words, and they'd talk about what he'd read the next time they met.

The following week he arrived unprepared and she blinked but seemed otherwise unaffected. She didn't tell him off, accuse him of wasting his parent's money or report him. She addressed him as an equal, discussed international politics, business, science, literature and music. When he ventured opinions, she asked him to explain why he held them. He came to look forward to the lessons and began studying the weekly magazine in the way she had suggested. He occasionally discussed what he read with his father. His mother listened but rarely contributed. He once found her reading an article in the magazine with the help of her dictionary; it was about Germany's economic situation. He felt he'd entered the adult world.

———————

At school, Helena learnt about the structure of the leaf, about its pores and the role of chloroplasts. She listened to the teacher and understood and was enchanted by the way the leaf took in water and carbon dioxide and exuded oxygen, which people could then breathe; she enjoyed the thought that the plants and people helped each other; she understood the process and felt comfortable with her knowledge. Later in the week, the teacher set an exam on the leaf, and again, she was confident and happy. This was fun, and she wrote everything she knew, feeling knowledgeable.

The exam papers were returned the following week. Hers came scored all over with red and a low mark. She held it in her hand, which trembled a little and the paper trembled too, a shiver like a leaf. She looked up at the teacher, who said to her in exasperation, "The pores have a name you know; you can't call them 'little holes'; you must use the right words. Your essay is nonsense."

Helena sat without moving, looking down at the sheet of paper in her hand without seeing it, not joining in the usual classroom hubbub which arose after exam papers were returned: people comparing marks and getting ready for the next activity. She understood now that though she'd thought she understood, that she was clever, she was in fact stupid. It had been stupid of her to think she was clever: it was clear to her that she was very stupid.

She did not talk to anyone except to say yes and no. When she got home, her mother was out at a meeting of one of her congregational committees. Helena sat and looked at her afternoon tea which waited on a plate in the middle of the kitchen table, and the face of the teacher kept coming to mind, disapproving of her and her work, with the teacher's words, "This is nonsense, nonsense." The afternoon tea did not seem satisfactory, though it was special, *Linzertorte*, which she loved. It stuck in her throat and she didn't finish it.

By the time her mother came home, Lore had arrived and Helena was playing a crazy game with her in the garden, a game which involved wild shrieks, jumping and running. Her mother discovered that Helena had failed to complete her homework and Lore was sent home, with Helena consigned to her room, to stay there until the work was done. She sat at her desk which faced the wall, holding the pencil. She longed for things to be different and looked sideways out of the window at the shapes of the trees and the darkening blue of the evening sky. The birds were finishing their goodnights. After a while the only sound was the rustle of a breeze through the trees. She sank into a blankness which was a kind of not being there. Her mother came in to see how she was doing and said, "What's the matter with you?" turning on the light. Helena blinked in the sudden glare. Her mother asked what the homework was.

"English."

"That's all?"

"Yes."

"Get on with it, Helena – I can't help you now, I'll check on you later."

But later her father was home and it was dinner time. He asked her how school had been today. She didn't want him to know. She hesitated, and Max interrupted, talking about football at the club and her father was immediately interested, turning to him and forgetting her. Helena tilted her chair back. Her mother told her not to, but she didn't want to stop. If she just tilted the chair a bit more, she might balance it on two legs: a seductive, irresistible idea, only just out of reach. The crash came suddenly: she went over backwards in a heap, her legs flung wildly upwards and over her head. Her mother quickly helped her to her feet, smoothed down her skirt, and established that Helena was unharmed except for her shoulder, which hurt. She said it would probably become a fine bruise.

"Please take your plate to the kitchen! No dessert!"

As Helena left the room, she dared to say through the closing gap, holding the door handle tight, "I don't care, it's only stinky old apple compote."

Helena sat at the kitchen table with her plate; Greta didn't say anything. Then Greta left the kitchen for a moment. The big bowl of apple compote was nearby, so Helena leaned forward and used the big serving spoon to slurp some into her mouth. She had to gobble it down quickly before Greta came back and barely had time to taste it, wiping her mouth on her sleeve to remove the juiciness. Some apple compote dripped down the front of her blouse. She hurried to the sink and dabbed at it with a wet cloth, which left a dark mark on her chest. Luckily Greta didn't notice.

FOURTEEN

The proprietor of the Blaue Traube made his way to their table and stood beside Walter, watching the card game. He didn't say anything at first, didn't move. His big hands hung loose by his sides. Everyone heard him clear his throat. Walter looked up. The others stopped playing too; the men at adjacent tables noticed and paused in their game, the pause and the silence spreading in the crowded low-ceilinged room. Walter caught the sly glance of the young waitress, her avidity, heard the scraping of chairs as those furthest away stood up to watch. They knew something: they knew whatever was coming. The tendons at the back of his neck went taut.

"It's time," said the proprietor, looking at each of them in turn. His expression was impassive, the tone of his voice flat, unapologetic. "Time to go. Don't come back."

They knew that nothing they might say would make any difference. The four of them pushed back their chairs, which grated loudly on the stone floor. Not a word was spoken. Turning their backs on the table which had been their *Stammtisch* for more than twenty years, they left their beers and cards and walked out under the crowd's intent gaze. Walter knew many of them by name – from the war and from living in the same town their entire lives. No one said anything. Many avoided his glance.

This had happened three years ago, during the regime's first week. Since then they'd taken turns to host the game at home. It was a simple affair: they played in the late afternoon and the wife brought in sausages and sauerkraut, potato salad, gherkins and beer, and they ate, smoked, told tall tales, drank and played some more. The household's older children would slip in and hang around until bedtime, listening to the jokes and laughter. Besides Walter, the regular players were Robert Loewenthal, Fritz Klein, Fanny's Otto and Kaspar Kretsch. Kretsch and Walter's friendship dated from the war, Kretsch a little younger than Walter. Frau Kretsch was pink and fair, a traditional dirndl-wearing *Hausfrau*; they had three little girls, also pink and fair.

Kretsch had been doing well at one of Nuremberg's better known law practices. When he joined the legal department of a pharmaceuticals manufacturer, Walter told him he was wasting his talents. But Kretsch shook his head; he didn't want independence. He was content within the safe folds of a large organisation, a solid body able to withstand the vagaries of a fluctuating economy. It was, thought Walter, a valid consideration for a family man.

Kretsch was late and the three of them began to play, but Walter remained alert, waiting for the doorbell to ring. At first, no one mentioned Kretsch's absence, but after half an hour had gone by, Robert said, "Someone will have warned him off."

Fritz said, "His job at risk, maybe."

Walter didn't speak. They went on playing without much enthusiasm; he knew this was it, the end of a friendship, but he hoped he was wrong, that a message would arrive, the phone would ring and the familiar voice would say, "So sorry, folks," and there'd be a good reason.

They broke up early, Robert giving Walter a pat on the shoulder on his way out, by way of silent commiseration. They had all suffered similar betrayals, old friendships suddenly breaking, people disappearing from their lives.

As Fritz was buttoning his overcoat, he peered at Walter. "Getting enough sleep?"

"Not really. The old story, nightmares, you know what it's like."

Fritz nodded.

"It's worse at the moment. Like a minefield, you never know when it'll blow up in your face."

"What happens?"

"Explosions, flying debris, bodies, screams..."

"How often?"

"Too often. Over and over. Sonia says that I shout and throw myself around. It frightens her. I wake up in a sweat; my heart pounds as if it might burst out of my chest."

"Ghosts can take some time to fade."

"I dread the nights... Sleeping pills make me groggy."

"Addictive too. A stiff drink and a good book work for me. And a short nap in the afternoon, if possible."

Walter watched Fritz disappear into the dark towards the back of the garden. The little gate squeaked.

Before the Nazis took power, there had been no reason for Walter to examine his life as a lawyer, to evaluate the amicable relationships he maintained as a matter of course with colleagues and with the judges at the new Palace of Justice. Some had known his father before the war, before the imposing building on Fürtherstrasse was built. Walter had taken his social milieu for granted, like the air he breathed.

A different world had emerged; one where people he'd known all his life shunned him, no longer acknowledging his existence. Jewish lawyers too young to have served at the front during the war were forced to retire, but veterans like Walter remained, ostracised by even the oldest clerk, an unofficial patriarch of the Law Courts, who until then had always seemed kindly and wise. It threw him at first– he was apparently invisible until the court got down to business. Then he seemed to rematerialize, the courtesies of judicial ritual punctiliously observed. He was bowed to, addressed as "esteemed colleague". More surprising was that he continued to win his cases. Sonia was very proud of his success. The issues he dealt with were different, personal; he would once have regarded them as tedious. Today he'd represented Chait, a small tailor, an *Ostjude*, whose supplier had sent him inferior material. The Nazi infection had not yet damaged the legal process, even in Nuremberg.

The phone rang in Walter's office and he picked up the receiver. Sonia's voice said, "Walter? Can I talk?"

"What is it, my dear?" She rarely rang.

"The Gestapo sent an urn with Frau Bauer's ashes to her family. They knocked at the door and handed it over. No explanation. Just like that." Her voice was low.

There was a long pause before she said,

"They sentenced her to death and no one knew. The family didn't know. This is their first news since she was taken away."

"Sonia, I'm very sorry."

He listened to her breathing.

She knew better than to mention Benno Martin over the phone. Benno had not responded to the request for help.

"I wanted to tell you." She sounded distant, forlorn.

"I understand," he said. "I'm very sorry, my dear."

"The children..."

"Indeed. No need to tell them."

"If they ask, I'll say we don't know where she is."

Around them, people disappeared; friends were arrested. A few were let out again, others were sent to Dachau. Some killed themselves or died of ill-treatment in prison or in the camp. Still others left the country. The Mannheims's life continued with a constricted routine. In the park where Sonia used to meet Elise, a bench was painted bright yellow, a "Jew's bench". No one sat on it. Elise and Sonia felt safest meeting at home.

Another washer woman was taken on. Sonia dismissed her almost immediately; a few more were tried and found lacking, until Walter pointed out how unlikely she was to find another Frau Bauer.

He stirred beside her in the dark and she woke. He moaned, threw his arms about and shouted, a long open sound without articulation, getting higher and stronger, a sound of resistance and defence, his legs kicking. She shook him to wake him up, to cut short the agitation and distress. He woke enough to embrace her. Their bodies intertwined. "You were shouting," she murmured into his chest. "There was a reason," he mumbled.

"Something bad?"

"Yes, they were attacking us, attacking the children."

"The children? Walter?" She sat up. "What is it?"

He gave in and said, "There's a possibility that they may forbid Jewish children to attend school."

She pulled away from him and asked, "They can do that?"

"Someone in Streicher's damned hierarchy would like to. They were discussing the odds at our last board meeting."

"Then they'll do it," said Sonia. "They will! Each time we're surprised and amazed at the new torment they invent for us, but no one defends us. That man is free to do with us what he wants, and then we get used to whatever it is and say proudly and so stupidly, so *stupidly*, 'We can cope!'"

She switched on her bedside lamp, got out of bed and slipped on her dressing gown, tying the belt with quick sharp movements. "I need to think about this," she told him, standing at the foot of the bed. "What will become of them? Not just ours, all of them, we'll have to start our own schools, in addition to the ones for the Orthodox, I mean."

"Yes," said Walter.

Then Sonia said, "Maybe it's just as well. The children don't always tell us what happens there. I heard about a child who was called up in front of the class for a demonstration, a lesson in what a Jew looks like, and described using the most appalling terminology."

"I'd heard about it too... They're unhappy."

"An understatement if ever there was one!"

She paused to gain control of her rising temper, and then added in a calmer voice, "Irene wants to send Lore elsewhere. She says it's only a matter of time before Lore refuses to attend school altogether.

Helena would miss her dreadfully. You know she hates school. She's becoming wilder and wilder. We must find a Jewish school."

Then she said, "Irene's thinking of a Jewish *Landschule* in Brandenburg."

"A *Landschule*? Where they teach about farming?"

"Not really – though I heard that the children learn to grow vegetables. There's an emphasis on a healthy outdoors life, back to nature, that sort of thing. It's by a lake and they swim a lot."

"She'd love that – where is this?"

"In Caputh, a village near Potsdam."

"Is it any good?"

"Walter, it's not as if she's learning anything now. She needs to get away, to be among Jews, not among people who... who behave as if they despise us. Everyone says the situation in the countryside is not as bad as it is here. As far as the school is concerned, I'm told it follows modern educational guidelines."

"Which means?"

She hesitated and then admitted, "You won't have heard of it, something called the Froebel Method."

He said, "As a matter of fact, I have heard of it: the Nazis burnt this Froebel's books with all the others. Not because he's Jewish, he's not – but because of his ideas. What else do you know about them?"

"He says that our approach is wrong, too authoritarian, that each child is different and has different needs and that they should learn to use their hands as well as their heads and their hearts."

"Their hearts? Sounds mushy."

"It does, and yet I'm told that what happens is extraordinary – the children rise to the occasion and work on projects of their choice such as drama, sport, languages or maths. They study whatever they've chosen in depth, so that their project encompasses other fields. The school is small – only about one hundred pupils. They love it there. Irene has heard that children are reluctant to come home during the holidays. They call it a paradise – a paradise! Can you imagine, with everything that's going on at the moment?"

She appealed to him, "Helena is difficult because she's miserable. Let me enrol her. Let her at least be happy. They might even manage to teach her something."

"I'll think about it… we must find something for Max – if all else fails, an apprenticeship until this is over."

"Until this is over?" She struggled to keep her voice low. "You're incorrigible! Can't you see that there's no future for us here? None, none at all! Surely there's a limit to your… your optimism?"

"We mustn't give up."

"Walter, we should be leaving, and you refuse to do so! Let our children be where they can feel at ease. Nuremberg's streets are not safe. Nobody is safe here. Whenever anyone of you is out, whether you're at work or the children at school, I'm worried, frightened even. An unexpected knock at the door sets my heart racing."

"Nobody is attacking your children. They are children, and a child should live with his parents, not among strangers, where anything might happen to them. They're safe with us."

They were going round in circles. She sighed, slid her feet into her slippers and went quickly down the stairs to the kitchen where she turned on the light, measured a cupful of water into the kettle, put it on the stove to boil, and leant back against the table, her arms crossed, deep in thought. The water boiled and she made herself camomile tea, a soothing ritual. She added a small spoonful of honey, watched the golden colour spread in the depth. She sat down, elbows on the table, holding the hot cup between her fingertips, alternately blowing and sipping.

She loved this house, this town, but they had to leave. She was determined to make Walter see sense. Fanny and Elise faced a similar quandary: their husbands felt one hundred per cent German and remained loyal to the state. Having risked their lives for the country, having managed to survive, returning relatively unscathed, they said that now, when their beloved Germany was in the hands of thugs and thieves, now was not the time to abandon her. They would not allow the fascists to win. The German people as a whole were honest and good. In due course, this rogue regime would be overthrown, and order would return. Walter had experienced the Western Front, the terrible losses, the dead, the wounded, Leo's suicide, all for the sake of the Fatherland. His decorations were for valour; many of those who scorned him now knew very well how he'd fought; they knew about the Iron Cross and the other honours. That did not protect him. Were it not for Hindenburg's gesture to his Jewish veterans, Walter would be prohibited from earning a living, like all the other Jewish men.

How could she protect the children, ensure their spirit was not crushed, their future not jeopardized? Elise, Hilde, Fanny, Oma, Irene, the women, the mothers, they all knew it was urgent to move their children and grandchildren to a safer place. Frau Koslovski told stories about her grandfather, who had taken his family and fled the pogroms in the East, abandoning everything: house, land, synagogue, the ancestors in the cemetery. It seemed to Sonia as if the entire German nation was now waging a vast, irrevocable pogrom against its Jews "who should get out while they still could," said Frau Koslovski.

But Herr Koslovski had also fought in the war. He owned a bicycle workshop set up by his father which still brought in just enough money, and he was reluctant to lose it, to become a refugee, suffering a fate of pennilessness in yet another strange land. So they stayed, trapped in the same dilemma: to stay was to court disaster, but leaving meant losing everything, because one had to pay to get out. The Nazis called those payments taxes. In the end, those who emigrated were left without a penny. "Be patient," said the men, but Sonia felt with every bone in her body that the danger was increasing day by day.

She washed her cup under the tap, dried and put it away, turned off the light and climbed the stairs on quiet feet. Helena's door was ajar; Sonia slipped in to look at her in the dim light: she was lying on her back with her arms flung out, her mouth a little open, a beautiful child on the verge of womanhood. Bärchen was half under the pillow. She resisted the urge to kiss her, and returned to her own bed, settling down under the eiderdown beside Walter who was snoring lightly. When she finally slept, she dreamt she was running through dark winding cobbled streets pursued by an inchoate evil which was closing in on her, the children in danger though they were not there. Walter woke her when she screamed.

FIFTEEN

President Hindenburg died in August 1934, and Germany became a dictatorship under Hitler. Shortly after the funeral, national elections to the Reichstag confirmed what Sonia believed and Walter had long denied, that the German people had given up fighting for democracy and had completely surrendered to Hitler's will.

Walter was on his way to a meeting one afternoon when a hand in a fine leather glove, a female hand, touched his arm. He looked down, for she was very short. There stood Frau Schinkel who had taught him the piano when he was a boy, for a year or two, to no avail. They'd both been young then, only about ten years between them; she'd been about to get married.

"How are you, Rechtsanwalt Mannheim?"

"I am well, and how are you, Frau Schinkel?" He was polite but ill at ease, afraid of attracting attention.

"We haven't seen each other for such a long time, maybe four years. Do you remember? We met at the opera, with your lovely wife. *Die*

Fledermaus, I think it was." She beamed at him, good will personified.

"We have not attended many operas of late," he said.

The city council still allowed Jews into the Opera House but Sonia preferred to stay away. Not fond of Wagner.

"How is your family?" He remembered she had children, probably in their forties by now.

"My son," she said, and he could tell she was very proud from the way she spoke, "my son is doing very well."

"Excellent! What does he do?"

"My eldest," she said with satisfaction, "is rising in the Party. They're giving him more and more responsibility and it's said that he'll go far. They have encouraged him to apply for a job in Streicher's office, with Streicher himself."

Bemused, he lifted his hat to her as politely as he could and took his leave. She would think him rude, no doubt, walking away in mid-conversation. Sweet and innocent. She knew he was Jewish but understood nothing. She had no idea of what was happening to them, no idea of the impact of Nazi policies. Yet the information was there in the newspapers, in the newsreels at the cinema, not to mention the notices in shop windows – Jews *unerwünscht*, the harassment, the theft of their property in various ways. Could she not see?

He wondered whether it was an inability to think things through, to imagine the consequences of what she read in the paper. Maybe what she was told did not translate into reality. Or did she believe that what was happening was inevitable? Whatever the reason for the German population's passivity, the Jews were suffering greatly because of it.

When he got home that evening, Max reported that the other Jewish boy in his class was leaving for Argentina. Hans's absence would leave Max alone, "in a sea of contempt," said Sonia later that night. Really, her language was unnecessarily powerful at times.

It was December 1935. The weather's cold bite intensified; Walter tucked his scarf into his overcoat against the sharp-edged wind. The streets were dull except for a few red flags remaining from the September Rally, unwelcome reminders of an abrupt decline in the fortunes of German Jews; for on the occasion of that rally an exceptional session of the Reichstag had been held in Nuremberg which had enacted the most appalling racist legislation.

As Walter made his way through the streets, insults might be muttered, sometimes shouted. Even Heinz, stepping outside his pub, emptied a bucket of filthy water into the street which he was unable to sidestep in time. Walter had become more or less inured to being shunned, but since these new Nazi laws, the rejections were more ostentatious, more frequent. It could be difficult to maintain one's composure.

Marriage to a Jew was forbidden, as was a sexual liaison or an innocent friendship. The isolation of the Jewish community was to be complete. Any contact between Jew and non-Jew was labelled 'racial defilement', both sides liable to be punished. Leo Katzenberger, an influential figure in the Jewish community, had been arrested for his friendship with a young woman he'd known since she was a child. If the charge of sexual liaison held up in court, she might be sent to prison; he risked a death sentence.

Reaching Pierckheimerstrasse, Walter passed a well-dressed woman whom he recognised, the mother of an erstwhile friend of Max's who lived in the neighbourhood. She swept by in a wide arc, with an exaggerated grimace of disgust. He noticed a Nazi badge pinned to her coat's lapel, a common sight these days.

Some were indifferent to the Jews' segregation and victimisation; others rejoiced. But under the vigilant scrutiny of their peers, they were all wary, afraid of transgressing the new laws through an inadvertent lapse or apparent wrong-doing, afraid of being reported to the authorities. They denounced Jews for all manner of misdemeanours, mostly fabrications designed to establish their loyalty to the Nazi regime. The Gestapo did not lack for informers.

The second law passed by the Reichstag that day had revoked the Jews' German citizenship; they were deemed 'not of German blood' by the racist regime. From one day to the next, they were labelled alien, foreign, though Jews had lived in Germany for over a thousand years. They had become stateless.

The repercussions of statelessness were not clear to most people. As Walter explained to Sonia and Max, the news was bad: "When these laws are enacted, we'll lose our right to justice, to ownership of property, to security. Our right to vote. No right to any rights at all."

Max asked, "Can't the League of Nations do something?"

"They're weak, not interested, ill-informed; their own Commissioner for Refugees resigned last month in protest. They yearn for Hitler to bring Germany back into their League, to rejoin the club."

Sonia asked, "So will no one speak for us?"

Walter said, "We're a tiny minority, like the Germans from the Sudetenland or the Russian refugees in France. But unlike them, we've no country, no state, no territory to return to. We're from nowhere, belonging nowhere. We can only rely on our own." He felt an upswelling of emotion and paused till it receded. Not twenty years earlier, one hundred thousand Jewish men had sworn an oath to protect the Republic. They'd fought in the war, most of them at the front. Twelve thousand had died. Eighteen thousand were decorated for valour. Now their homeland had disappeared from under their feet, since Nazi Germany refused to recognise that they belonged there. "A man without a state does not exist legally," he said. "If he leaves Germany, he becomes a refugee in a foreign country, whose language he speaks badly, if at all, where he cannot work or take up permanent residence. He's on his own, without community support. No one cares about him."

"However," he added, "there is one anomaly; should a stateless man stand accused of any crime at all, even stealing an apple from a market stall, he immediately regains a legal status: that of a criminal. In principle criminals have defined rights, the right to decent treatment in prison and the right to a fair trial, for instance. This means that all the baseless accusations levelled against Jews these days will result in court appearances following normal legal procedure. A stateless person can be thrown in jail and tortured, or allowed to die of neglect. Not so a petty thief or swindler"

Sonia asked, "But who will defend them against those accusations?"

Walter said, "A Jewish lawyer. No one else will touch the case."

It turned out that the new laws would only be fully enforced the following year, in autumn 1936, after the Berlin Olympics were over and done with and the eyes of the world were no longer focussed on Germany and her Nazi regime.

All over Germany the Jews turned to the only companionship available, that of their own community; these days, Walter, Oma and Sonia attended most services at the synagogue, despite the officious presence of Nazis monitoring every word spoken from the *bimah*.

———

Fritz and Frieda Klein came for coffee and cake on a Sunday afternoon, Frieda as elegant as usual, her silver hair cut fashionably short. Sonia poured the coffee and wondered whether Frieda had lost weight again; reaching for her cup, her hands seemed skeletal, the skin almost transparent. She'd eaten very little. "How are things in England? How is dear Alicia?" asked Sonia.

"Studying hard," said Frieda. Alicia was preparing for the entrance examination to an English medical school. "We hoped she would come home for a week or so, but she's about to sit exams. We shall have to wait until they're over."

Nothing more was said on the topic. Sonia thought of Walter's objections to sending their children away; it was true that they were younger and less disciplined than Alicia; besides there was no trusted friend in England to care for them. But she wished she could protect them from the harm which was inflicted on them daily.

Walter coughed. He was about to change the subject, she could tell; the topic made him uncomfortable.

Walter said, "I had a strange experience the other day, a kind of revelation."

She was surprised and a little irritated; he hadn't mentioned anything.

"I was working in my study, the window open," said Walter. "I could hear the children in the garden, shouting and laughing; there occurred from time to time a pinging noise which I couldn't identify. They were out of sight, and they appeared to be having such a good time that I became suspicious, as any parent might."

They were all smiling.

"I went to see what they were up to, and discovered that my military helmet, my *Pickelhaube*, was anchored to a low branch of the cherry tree. Max had pinched it from the basement. He and Helena were taking turns, throwing pebbles at it, aiming for the coat of arms: it pings when it's hit. That was that high note." The familiar emblem appeared in countless settings all over Bavaria – lions prancing over the motto *In steadfast loyalty*.

Walter said, "We were all taught from childhood to revere the flag, the emblem and its words, weren't we. Once upon a time, I swore loyalty to this country. I fought for it. My children were educated in the same tradition at home and at school – and here they were, casting stones! To my great surprise I experienced no outrage, no anger! I felt nothing at all! Complete indifference."

He addressed Fritz. "As I stood there, I realised that everything, everything those symbols represented has disappeared."

None of them spoke. Sonia felt fury gather and swell in her chest like a storm about to break. She looked down, staring at her hands which were clenched in her lap.

Fritz said, "It's true that the Germany we once knew has vanished. But one day, a day hopefully not far off, real Germans will emerge again, worthy of our love and respect."

Exactly what Walter believed. Sonia bit her lip, and asked Walter, "What did you say to the children?" Her voice sounded flat.

"I didn't speak to them. They didn't notice me, so I went away."

"And what did you do, following this epiphany?" asked Frieda. Was that sarcasm? wondered Sonia.

Walter said, "I sat in my study for a long time, unable to work. The end of my commitment to this country – and I felt nothing at all."

Sonia picked up the empty coffee pot. She said in what she hoped were normal tones, "More coffee, anyone?"

As she went into the house, she heard Fritz say, "A kind of liberation."

Alone in the kitchen, she poured herself a glass of water from the tap, watching the water rise, willing her hand not to tremble with the rage flooding her body. She drank slowly, forcing herself to concentrate on the water's coolness. She put the glass down and stared blindly out of the window, waiting for the emotion to subside. Having at long last relinquished his attachment to Germany, might he at last see sense and agree to emigrate?

When she returned, the men were discussing an eventual war.

Fritz said, "They're preparing."

"Who is?" asked Sonia.

"The German government," said Walter.

"The signs are there," said Fritz. "A man arrived at the hospital with a leg broken 'during an exercise'. He was fit, bright enough, the right age, an SA stalwart. He'd received competent care on the spot – but not in a German hospital, one could tell from the cast. I chatted to him and he let slip that he'd been in Russia. Most likely military training. Probably an officer's training course."

"But the SA's only weapons are spades," said Frieda.

"Germany is manufacturing arms; it's an open secret," said Walter, "Thereby reducing unemployment, an added benefit, the Versailles Treaty notwithstanding."

Fritz said, "Another two years, and they'll be ready."

Sonia said nothing. She wondered where the family would be in two years' time. For all his changed attitude to Germany, Walter had said not a word about leaving.

Helena was lonely. Lore had left for a Jewish boarding school near Potsdam, a Land School. She'd written that it was in a beautiful park by a lake where the children swam. She sounded happy. Helena had difficulty imagining happiness at a boarding school, but she did envy Lore for leaving home.

These days, Helena walked back from school with an older girl called Inge, who lived nearby. Inge had told Helena that her parents would leave Germany as soon as "a big fat Nazi" made a decent offer for her father's workshop. This workshop produced a new-fangled invention called a "zip fastener". The only zip fastener Helena had ever seen was on Inge's jacket: its sharp shiny metal teeth reminded her of the crocodile at the zoo. Inge said that her father could make zip fasteners in all sizes and colours. They would revolutionise the world of fashion: no more hooks-and-eyes, no more buttons! Much simpler, she said. Helena listened politely. Even supposing Inge was right, she wondered how the rest of the world would come to hear of this strange invention. How would one convince people to use it?

As they walked towards the tunnel in the fortifications which led to their neighbourhood, they heard laughter behind them, girls' laughter and giggles. Glancing back, Helena recognised a girl she knew from primary school, who had come to play in the garden once or twice – in the distant, cheerful time when no one cared who was Jewish and who wasn't. Helena hadn't seen her since. The giggles turned into jeers, which grew louder, threatening. The group was catching up with them now, intoning something Helena didn't understand, though they seemed to want to be heard. They were chanting it in unison, a threat combined with the laughter. Helena shivered. She had a knot in her stomach, and she felt her heart beating furiously.

They walked faster but the girls closed in on them, their chant now unmistakable: *Juda verrecke! Juda verrecke!* over and over, hissing and spitting, echoing in the confined space. They were right behind them and one of them trod on Helena's heel. Helena turned to face a tall girl with a spotty face and greasy hair standing over her, gloating, poking hard fingers into Helena's chest, baying the horrid words. Another girl grabbed Inge's long hair and pulled, and Inge roared – like a lion, thought Helena – and slapped her hard. Helena kicked her assailant in the ankles, and swung her school bag at the other girl, losing her balance and stumbling forward – she pulled back her arm and thrust, punching the tall thin one in the stomach with her clenched fist; the girl gasped and folded up, emitting a high-pitched scream, which surprised and frightened the others, who yelled more horrid things about Jews, their eyes cruel and their mouths like gargoyles, spraying spittle, their teeth glistening. Helena fought beside Inge, both of them kicking and hitting like furies, until the attackers ran away and the two of them stood dishevelled and shocked. They looked down the empty tunnel and laughed crazily, their shrieks echoing back, tears running down their cheeks. Still giggling, they tidied themselves up, tucked their blouses back into their skirts; Inge found her hairclip on the ground and combed her hair with her fingers. They checked each other's appearance and walked arm in arm out onto the wooden bridge across the moat, the sound of their steps like a drum-beat. Pierckheimerstrasse wasn't far, and they were still tittering when they reached Helena's house, where they told her mother what had happened. She shook her head without saying much and phoned Inge's mother, asking her to come over. She fetched the brown disinfectant and dabbed it on Helena's arm where there was a long scratch and on Inge's grazed knee. Helena didn't feel well by now, sort of wobbly, and rather cold, and her mother sat her in her father's big armchair and tucked a blanket around her. Inge's mother arrived and Inge cried while her mother held her and said "There, there." The mothers had a quiet talk and then Inge's mother took Inge home. That evening, her father told Helena she'd been brave; Max was impressed, though by then Helena felt as if the attack had happened to someone else. It was arranged that from now on, her mother and Inge's mother would take turns waiting for Helena and Inge at the entrance to the tunnel.

Helena disliked that idea. She didn't want her mother to stand and wait; her mother would look sad and sigh and sigh as if she couldn't breathe deeply enough to fill her lungs. Helena longed for the old life, when events had been predictable, when mothers stayed home and entertained other people with coffee and cake in the garden.

The next day, her father announced that Helena was to attend the Land School near Potsdam, Lore's school, and Helena was enraptured at the thought of leaving Nuremberg and changing school. "What about Inge?" she asked. Her mother said Inge had been offered a position at a Jewish primary school to help teach the younger children. She was good with the little ones.

SIXTEEN

On the tram to Miss Winteringham's Max stood swaying, clinging to a strap. At the Plaerrer, many people got off and the crowd shifted. He found himself face to face with a beautiful girl.

Every single item belonging to Helena was labelled with her name. Her mother sat up late stitching tags onto her clothes – every last sock, all her underwear and her towels. The tags came in a thick white roll on which *Helena Mannheim* was embroidered in slanting red letters in endless iteration. At first Helena had welcomed them as an omen of independence. But her mother wouldn't allow her to help with the sewing, saying, "You'd only make a mess of it." Everything was packed by her mother herself into two suitcases, a large one and a small one. Helena inserted Bärchen into the big suitcase at the last minute. No tag on him.

The next morning, after goodbye kisses and big hugs from Father and Max, Helena and her mother took a taxi to Nuremberg's central station and embarked on the train trip to Berlin. Forbidden to stand in the corridor or wander through the train, Helena was reduced to reading or staring out the window. Around midday, the situation improved when an elderly waiter came by to announce in ceremonial tones that lunch would be served in the dining wagon in ten minutes' time.

After the confinement of the passenger compartment, the dining wagon seemed exciting and luxurious, with its maroon leather seats, silver cutlery, cruets and folded napkins laid out on white tablecloths. Helena leaned back in her seat, smiling in delight at her mother, who smiled back and reached over to pat her hand. Outside, the world streamed by, hills covered in forests, fields with and without cattle, here and there people at work, red-roofed farms, villages with traditional timbered houses. She was leaving home for a long time and she did not mind at all. There would be Lore, and the lake. Father didn't think much of the school, but her mother seemed sure Helena would be happy. Helena had noticed her mother sighing repeatedly that morning and wondered why. She enjoyed the luxury of unfolding her starched napkin, laid it on her lap and picked up the menu.

They spent a night in Berlin at Tante Liesel's. Tante Liesel always made a fuss of Helena, perhaps because she only had a son, no daughters. Helena loved the grand apartment, the third-floor view of the great trees lining the street, but they didn't stay long. In the morning she and her mother caught an early train, a humbler one, painted red and cream, lacking a dining wagon. It was one of the new electric trains launched only recently on the suburban line, which Max and her father had once discussed enthusiastically. They were reputed to be modern, cleaner and more spacious than the steam trains. That was exciting, though the trip to Potsdam was brief; a man with a car was to meet them at the station.

When they found him, she was surprised how young he was. He introduced himself. "My name is Egon." And to Helena's further surprise, for he seemed only a few years older than she was, he added, "I teach biology."

The car was ordinary and rather dusty. Egon placed Helena's suitcases in the boot. She found it strange that he was someone who carried your luggage and expected to be called by his first name, that he was employed as both a driver and a teacher. She was aware of her mother not saying anything, probably thinking similar thoughts. Her Nuremberg school had been for girls only, the teachers mature women who were always addressed formally, their first names unknown, hidden. Helena was embarrassed to call Egon by his first name within earshot of her mother. He asked her, "Would you like to sit in front?"

"Yes please!" she said, while her mother frowned.

As they drove off, her mother asked him about himself and he said that besides teaching, he drove the car when required and helped around the school and garden.

The road ran through a forest, tall trees with shimmering leaves. Helena soon saw the brightness of the lake shining and flickering between the trees; she sat bolt upright, almost bouncing with excitement. From the back seat came her mother's voice, "Do sit still, Helena!"

At the entrance to the village, the road became a cobbled street. She caught glimpses of the shimmering water between the houses; she saw windows trimmed with bright geraniums, tidy gardens, a sturdy church, a few shops and a pub.

"The village is out of bounds to students," said Egon. "The main school building is on the hill above the holiday homes. There's a path leading straight down to the lake."

"How often may people swim?" asked Helena.

"With the weather warming up, we're swimming most days before breakfast, though some people prefer to walk in the woods."

Her mother asked, "So early?"

"Officially at a quarter past six. Some rise earlier. After swimming or walking, we work in the vegetable garden for a spell – mostly weeding."

Helena asked, "Before breakfast?"

"Yes," said Egon with a grin.

Helena mulled over the information.

The street turned away from the lake, became a dusty lane leading up towards the wood. They reached tall gates framing a drive. The car turned in and drove up to a large house, a kind of manor house with a peculiar turret. They'd arrived.

The office of Fräulein Gertrud Feiertag, the school's founder and director, was a comfortable room with a large desk in a bay window overlooking the park. In the distance, Helena could see a radiance which she thought must be the lake. A large sofa and several armchairs were arranged around a low round table with a steaming teapot and a plate of biscuits. Helena was invited to sit on the sofa, and Fräulein Feiertag sat beside her. She said that everyone at the school called her Tante Trude. She was interested in hearing what Helena had to say. Helena looked into Tante Trude's bright brown eyes and to her great surprise felt welcome. She was asked how she felt about the separation from her family. Helena explained that Lore was a close friend and that her mother had predicted she'd love the school. With her mother's nodded approval, they agreed that Helena would study both English and French (Like Max! thought Helena with a surge of delight); many children were learning languages in preparation for emigration. Tante Trude said that Tante Sophie would be Helena's house mother as well as her English teacher. Tante Sophie arrived, another surprise. Sophie was as young as Egon, with a shock of dark hair, a vigorous handshake and a friendly greeting. More like a sister than an aunt, thought Helena, astonished. She could detect equal surprise in her mother's polite demeanour. She was relieved when Tante Trude mentioned Sophie's "outstanding" teaching qualifications; that would put her mother's mind at rest.

Sophie took Helena and her mother to see the house further down the lane where Helena would live with Lore and other children. "This is a classroom, and this," said Sophie, opening doors to a large room on the ground floor "is my room. If I'm not at the main house, I'm here most evenings. You can call on me any time, Helena."

Helena and Lore's room was on the third floor, under the roof. Lore herself was away on a walk with her class. "They'll be back for afternoon tea," said Sophie. They were served lunch at the main house, in the dining room in the company of a gaggle of younger children. Sophie explained that the lettuce was home-grown and that they also grew carrots, spring onions, beans, potatoes, and even pumpkins. Helena had never eaten pumpkin: pumpkins belonged in Grimm's fairy tales, as far as she was concerned; in the real world it was poor people's food, she thought. After lunch, her mother took leave of Helena with a kiss and Egon drove her away, her gloved hand waving goodbye out of the car window.

Helena returned to the room under the roof and unpacked Bärchen from the suitcase, laying him on her pillow. She went out and wandered up the lane, around the deserted park, orchards and vegetable beds. She discovered a path which she thought might lead to the lake. Running down the hill, she reached a pebbly beach by the water and paused to take in the view. The lake lay cradled among green hills. Further along the shore, by a boat shed, several small boats were moored off a wharf, bobbing gently. In the distance, she could see triangular white sails on the water.

Near the edge of the water, the pebbles turned into sand. The rippling waves seemed inviting, so she removed her shoes and socks and paddled, the water flowing gently round her toes. Little waves splashed onto the beach, a few birds – gulls? – cawed and wheeled above her. Tentatively, she inched deeper, bunching her skirt up around her thighs. There was no other sound except for the lapping water and the birds. She felt alone, but not lonely. She breathed in deeply. She was aware of the beautiful landscape. I am lucky, she thought. I only have to wait for Lore to arrive and everything will be perfect.

When she thought it was time for afternoon tea, she made her way up the hill on bare feet, carrying her socks and shoes, wincing over the gravel. She reached the lawn by the main house, wiped her feet on the grass and struggled to pull her socks over damp feet. Peeking into the empty dining room, she saw bowls of apples and plums, and jugs of water on one of the tables. The clock on the wall showed four o'clock. She sat on a bench outside, waiting.

She heard their chatter and laughter before she saw them: a crowd of teenagers turned the corner of the house, Lore among them. Lore waved and rushed over to Helena, and they hugged and kissed. They went in and sat down to eat, side by side at one of the big tables. Lore introduced her to everyone. Afterwards, they walked over to the other house with the room under the roof. Lore sat on her bed telling Helena about life at the school, watching Helena unpack and arrange her clothes in the cupboard and chest of drawers. Lore said this was heaven. She said everyone's favourite time was Saturday morning, when they all gathered for a talk with Tante Trude. People could discuss anything with her, whatever was on their mind. It was the best thing ever.

That evening after dinner, one of the older boys stood up and welcomed Helena in the name of the whole school and everyone looked at her, which was both nice and embarrassing. She was asked if she wanted to say anything in reply and she stood up and said quickly, "Thank you," before sitting down again beside Lore. A group of children then played scratchy music on the violin and the flute, a man helping them along on the piano.

The next morning, the wake-up call came shockingly early, though it was already light outside. She and Lore joined the children running down to the lake in their bathing suits. Everyone splashed straight into the water despite the cold. Lore said they had twenty minutes before the whistle. Swimming in the clear water among the gentle hills, Helena felt the happiest she'd been in a long time. Then she thought about it again and realised that she could not remember ever being so happy.

The whistle blew and they ran back to the house to wash and dress, before joining everyone at the vegetable beds, where Helen was introduced to her first pumpkin plant. She was surprised at the size of the leaves – bigger than her hand. It was not difficult to tell which were weeds and which were not. The earth was loose and damp and they came out easily. Very soon a bell clanged and they went to wash their hands before filing into the dining room.

Everyone stood by their chairs until Tante Trude gave the sign to sit down. Rolls and slices of bread were on the table, with butter, cheese, honey and jam. Helena reached out, but Lore stopped her with a gesture. In the pause that followed, Helena realised that no one was moving or talking. The big hall was quiet, very quiet – a hundred children and many adults sitting still, silence settling around them. She noticed for the first time the ticking of a large clock on the wall. Then the man who had played the piano the previous evening played again. The notes flowed into lovely harmonies and Helena listened intently, wanting the music not to end.

When it was over, there was again a prolonged silence before people began to eat. They did not talk much, as if some of the silence remained inside them. Lore told her they listened to piano or violin music every morning. A violinist from the Berlin Philharmonic had visited once and played a piece by Bach. So beautiful, she said. He'd gone overseas, leaving the orchestra and Germany for ever.

After breakfast, Helena attended Lore's history lesson. The children sat in a circle with the teacher to discuss their projects. Lore was researching the life of Alfred Einstein, who owned a holiday villa nearby. Einstein himself had left for the United States and the villa was rented to youth groups. Helena who had no such project was soon bored; the teacher told Lore to take Helena to the kitchen to see if she might help there.

In the busy kitchen Helena was given a spotless apron by a woman introduced as Tante Klara, who was peeling a mountain of apples. "For a strudel," she explained. Helena helped peel the apples. She didn't think she was very good at it – too slow. When they'd finished, she was given a broom to sweep up all the pieces of peel she'd dropped on the floor. Her mother would have called it a great mess, but Tante Klara didn't. She just gave Helena the broom. As they chatted Tante Klara measured and mixed the ingredients and Helena discovered that she also taught German literature and Hebrew. With the strudel in the oven, she asked Helena if she wanted to copy the recipe. The school recipe was for fifty people, which had been tripled to one hundred and fifty. Helena sat at the high bench; she had to work out the quantities for four people, the size of her own family. She enjoyed imagining her mother's surprise when she baked them a strudel! Then the same old struggle arose when she had to divide or multiply numbers, with the zeroes and the comma – by how many places to shift the comma? While peeling potatoes, Tante Klara guided Helena through her confusion. At the end of the morning, to Helena's amazement and gratitude, Tante Klara asked whether she would like to assist her in the kitchen for a couple of hours in the morning, once a week, providing Tante Trude agreed.

Before lunch, Helena and Lore returned to their room to make their beds. This consisted of giving the feather eiderdowns a good shake and letting them settle again, which they did soundlessly like big soft birds. One of the children swept the room and another came by to check that it was tidy. Helena's name was entered onto the roster for housekeeping. She felt apprehensive about this new role, but Lore said there was nothing to it. Lore promised she'd help.

―――――――

The following afternoon, the sky was brilliant and cloudless, the sun hot, and all lessons were officially cancelled in favour of swimming. Students and teachers in bathing suits trooped down the path to the lake, white towels round their necks. Helena was disconsolate; her period had started and she would have to stay behind. Tante Sophie left her with two older girls for company, before disappearing down the path with the other children. Lore ran to catch up with them, waving goodbye.

The other girls lay sprawled on the lawn, gossiping about boys and giggling. Helena longed to be on her own. There had been no respite since her arrival, every minute crowded with strange people, except for Lore.

"I think I'll go to my room," she said, standing up.

They looked up at her, a little shame-faced. "Would you like us to come with you?"

Helena shook her head and they didn't insist. She went down the lane to the house and slowly climbed the flight of stairs to her room. Light streamed in through the two attic windows. She kicked off her sandals and curled up on the bed, hugging Bärchen. The faded blue wallpaper by the bed was patterned with delicate flowers, mushrooms and fairies. Might the room once have been a nursery, she wondered, or a young girl's room, someone younger than herself? From her bed, she could see through the window a luminous blue sky and the crowns of trees. She had noticed the tall trees in the nearby forest, the sparse undergrowth, the sandy ground, a light colour, with occasional drifts of crisp brown leaves; they seemed to invite one to run and play. She thought of the lake. Another few days and she'd be able to swim again.

She woke up unsure how long she'd slept. Tip-toeing out to the landing, her naked feet were soundless on the wooden floor. The doors to the other rooms were open and she peeked in cautiously. No one was there. Someone had said the house was rented from people who had emigrated. Emigration was often mentioned here, more than at home. One of the boys studied Spanish because he was going to Chile. Everyone learnt English.

Things were different here, thought Helena. Her parents didn't talk about leaving Germany, though many people they knew had left, even close relatives like Tante Gusti and Uncle Hugo. And every single person at the school was Jewish – the children, the teachers and the young women who helped in the houses. Lore had pointed out the mezuzahs on every doorjamb in the main house – a Jewish house. The food was apparently kosher: it didn't seem much different from what she ate at home.

Helena went down the stairs, exploring the second floor. One room was set up as a classroom with chairs and tables and the others were bedrooms with three or four beds each. On the ground floor, the door to Tante Sophie's room was closed.

The house had a kitchen which did not seem to be in use – all the cooking probably took place at the main house – except for a large bowl of plums on the scrubbed wooden table. They were plump, dark and shiny, and she couldn't resist. She took only one; it wouldn't be missed. The plum was as good as it looked, sweet and luscious. Juice ran down her chin. On to her white blouse.

Spots should be washed out immediately, her mother said. Helena tore up the stairs to her room. Sucking on the pit of the plum, she changed into a clean blouse. She spat the pit into the palm of her hand, admiring its perfect oval shape. She couldn't see a wastepaper basket, so she put it down on the low cabinet between the beds. She rushed to the bathroom and ran water over the spot: it seemed to glow all the more. She dabbed a nailbrush with soap and scrubbed. The soap failed to foam and there was no change. She scrubbed and rinsed, but the spot was impervious, bright as ever. Such a beautiful colour, in the wrong place. By now, the entire blouse was soaked and dripping, and she realised there was also a wet patch on her stomach and a puddle on the floor. She thought of hanging the blouse up to dry, but didn't know where a line could be found. She didn't want anyone to know what had happened, so she squeezed the blouse as dry as she could and hung it out of sight on a hook behind the bathroom door. It wasn't the right place, but she didn't know where else to put it.

The house was utterly silent, and she began to feel as if she were the only person in the world. She lay on her bed and held Bärchen, buried her face in his belly, sniffing him to get the smell of home. She longed for home so much that she began to cry.

"Helena, my dear, what is it?" Tante Trude stood at the door.

Helena wiped her tears away, but more kept coming.

"No swimming today?"

"I'm not well," said Helena. The words came out croaky.

"Your period, is it?"

She nodded and sobbed harder. Helena had never discussed her period with anyone, not even Lore. Her first period had been frightening and unexpected. She'd gone to her mother thinking she might be dying of some disease, but her mother had said, "It's just your period," and explained that it would happen regularly from now on and that she shouldn't swim or exercise during this time. She was sent to wash and change. By the time Helena had finished cleaning herself up, her mother had disappeared and pads and pins had been neatly laid out on Helena's bed. She'd had trouble working out how one used them. Her mother appeared to believe that Helena would know about periods and pads, but she didn't; nor did she know from whom she could learn. Something was wrong and it seemed to be her fault.

Tante Trude asked, "May I sit on your bed?"

Helena nodded.

"Missing home?"

She nodded again, trying not to cry. She found a handkerchief in her drawer, a handkerchief her mother had ironed and named for her. She blew her nose and cried more. Tante Trude sat without speaking. The plum pit lay on the cabinet; Helena braced herself for the reprimand which was sure to follow.

But the plum pit was not mentioned, though she was sure Tante Trude had noticed it.

"Are you hungry?" asked Tante Trude. "It's time for afternoon tea and there are some lovely plums from the orchard."

"I saw them in the kitchen," said Helena. "I took one. It was very nice."

"They're so juicy, they're tricky to eat!"

Helena then told Tante Trude about the spot, and Tante Trude took Helena's blouse down to the empty kitchen. She poured some milk into a cup, and dipped the stained fabric into it, explaining to Helena, "The milk may draw out the colour... we'll leave it immersed for half a day or so. I'm not sure how well it'll work, but I wouldn't worry too much about it, Helena. Isn't the colour beautiful?"

Children's voices could be heard outside.

"They're back from the lake," said Tante Trude. "Time for afternoon tea."

With strudel, hopefully, thought Helena as she ran out to look for Lore.

Max was on the tram on his way to his English lesson when he saw the girl again; he'd been watching for her and he suspected she'd noticed him too. He saw the corners of her lips rise a little, the shadow of a dimple, the hint of a smile as she edged past his seat.

A week later, they met again. When she happened to drop one of her books, he was quick to pick it up. That day he sat next to her for the first time. Her name was Marlene. Thereafter they sat together on the tram every week, talking until he reached his stop. He tried to find a way of meeting her elsewhere at a different time, but both his parents and hers always knew where they were and what they were supposed to be doing. He would have lied about where he was, but Marlene didn't think she could do that.

Miss Winteringham had introduced him to Shakespeare's love sonnet, "Shall I compare thee to a summer's day?" She was surprised that he'd learnt it by heart.

SEVENTEEN

Sunday afternoon at four, and it was Tante Suzi's turn. Max was scheduled to call on a series of aunts in rotation, one a month. He thought how Helena's departure for the Land School had liberated her from this chore, though she had never minded as much as he did. His mother assured him often that the tantes *loved* the visits, as if that made any difference. Time was deadly dull in those hushed drawing rooms, reminding Max of lifeless china cabinets. The framed photograph of a soldier would be on display, a fiancé or a husband who had died in the war. Had that man ever wanted the tante as much as he wanted Marlene? Considering the corseted old woman sitting across from him, it seemed unlikely.

Tante Suzi had a broader outlook than most. He could discuss what he read in *The Economist* with her. She'd travelled as far as Australia and New Zealand. All the aunts enquired about his schoolwork, his latest marks, the books he'd read, films he might have seen and the tennis, and then they'd run out of things to talk about, while he sat and tried not to fidget. There was no escape. His father was strict. "These women must not be forgotten," he'd declare and would add every time that he had known the men personally, they had been "brother officers", and every time his mother would nod primly and purse her mouth, so annoying. He chafed at his parents' perfect agreement in running his life, maintaining discipline and duties. Before he left home, his mother would remind him that the visit must last at least half an hour. The only redeeming feature was the cake which came with the tea.

Tante Hannelore's cook made a terrific chocolate cake, the genuine *Sachertorte*, and he'd once been unwise, accepting the second piece she'd offered him, topped with a voluptuous whirl of whipped cream, though he knew his mother would disapprove, and by the time he'd cycled home, Tante Hannelore had phoned to report everything he'd said and done, including treacherously, "He liked my *Sachertorte* very much – *two* pieces." His mother's diatribe began as soon as he walked in. He avoided listening, waiting for her to finish so he could go, and when he failed to answer or argue, her annoyance increased and she punished him as if he were a child, depriving him of dessert. He left the table gladly, fled to his room, on his own at last. When would he be able to see Marlene and spend time with her?

He learnt from the gossip at the sports club that his father had a mistress. At first, he hadn't known what to make of what the boys were saying, and when he understood, it came as a shock. His father was old, too old for passion; his mother he couldn't think of at all in that context. He was hurt in some way he couldn't comprehend. He'd wanted to hide his embarrassment, to pretend he knew, that he didn't care. The others had observed his discomfiture with something akin to glee, even those he thought of as friends. He wondered whether there was a secret, separate set of rules governing a man's behaviour, different from the one taught by parents and teachers?

In the Loewenthal's living room the windows were wide open to let in the evening air as the sweltering afternoon drew to a close. The men had gathered for their weekly game of skat.

Fritz took the final trick.

"Clever bastard!" said Walter. He stood up, stubbing out his cigar and stretching.

Robert yawned and said, "I walked by Heinz's pub yesterday, clean as a whistle."

"Clean as a whistle?" inquired Otto, pushing back his chair.

Hilde appeared at the door. "Do come. The food's on the table."

"No *Juden unerwünscht* in the window," said Robert. "And the *Stürmer* box was empty. Orders from above, according to Heinz: all appearance of antisemitism to disappear during this single August fortnight, concealing Nazi Germany's true nature from the tourists flocking to the Olympic Games."

Swastikas and red flags remained overwhelmingly in evidence. A year ago, long before the Games, the Bar Kochba sports club had searched high and low for soccer balls free of Nazi insignia, in the end importing them from Switzerland. These days, the multicoloured Olympic rings appeared with the swastika on most tourist bric-a-brac, in combination with XI Olympiade, Berlin and 1936. The Games were impossible to ignore.

Walter said, "The newspapers are celebrating the Mayer girl's return from the US, in anticipation of a gold medal. No mention of her previous expulsion from the fencing club."

"She's not really Jewish, is she?"

"Half-Jewish," said Walter.

"Nazi definition," said Otto. "No such thing. Like being half-pregnant. The mother's not Jewish, neither is the daughter."

"That's according to our definition, not theirs. The Nazis considered her Jewish enough when they threw her out."

"Indeed, they treated her like a Jew."

"Despite her Aryan looks," said Hilde. "Please come and eat."

"The girl's looks allow them to disregard her Jewish father. You'll notice a dearth of sausages," she announced as they took their seats at the table. "The butcher wouldn't sell me more, not because he's a Nazi – which he is – but because meat has apparently been requisitioned from the entire country to feed Berlin's Olympic visitors."

Otto slowly poured beer into his glass, holding it at a slant. He carefully took a first sip and wiped the white foam from his moustache. "Have you seen the newspaper? The Black Americans?"

"One of them is a fantastic runner, apparently. Black as pitch."

"They think he might win."

"It seems likely."

Hilde said, "An interesting conundrum: one of the Nazi top brass will be obliged to congratulate a Black man for his superiority, hang a medal round his neck, shake him by the hand, be photographed with him, on behalf of the racist German Volk."

"Hitler won't do it," said Walter.

"Whether the Black man wins or not, the Nazis will continue to hug their myth of innate superiority to their bosoms," said Robert, helping himself to two sausages and a dab of mustard. "A denial of reality which should contribute to their downfall."

"That may yet take a while."

"Unfortunately."

"People easily believe in their innate superiority; no need for supporting evidence," said Walter.

Fritz asked Walter, "How do you think your clever Dr Martin copes with these contradictions?"

"Not *my* Dr Martin," said Walter.

Otto asked, "You're still meeting?"

"We've not spoken for a long time, neither face to face nor on the telephone. He walked straight past me in the street the other day. No acknowledgement, too risky. We saw him at the theatre last week, Sonia and I, with Streicher and his gang, and the usual gaggle of dubious females. He seemed at ease."

"I don't know how he does it."

Walter shrugged and said, "A political animal, through and through."

Fritz asked, "But can you count on him?"

There was silence round the table.

Walter said, "I believe I can. He'll do what he can for us."

"Providing it doesn't put him at risk," said Robert.

The others shifted uncomfortably in their chairs.

Walter looked at Robert and said, "If it were really important, I believe he'd risk it."

"I hope you're right, Walter. I truly do."

As far as Max was concerned, the year went by without much change. His isolation at school was briefly interrupted by the news of the Hindenburg Zeppelin disaster in America, when the boys were united in their desire to learn every detail of the fire. He remembered it well, because it happened in May 1937, a few months before he experienced his own personal disaster.

At the end of the school year, a letter arrived from the school, with a certificate. Father read it and showed it to his mother without a word. She read it, pursed her lips and shook her head. She put her hand on Max's shoulder and said, "It's bad news, Max," before passing him the paper. Bad news?

His mother pointed to the sentence written below the list of his marks: "He leaves the school of his own free will." It was signed by the headmaster. Not Dr Staehlin, who had been replaced by a Nazi sympathiser. Max read the words and read them again, incredulous.

The lie and the rejection were like body blows after the misery of the last years, particularly since Hans's departure. He experienced afresh the sense of betrayal, the disbelief and the confusion he'd felt four years ago, when no one turned up to play football. He'd known he would have to leave school without completing his studies. Why the lie? Why did they dissociate themselves from their actions? His school didn't want him, not him nor any other Jew. They wanted to be *Judenrein*. Let them at least be honest about it! Let them tell him to his face! He paced the room, feeling as if he might explode with frustration and rage.

His father stood up. "Come Max, let's go for a walk."

Max followed his father without enthusiasm. It was early evening. In the fading light, they walked side by side through the familiar neighbourhood. His father didn't speak. Max dug his fists into his pockets. Finally he said, "It's so unfair!"

His father nodded. "You've done nothing to deserve this."

"How can they lie like that?"

"Indeed," said his father. "It's very disappointing, but not unexpected. I promise you we'll do everything we can to enable you to study."

They walked on as evening fell, the shadows deepening. His father said that work might be found for Max at Uncle Robert's publishing house, until something better came up, whatever that might be. "It'll keep you busy," he said. "Who knows, you may even be of some use. I know you would choose something different if you could, but it will have to do for now."

To Max, the thought of working at the publishing house felt like a prison sentence. The job was bound to be menial and boring. Anger welled up again and he clenched his teeth. His father touched his shoulder and Max had to restrain the impulse to shrug off his hand. "There's nothing to be done right now," said his father. "Your mother and I are examining other study options for you. Something will turn up."

His father stopped and turned towards him. Max could just make out his features in the dark. He said, "Max, remember this: never give up hope. Never."

———

In preparation for his interview with Uncle Robert, Max was dispatched on his bicycle to the barber on Essenweinstrasse, the same street as the Orthodox synagogue. He rode along the moat's parapet, past the Opera House. Until a year or so ago, he and his father had gone to a barber in the city, but a sign in their window now said: "No Jews and no dogs."

Many *Ostjuden* lived and worked in this neighbourhood. Some people – not his parents – didn't like the *Ostjuden* much, spoke ill of them. He wasn't sure why.

A barber's chair had been squeezed into the small shop crowded with goods stacked against the back wall – baskets and boxes containing china, enamelware, clothing and books, none of them related to hairdressing as far as he could tell. An odour of fried food drifted in from an open door at the back, at odds with the sweetish smells of the barber's lotions and pomades. The barber himself wore the black kippah, beard and *tzitziot* of the Orthodox. He'd been trimming the hair of a large man to whom he talked in Yiddish. To make room for Max, he swept a pile of newspapers off a chair and shooed away a small child with ringlets who scuttled out through the back door. The child wore a kippah too, bright blue embroidered with gold stars. Acutely aware of his own uncovered head, Max picked up one of the newspapers and opened it wide to hide his embarrassment. It was in Hebrew. He had trouble making sense of the words, which seemed longer than usual. They resembled German. He realised this must be Yiddish. He didn't know Yiddish, had never seen it in print. He'd thought it was an unwritten dialect.

A thin woman wearing a long dress and a headscarf emerged from the back, carrying a basket. She squeezed past him to get to the front door. When his turn came, the barber beckoned to him. He was talking in Yiddish to a new arrival, another bearded man. Max climbed up and was swathed in a white cloth, clean but rumpled; he missed the Nazi barber's freshly starched sheet, his tidy, spacious premises. This is what gives Jews a bad name, he thought. He watched the hairdresser work and felt ashamed of his disloyal thoughts, averting his eyes from the mirror, afraid the man might guess his distaste. He was glad when the job was done, though he felt shorn, his hair considerably shorter than usual.

The next morning, Max rode his bicycle to the centre of the city, to the tall grey building with the words 'Loewenthal Publishing House' painted in elegant blue letters across the facade. He leant his bike against the wall and locked it before smoothing down what was left of his hair and tugging at his jacket. The interview was a formality, his father had said.

He felt lost. He belonged nowhere except at the sports club, and this meaningless job would prevent him from playing football in the afternoons. His English lessons now took place in the evening and he could no longer meet Marlene. He was powerless to change anything but he was certain this was the wrong path, even if only for a short time: wrong direction, wrong work, wrong country.

In the wood-panelled hall, books were on display in glass showcases. The uniformed receptionist sent him up to the first floor where a woman ushered him into Uncle Robert's office. The door closed behind him without a sound.

Uncle Robert sat at a large antique desk between two tall windows. Bright light poured in. Books were everywhere: on the polished shelves rising to the ceiling, piled on a long table, on the desk itself. In this setting, Uncle Robert looked imposing, unlike the easy-going man Max had known all his childhood.

Uncle Robert laid down his pen and closed the file he'd been reading. He indicated one of the chairs in front of the desk, "Take a seat, Max."

He leant back. "How do you feel about working here?"

Max hesitated. Since he was barred from German universities, what he most wanted was to emigrate and study at a foreign university, like Alicia Klein. Uncle Robert's own son Emil was at the Sorbonne in Paris, on his own. Admittedly, he was three years older than Max. Father wouldn't hear of sending Max abroad.

"You'd rather be studying, wouldn't you?"

Max nodded. He wasn't sure what field to choose, but he had no doubt that he belonged at a university. Right now, he was trapped in a constricted world, afraid that the present blight on his life would injure him beyond recovery, so that he'd become unsuited to any profession, forever. He didn't know how to escape.

"Your time will come. Your father has important work to do here. You have to be patient." Uncle Robert's grey eyes were kind.

The same rhetoric! Patience was like a prison, a grim dark place, thought Max. Nothing grew there, nothing. His father blocked his way.

"Max, you may have obtained this position through our family connection, but make no mistake. I expect the same commitment from you as from any other employee. Not that it should worry you. You used to work hard at school, did you not?"

He peered at Max over his rimless glasses. "On Monday, you'll report to Herr Keller in the accounts department. The work is easy for someone of your ability. You'll get the standard basic wage for a trainee. Pay attention and you'll learn how companies are organised, what makes a business successful. The product doesn't matter: books, beer or toys, the basic principles are the same. If you want to talk to me, let my secretary know."

"Thank you," said Max. He stood up.

"Sit down, sit down."

Uncle Robert removed his glasses and rubbed the bridge of his nose. The skin around his eyes was creased and pale, worn-looking. "Max, Herr Keller and I both started here as apprentices almost thirty years ago. He's as trustworthy a man as can be expected under the circumstances. Because we are what the Nazis call a 'Jewish firm' our employees may experience some... difficulties at times. Herr Keller is one of our best employees; he's hard-working, reliable, intelligent and loyal. As far as I know, that loyalty has not been tested. But I'm aware, as I'm sure he is himself, that sooner or later he'll have to choose." Uncle Robert sighed.

"Two of our employees chose early on; it's obvious who they are. They're proud of their allegiance and make no effort to hide their association with the party. We don't know who else might be supporting the authorities on the quiet. Please be careful about what you say and do. Be very careful."

"I'm going for a bike ride," said Max to his father in as casual a tone as he could muster. It was Sunday morning and his father was reading the newspaper at the breakfast table, taking his time. His mother was in the garden. His father nodded without lifting his eyes from the page.

Outside, the air was fresh and cool. The trees lining the street had sprouted tender green leaves; spring was here at last. He wasn't sure when services started at Marlene's church, 9:30 or 10:00 probably. She went to the Catholic school nearby and had mentioned the church once. He'd avoided telling her he was Jewish.

He cycled fast through the quiet streets to the small church square with its double row of plane trees. He found it deserted – had the service begun? He leant his bike against a tree and ran up the steps, opened the external door, and stepped into the vestibule. With some caution, as if transgressing, he opened the inner door to the nave. The church was empty, dark and chill; he hesitated before going in. He wandered along the rows of benches, examining the statues and the paintings on the walls. He recognised the Virgin Mary with the infant Jesus, and St Sebald, Nuremberg's patron saint, but he couldn't identify the others; in Switzerland, he'd seen similar images in churches. "Some might call this idolatry," his father had said, but his mother admired the works of art.

On the altar stood massive silver candlesticks; above it, an agonising Christ nailed to a cross. He preferred Lutheran churches – sober, devoid of statues and paintings, like a synagogue. He'd been told that

Luther had hated the Jews because they resisted conversion. Max stood looking up, contemplating the contorted figure.

A quiet voice behind him said, "Can I help you, young man?"

Startled, he turned to meet the clear-eyed gaze of a young priest in a black cassock. Max stammered, asked when the service would begin and the priest answered, "In about an hour. You must be a visitor to our parish, I've not seen you before, have I?"

Max acknowledged that he was a visitor and the priest welcomed him. "What is your name, my son?"

Max fled with a muttered apology. He ran to his bicycle and rode away as fast as he could, thoughts racing. If that priest had known he was Jewish and pursuing a Christian girl, there would have been trouble.

Nevertheless, he returned the following week, later in the morning, and waited under the plane trees.

He saw her arrive in the company of two other girls who wore similar dresses – best friends, or maybe her sisters. He waited for the service to start, slipped in among other people and sat down at the back. He watched the ritual, liking the smell of incense; he seemed to recall that the rabbis forbade it. He watched the crowd rise and kneel again, bowed heads over joined hands, an alien piety. While they were absorbed in prayer, he left and went out to stand by his bike, half-hidden under the trees. He didn't think Marlene had noticed him. When the service ended, she appeared in the company of other young people, including a few boys his age. No one from his school, fortunately. He willed her to look his way – could she not feel his gaze upon her? And then she saw him and hesitated briefly and glanced at him again, but went on talking to the girl beside her, telling her something; she turned back to the church on her own. The group she'd been with lost its cohesion for a moment and then rallied and carried on down the street without her. Max wheeled his bike to the church, leant it against the wall and ran up the steps to the side door through which she'd disappeared. He opened the door cautiously, frightened of meeting the priest but she was there, waiting in the space between the inner and the outer doors; everyone else had gone.

He said, "I had to see you," and she said, "I missed you on the tram." Her cheeks blushed pink.

"So did I."

And they paused.

He started again. "Can I meet you somewhere else, I mean properly? Where can I leave a letter for you?"

She spoke hesitantly about piano lessons, a teacher in the centre of town. She might leave early once, but she dared not miss the lesson completely; the teacher was sure to let her mother know. Taking her hand which felt warm and assenting, he said, "How about Sundays?"

They stood close.

She whispered, "I can't give them the slip again, I told them I'd dropped my handkerchief in church."

He said slowly, looking into her eyes, "Well at least I'll see you..."

"I must go," she whispered.

He leaned forward and put his arm around her waist, kissed her gently, her lips warm and soft, yielding.

She pushed him away and said in a low voice, "Are you mad, the priest..."

Then the inner door opened and the priest was there. Max turned on his heels and ran out through the door and down the steps, to his bike. He glanced back as he rode away, afraid for some reason, but there was no one to be seen. The kiss was on his lips, delicious.

EIGHTEEN

Another year went by. At sixteen, Helena belonged to the Landschule Seniors, a group which carried some of the responsibility for running the school. She'd been taught the basics of first aid, she monitored younger children's activities, and helped to host guests, some of whom were eminent. Artists visited the Landschule regularly; unable to work in Germany, they were often on their way to another country.

An opera singer joined the staff, a famous prima donna who had sung at the Opernhaus in Berlin. "A great privilege," said Tante Trude. The singer wore flowing, colourful dresses, shocking red lipstick and smelled wonderful. She allowed the girls to sniff her French perfume, a golden liquid in a beautiful round bottle with a glass stopper.

She talked to the children about composers as if they were still alive, sang the songs differently, in ways that made Helena want to laugh or cry. The choir rehearsals became more popular and the singing evolved, at times powerful and soaring. The melodies lingered in Helena's mind for days. The singer taught at the school for three months, and then her agent signed a contract in New York. A contract in New York! The sentence had a mysterious cachet.

The school celebrated her success with a party and she gave a recital, standing by the piano in the dining room in a dark-red full-length dress which left her shoulders bare, so that she looked like a queen. She kissed the children goodbye; she was smiling and laughing and Helena could tell she was glad to go, that she was looking forward to leaving the school, to leaving Germany. Considering the beautiful forest, the lake and the swimming, the day-long walks with her friends, everyone's kindness, Helena thought she was as happy as she could ever be. She had no wish to be anywhere else.

In the house on Pierckheimerstrasse, the phone rang.

"Can I come by?" asked Robert.

"After dinner?" asked Walter. "Has something happened?"

Robert said, "We're selling the firm."

"Tell me," said Walter. They were in the study and he'd poured them each a brandy. Robert looked into his glass, gently swirling the liquor. "As you know, we've been struggling for several years, since the Reich Citizenship Law was passed. Less and less business, old contracts not renewed, no new ones. Since the *Anschluss*,[1] Austria's as bad as Germany. One of our resident Nazis tried to help when our paper supplier defaulted." He laughed. "For our man, the equation was simple: no paper, no books – no books, no job. He sorted things out, at least in the short term. That was only a reprieve. From next week all publishing firm owners are obliged to register with this so-called

German Chamber of Literature. It's been around for some time, but fortunately for us they were at odds with themselves until now."

Walter said, "Jews *unerwünscht,* of course."

"Indeed. We've reached an impasse. The end. Buyers are waiting in the wings like vultures. They'll argue the business is worthless. "Your sales are in decline!" – which is true, because my traditional customers are terrified of ordering books from a so-called 'Jewish' publisher. In Switzerland they don't care, but as you know, my travel plans have repeatedly been stymied, the necessary documents delayed or refused."

"You've done everything you could," said Walter. The scenario was familiar. All Jewish-owned firms faced the same threat.

Robert said, "The merry-go-round grinds to a halt, the fun is over."

"I'm very sorry," said Walter.

They sat without talking, sipping their brandy.

"You don't seem that upset," said Walter.

Robert laughed, "I've been upset for years! I'm surprised myself at how relieved I am. As you know, we left no stone unturned, Hilde and I. That part of our life is completely done, finished."

Walter said, "Consider what happens to people under this damned regime – arrested, tortured, maimed, shot, guillotined, hanged... In that context, losing the business still allows hope for the future."

"It does."

"Robert, what will you do now?"

"We're leaving. You may remember some years ago, I transferred assets to France? Hilde and I will join Emil in Paris."

"When?"

"I don't know how long it will take to conclude the sale. But otherwise, as soon as possible."

Walter sighed, "I can't imagine our lives without you. I know Sonia will feel the same." He felt that the family was disintegrating: Hugo and Gusti had emigrated to America; Georg and Senta would soon be leaving for Palestine.

Robert's voice became a little hoarse. "We shall miss you too, Walter, very much, very much."

He added, "I'm sorry Max will lose his job. Hilde mentioned that Sonia had something in mind for him?"

"Yes, a language school."

"Nearby?"

"Not as close as I'd like – Hamburg. We've relatives there."

"Walter, surely it's time you went too?"

Walter shifted in his chair. "I'm not ready. There's still work in court. People need help."

"Sonia thinks you're obsessed with Streicher," said Robert.

Walter said, "Streicher's a criminal – transgressing is in his nature. He's cunning, but he'll blunder one day, infringe some rule or law. Of that I'm certain. So, no, I'm not ready to leave! Benno may appear to side with him, but should an opportunity arise to purge Bavaria of Streicher he'd not hesitate!"

Max lay in the dark, brooding. He'd known everyone at the party that night, had known them forever; they were almost like family; there was no one new, no chance of meeting someone interesting. The next party would be at someone else's home, but the same crowd would turn up. He missed Marlene.

The parties were not altogether bad. He liked the pretty girls who watched him out of the corner of their eyes, he enjoyed dancing, feeling the smooth firmness of their flesh through their light party dresses, breathing in their scent. From time to time, beaming parents peeked through the doorway. Couples would slip out to the dark garden for a cuddle. He'd kissed little Ella; nice, but not as exciting as kissing Marlene.

The Mannheim parties had been legendary, with a crowd of children invited from all over the neighbourhood. Now they were sealed off from everyone else. They could barely keep track of what was happening beyond Nuremberg – his father said the *Frankfurter Zeitung* was hardly worth reading and that the evening news on the radio was "all lies and propaganda." They tried listening to the news from France, which his mother understood quite well and his father a little. Occasionally, they managed to catch the BBC, and Max translated what he could hear as the sound waxed and waned. The crackling sometimes almost obliterated the broadcaster's voice: civil war in faraway Spain and in France, Leon Blum, a Socialist prime minister and a Jew, unimaginable.

All his friends planned to emigrate – on their own or with their families, excited and hopeful, without regret. They were leaving for Paris, Amsterdam, Lisbon, Toronto, Buenos Aires, even Shanghai, wherever relatives were willing to vouch for them and friends could help. He had no future in Germany. He kicked at his bedding. He feared becoming a man without status, a nonentity. The little he'd learnt about commerce at Uncle Robert's was irrelevant. On his last day there, Max had taken leave of the people he knew. They had shaken his hand, expressing conventional wishes for the future, but they had trouble meeting his eye. What could they say? They knew the business had sold at less than half its worth because Jewish businesses were on sale everywhere; a buyer had only to choose. "Let the Jews squirm," said the Nazis. The sum Uncle Robert received would then be taxed by the state at more than 90 per cent. "Theft," he'd said with a shrug. Max couldn't understand how he maintained such equanimity.

His father persisted in refusing to consider other educational possibilities. "All in good time, Max," he'd say. "We'll get you out in due course; we might send you to Hans." Uncle Hans was a distant relative in America. "You've a good head on your shoulders, hard work will see to the rest, you'll soon catch up."

Now was the time to leave, thought Max, but his father was unrelenting. He wanted to keep his children near, to watch over them. Max was only allowed to move as far as Hamburg, to study languages – English yet again and French – under the vigilant eye of an unknown, distant aunt. Unable to sleep, he got out of bed and went out onto the landing. In the hall below, a crack of light shone under the living room door. He went down on bare feet.

"Still awake, Max?" said his mother as he went in. The curtains were drawn; his parents seemed content, almost happy. They were listening to a record, a deep contralto singing Mahler's *Lieder*. They smiled at him. His mother held up her glass and asked, "Like some?"

"Time to drink up," said his father.

Max knew they had decided to drink the good wines, those laid down for special occasions, a glass or two every evening. Tante Fanny and Uncle Otto were doing so too. His father fetched a crystal glass from the cabinet and poured the wine for him.

Dutifully, Max held the glass up to the light and swirled the wine gently before sniffing it. His father nodded approvingly. Max wished he wouldn't. He sat down and took a sip. The wine was velvety, smooth.

"Taking leave of Germany, little by little," said his father.

His mother said as if in warning, "Your father believes he can still be useful here."

On cue, the telephone rang in the hall.

A month or so later, as Sonia was preparing for a welfare committee meeting one afternoon, she heard the front door open and Walter's unmistakable tread. The time was wrong – much too early – and she felt her heart race. Forcing herself to stay calm, she went to the hall. "What is it, Walter?"

He took her hand and guided her into the study, shaking his head as if to say that nothing was the matter. But there had to be; it was clear from his behaviour he'd come home specially for her, to tell her something. He was very concerned, she could tell. He closed the door.

"What is it?"

"Everyone is safe," he said reassuringly. "It's something different." He took her hand and said, "Jews are no longer allowed to own silver or jewellery." He guided her to a chair and made her sit down.

She looked up into his face which was full of concern. She asked, "Not allowed to buy any?"

"That too, and not allowed to own any, not allowed to have any."

"But what about what is ours?" She was thinking of her mother's pearls, the silver frame on her desk with the photo of her parents.

"We've been ordered to hand them over."

She said firmly, "Walter, please explain exactly what they want."

"The Nazis have commanded us to bring them our silver and our jewels."

"And there's nothing we can do?"

"Nothing."

"And no indemnification, I suppose," she said.

Sonia's jewellery had mostly been given to her by her mother and grandmother. With the birth of each child, Walter had chosen a new piece for her. After her mother's death, she and Fanny had inherited the rest. There wasn't much, except for her pearls; her mother hadn't liked wearing jewellery, finding it ostentatious. "I'm not a Christmas tree, to be hung with baubles." Since her mother's death, Sonia had always worn the pearls.

She put a hand up to her necklace and looked at him. He nodded. She glanced at her watch, which they had chosen together in Switzerland during their honeymoon, at the rings on her fingers. The brooches, necklaces and earrings were in the ivory box upstairs, and one necklace was at the bank, the nearest thing to an heirloom. She looked at the familiar objects in the room – a silver cigar box, the ebony walking stick with its silver knob leaning in a corner which had belonged to Walter's grandfather. She pulled herself together, straightened her back, clasped her hands in her lap. A tear rolled down her cheek.

"People will find out in due course," he said. "Now, please go and wash your face and make sure neither my mother nor Greta see you've been upset. The news will be announced soon to everyone. I want you to set an example of courage." He added, "We are powerless to prevent this robbery, that is a fact. But we can rise above the insult and injustice. We must do so for the welfare of the community. We must remain strong. You know this as well as I do. People will follow your lead. You must be ready."

NINETEEN

It was the summer of 1938. In Walter's office, the phone rang one morning with a message from the Jewish Community board's chairman, requesting Walter's presence at a special board meeting that very afternoon; not at the Community Centre, but at the chairman's chambers. No reason was given; this meeting was to remain absolutely confidential. The word urgent was not mentioned. The whole thing was so unusual that Walter was immediately alarmed. As a rule, the schedule of board meetings was planned for the whole year, with an established agenda. He cancelled his commitments for the afternoon. The chairman's chambers were nearby on Karolinenstrasse.

When all the board members had gathered – except for the rabbi, who had advised he'd be a little late – the chairman explained that a clerk from the Town Hall had been in touch with his office that morning and had asked for the prompt "collection of a statement" without explaining the nature of that statement. The chairman had asked board member Fechheimer to see to it. Fechheimer had returned with a verbal instruction – nothing on paper. Upon hearing this instruction, the chairman had decided to convene the board under conditions of secrecy which were necessary, he said, to protect the community from the undue fears and rumours liable to arise if people became aware of an unscheduled board meeting.

A secretary brought in a tray with coffee. Before she began to pour, the chairman requested she leave the room. That too was unusual. They were still waiting for the rabbi.

Walter watched as people congregated around the coffee pot. A few stood by the windows, staring at the busy street below. The two women members sat side by side. Walter knew them well; he had supported their campaign to join the board, the first women to do so. The prettier of the two, Elise, was an old friend. She kept folding and smoothing the fabric of her skirt in a nervous rhythmic gesture. Except for the chairman, people were restless. Little Kolb was there, his face sallower than ever. He didn't know anything: the Gestapo and the city council were separate entities. Rabbi Andorn arrived at last, a little out of breath, and they sat around the long polished table. Fechheimer checked the door and sat down. They waited for the chairman to speak. He said, "Streicher wants to demolish our synagogue. Fechheimer, tell them what they said."

Fechheimer explained, "They want us to donate our synagogue to the city in order for them to tear it down. They specified 'of our own free will' – immediately."

There was a pause, and then a flurry of comments rippled up and down the table, people reacting in confusion after the lengthy wait, reluctant to consider this new and horrifying reality.

"Of our own free will?"

"What do they mean?"

"Suddenly they care whether something is freely given?"

In itself, the wish to demolish came as no surprise. Streicher had been clamouring for the synagogue's destruction in *Der Stürmer* for the last couple of months; the call had been taken up and amplified by other Franconian papers. Only a few weeks earlier, the Munich Jewish Community, one of the largest, had been asked to hand over their synagogue to the authorities. To the consternation of the other Jewish congregations, they had complied with what could only be described as docility. (One shouldn't judge, Walter reminded himself.) The Nuremberg synagogue had been built at the same time as the one in Munich, in the prevalent Moorish style. They were confronting the same dilemma. Munich's synagogue had been demolished "in order to make room" for the renovation of Munich's Artists' House, next door.

"Why didn't they write what they wanted?"

"Couldn't they have let us know in the usual way, by messenger or by post?"

Fechheimer said nothing. The chairman waited. Beside him, the rabbi was pale. Walter wished old Rabbi Freudenthal were still alive. He'd been a man of action, a good fighter. Rabbi Andorn was in his mid-thirties, still young, relatively inexperienced. The commotion died down as they turned towards the chairman. Walter noticed Elise wringing her hands.

The building of Nuremberg's great synagogue had required a lengthy and sustained effort. Walter's grandfather and father had both been on the planning committee at different times and so had the forebears of several other board members, including the Josephthals, the Fechheimers, the Dormitzers, the Rosenzweigs and the Berlins. The search for a suitable plot had lasted years. Neither the city council nor the state of Bavaria had been willing to sell land to the Jewish community. In the end, two juxtaposed houses had been acquired, on the bank of the Pegnitz River in the city centre, with the aim of tearing them down. The consultant engineers warned that the ground was unsuitable to bear the great weight of a major edifice, but the committee went ahead anyway. They had already deferred too long. It was said that a synagogue had once stood there in the past, before the 1349 Jewish exile from the city. This was confirmed when an enormous stone was unearthed during the digging of the foundations; it was identified amid great sensation as the keystone of an old synagogue's ark. Simultaneously, the engineers were proven right: the only way to ensure the massive building's stability was to drive wooden piles into the ground. In a noisy, laborious and expensive process, one thousand oak piles, each ten meters long, were rammed into the sludge. Then the funds ran out, followed by the Prussian War; several years passed before construction could resume.

In September 1874, a few years before Walter was born, the synagogue was finally inaugurated and the ancient stone was reverently displayed in its foyer. In a glass case next to it lay an ornate gilded key, the key which chairman Gustav Josephthal had ceremonially handed to Nuremberg's mayor Von Stromer for the synagogue's official opening.

He remembered his bar mitzvah – the crowded synagogue silent and attentive while he chanted his *parashah* from the Torah scroll on the *bimah*. As he finished the last section, he'd looked up and seen the undisguised emotion in his father's face, the love and the pride. His father had died three years later, of a sudden, severe heart attack.

In recent times, a volunteer security team kept watch at night as a precaution against vandalism. He took his turn every couple of months. Stationed in the basement, they toured the building at regular intervals. They played cards to pass the time, recounting stories and jokes. He knew the men well; they'd grown up and served together during the war. He heard a few stories about his father which were different from those the family recounted. He thought of his father in new ways. Of course, he was much older now himself, almost the age his father had been when he'd died.

Sometimes after completing an inspection, he'd sit down at the back of the main hall; he'd once fallen into a kind of reverie, staring ahead through the obscurity at the ark with its little glowing light. What had he been thinking about? Had he been thinking at all? He'd become aware of quiet, of a sense of peace, had felt that it was entirely right for him to be sitting there, in this synagogue in this town, despite the murk of baseless hatred churning around it.

The chairman looked up at last and the exclamations died down. They waited. The word passed to the rabbi who stood and uttered a brief prayer in Hebrew. Walter understood the prayer's meaning – may God protect us from calamities – and wondered how the rabbi kept his faith. He didn't mind; the prayer would do no harm, might even provide some people with comfort. The rabbi then made a short speech, quoting from the sages, summing up his opinion in a final sentence: "The more we give in, the greater the ensuing demands," and sat down.

The chairman spoke, reminding them of 1923, only fifteen years earlier, when Jews in Germany had suffered attacks in the streets, vandalism in the cemeteries; when the refugees who'd fled the Polish pogroms were rounded up and dumped back where they'd come from, over the Polish border. At that time, the Nuremberg Jewish Community had written a letter demanding of the Bavarian state that it take the measures necessary to curtail these antisemitic activities, and the state had complied.

"The situation is not the same," said the chairman. "There is however a common factor: intimidation."

They thrashed the matter out over several hours, following the usual routine – considering all aspects of the problem – to agree forthwith, to delay, to refuse outright, the likely consequences of each option.

Walter looked at the people around the table: they were all worried. No, he had to be honest, they were terrified. On a personal level alone, not counting the danger to their families and to their livelihood – the risk was internment in Dachau or worse. People had been arrested for much less, had been brutalised, damaged, returning changed beyond recognition. Some had been murdered. Most of the board members had been subjected to SA abuse in the early days of the regime, dragged from their homes in the early morning, subjected to vicious humiliation, without knowing when it would stop, whether they would survive.

After they'd had their say and every single board member had agreed with the rabbi, the chairman summed up: they were going to stand together, to stand strong. The answer to the Town Hall was drafted with little argument as a single sentence reading, "No Jewish community surrenders their house of worship of their own free will."

The letter was dispatched immediately. They agreed to defer informing the community for as long as was possible.

Walter left the meeting with an unexpected sense of accomplishment. He noticed that several of the others also seemed pleased. An odd elation, given that this was a struggle which could not be won.

Sonia recognised something was wrong as soon as he entered the house and he did not hesitate to tell her – she would have worried more had he left matters to her imagination. Many of the others would probably also tell their wives – those who could be relied upon to keep it to themselves.

Messages came and went between the Town Hall and the board, the Town Hall increasingly imperious, hectoring; the board members resolute despite their fear, ranked staunch behind their chairman. Each of them was conscious of personally opposing the regime. To their amazement, there was no additional harassment; no threats, no repercussions. The daily persecution of Jewish citizens continued as before, no better, no worse.

Two weeks later, Walter phoned Sonia. "I've just heard. The inevitable has happened."

The expropriation was about to take place. The Town Hall bureaucrats had succeeded in identifying a law which could be twisted to suit their purpose: it concerned the urban development and beautification of Nuremberg, "the Führer's favourite city." The synagogue was declared an eyesore because of its foreign architecture, by which they meant its Moorish style, its turrets, domes and horseshoe arches. Therefore, they said, they were legally entitled to demolish it. They added – in their misguided wish for propriety – that the community would be compensated for the loss.

It was true that as one approached the city, the synagogue's great copper cupola was clearly visible on the horizon, a prominent landmark. Streicher hated it with a passion, referring to it as "a blemish on the landscape", proof of "Jewish impudence". Walter reflected on the many church spires and the giant cupola of St Jacob's Church, also visible from a distance.

A few days later, Sonia climbed the gloomy stairwell of an old house on the Hans Sachs Platz. Over the centuries, feet had worn a shallow depression at the centre of each tread. She proceeded slowly, the weight of the basket pulling her body askew. Besides her purse, it contained carrots and a lettuce, slightly wilted in the heat, and a metal canister of chicken soup, propped up between a round loaf of bread in a paper bag and a kilo of potatoes. Four eggs were wrapped in several layers of newspaper. She took care to keep the basket upright, to prevent the soup from leaking. In her other hand she held a small bunch of red roses from the garden.

On the third-floor landing she paused to rest. She peered through the narrow dusty window at the walled garden below. A pear tree grew in the centre; there was a tidy vegetable patch to one side; in the corner, a hut and a chicken coop leant against the ancient brick wall. She could see a couple of hens scratching the earth. A woman in a faded blue dress sat on a bench sorting dried beans on a tray, a wicker bassinet beside her. Sonia could see two small bare feet kicking in the sun. As she watched, the woman addressed the baby, cooing. On either side of the bench, a climbing rose grew up the wall, one flowering red and the other white: like one of Grimm's fairy tales, she thought, a tale of good and evil.

She picked up the basket, switching hands, and resumed her slow climb. A smell of simmering sauerkraut had become insistent. The fourth floor was the last before the attic. By the doorbell, the card with Frau Kühn's name in old-fashioned handwriting was slotted into a brass frame. Sonia put the basket down and wiped her forehead; she tucked her handkerchief into her sleeve and rang the bell.

She heard a key turn in the lock and the door opened a little. Seeing Sonia, the old woman welcomed her, "Come in! Come in!"

Sonia sidled into the corridor and allowed herself to be kissed, holding her basket away from her body so that the soup would not spill. The smell of sauerkraut remained blessedly outside. "How are you?" she asked.

"Fine, thank you," said Frau Kühn. "Brave of you to visit today." She hobbled into the long low-ceilinged room crowded with heavy furniture. At the far end two armchairs faced a wide-open window. A profusion of pink petunias bloomed from the window box. "Coffee?"

A rickety wooden trolley was parked between the armchairs. Pencils and stained paintbrushes protruded from an assortment of jars, beside a flat box containing contorted tubes of paint, and a palette covered in colourful blotches. An easel leant against the nearby wall. Frau Kühn painted flowers, in oils.

The food Sonia had brought was paid for and put away, the roses arranged in a vase, coffee brewed and poured. They settled by the window and exchanged news about family and friends. Sonia gave a brief summary of the congregation's status quo, recounting who was about to leave and who had recently left, where they were emigrating to, what was happening to their homes, as if this state of affairs, this terrified headlong flight of an entire community in every direction world-wide were a normal phenomenon. Afterward they sat looking out at the view of roofs and sky.

In the square below, an outsize bronze statue of Hans Sachs, Nuremberg's celebrated *Meistersinger*, rested on a massive granite pedestal. He wore the traditional cobbler's apron and was seated on a pile of books. His handsome face bore a remote expression as if in the throes of inspiration; his hand was raised in a conductor's pose. The Nazis adored Hans Sachs, the man and his poetry; they'd appropriated him into their mythology. Sonia had come to loathe the statue with its perfectly proportioned head and exaggerated noble features, the flowery profusion of beard and the powerful, manly legs.

"Much activity around the synagogue," said Frau Kühn.

Sonia peered out. At the far end of the square the synagogue rose, solid and serene. Several lorries were parked in front of a makeshift fence screening its base. Nearby, a group of workmen were dismantling a wooden tribune.

"I'm painting the synagogue while I still can," said Frau Kühn. "That fence went up this morning, before I could finish a preliminary sketch, but I found an old etching; I can work out the colours from what I see – the browny-pink of the sandstone and the pale green of the copper on the cupolas."

Tears came to Sonia's eyes and she clasped her hands tight. Frau Kühn leant towards her and touched her arm.

"We feel as if it's always been there, that it's permanent, but in fact it's only sixty-four years since that synagogue was built. Not even a century."

Sonia cleared her throat and said, "Walter's father was at the inauguration."

"So he was. A member of the board, wasn't he? I remember the occasion well; my sisters and I wore new dresses for the occasion," said Frau Kühn. "Lewandowski had been commissioned to compose the music. It was a good time for Jews, not only in Germany, but all over Europe – before the Dreyfus affair. Nuremberg had an enlightened mayor in those days, Von Stromer. And I was a silly young girl, impressed by the golden key with which he opened the synagogue doors."

Sonia had seen the key in its glass box in the synagogue's foyer. "When the demolition was announced, Walter helped remove whatever was possible. So did many others. He didn't say anything about the golden key. They've rescued as much as they could, the Torah scrolls first of all, the antique silver finials, mezuzahs, candelabras. They're hidden but he didn't say where," said Sonia.

"Better that way," said Frau Kühn.

Sonia sipped the remains of her coffee. "They had to leave many books in the library. The prayer books too."

Frau Kühn sat with her elbow on the armrest, her chin in her hand, gazing at the synagogue. "During Streicher's rally yesterday, that giant crane removed the Star of David from the cupola." The crane was huge and its arm was very high, higher than the synagogue. "The dome looks naked without it."

The newspapers had reported Streicher's vituperations. He had spoken for an hour and a half from the provisional tribune to Nuremberg citizens massed in the square, including a brigade of Hitler Youth lined up in military order. The crane had slowly removed the Star of David and lowered it to the ground. It was ceremonially presented to a delighted Streicher, to music from a band and cheers and hoots from the crowd; the headlines announced that the building would be "gone by September, in good time for the next Reich rally."

The crane's arm stretched out against the sky. "The sword of Damocles," said Sonia.

"That coffee must be cold by now, surely?" asked Frau Kühn. She began to haul herself out of the chair.

"There's no need for more, thank you, Frau Kühn," she said. "They managed to spirit away that huge old stone too, God only knows how, before Streicher's rally. Before the hordes descended."

"I'm glad," said Frau Kühn. "I watched the craziness from here. I was so petrified that I hid behind the curtains. SA men were leading the charge, yelling into megaphones, whipping up the crowd; the rest of them were ordinary Germans off their heads with hysteria – men, women, children yelling and howling in front of the synagogue in a kind of *danse macabre*. Frightening."

Sonia said, "I saw prayer books on the ground in the square, trampled into the dust."

"The people ran in, threw the prayer books and kippahs around, draped themselves in the prayer shawls; they were encouraged to do their worst. Of the police, no sign."

"That Benno Martin is in Streicher's pocket," said Sonia.

"Neither law, nor order," said Frau Kühn.

"To see the pages strewn in the dirt..." She was surprised at her feeling of desecration. She'd never cared for prayer or prayer books.

"The rabbi would say that these are only objects," said Frau Kühn. "The synagogue too... The commandment is to have no other gods. Since Streicher's performance the city council has been removing all manner of things from the building: benches, light fittings, banisters, tables and chairs. Our synagogue stands staunch. Look at it! Last week a team of road workers arrived. I heard pneumatic drills drilling away from morning to evening; I counted them as they came out, eight men, each with a drill. But the building remains strong. They can't destroy it!"

Sonia contemplated the synagogue. She wanted to fix the image of the majestic stone building in her memory: its great cupola framed by turrets, the round stained-glass window at the centre of the facade above the three Moorish arches leading to the main entrance. The wide steps up from the street were hidden by the palisade.

"Might they give up," asked Frau Kühn, "since the drilling failed?"

Sonia shook her head. "During the war, Walter worked with sappers, the soldiers who blow up bridges and buildings. He explained that they drill holes into the supports of the main structure. In our case, into the eight pillars which support the mezzanine floor and the roof. That's probably what they did last week."

"And then?"

"Then they carefully fill the holes with explosive material and cover them with piles of sandbags, to direct the force of the explosion towards the centre of the pillars. When the pillars collapse, so does everything they hold up, including the roof."

"Oh! No hope, then."

"None," said Sonia. "That crane will finish off the work."

"How so?"

"Walter was talking about it the other day; they're concerned to protect the houses round the square. It's difficult to blow up the entire synagogue without damaging them. The synagogue's outer walls are supposed to contain the blast which will destroy the pillars. Those walls are very thick, very solid. Once the interior has been destroyed, the crane will swing a massive ball against whatever remains standing and break it down completely."

They watched the workmen's activity in the square.

Frau Kühn said, "When the synagogue was inaugurated, Mayor Von Stromer said that a society's attitude towards its Jews reflects its moral and ethical status."

Walter had recently quoted that very sentence. She didn't repeat to Frau Kühn the rest of what he'd said: "When Fechheimer was at the Town Hall recently, he noticed a gap among the portraits in the gallery, where Von Stromer's used to be."

TWENTY

A week or so later, Elise and Sonia strolled round the garden, arm in arm. The gardener had immigrated to Holland a few months earlier and the plants had escaped control, weeds lush in the flowerbeds except for a space around every rose bush which Sonia kept clear. Since Max's departure for Hamburg, there was no one to scythe the lawn. Walter was hopeless at this sort of task. Besides, they both had more important things to do.

Elise was speaking about her maid, Käthe. "Both rude and lazy – she was always slow, but we were used to her ways."

"And now?"

"A paid-up member of the Nazi Party. She can do what she likes."

"She hasn't stopped working altogether, surely?"

"Not quite. She takes long breaks, drinks our coffee, smokes our cigarettes and makes antisemitic comments. As if her years of experience of us and our friends who have been considerate and polite, have been wiped from her mind and only resentment and Nazi lies remain. She'll only leave if we pay her an obscene amount of money. She already earns good wages. Anyway, I don't think she can imagine doing anything else."

"What will you do?"

"It doesn't matter anymore. That's what I came to tell you. That permit from the tax authorities arrived yesterday, the last stamp is in place. Our papers are in order, Sonia – finally complete. We're free to go."

"At last! I'm so glad for you, very glad! Though I'll miss you most dreadfully." She hugged her friend and kissed her. Losing Elise would be hard. "How soon can you leave?"

"We're leaving the day after tomorrow, via Holland. Käthe doesn't know; she'll find out on the day. And we'll be off to a new life. A brand-new career in Britain!"

"I can't imagine you as a housekeeper!"

"It's ridiculous, I know. I'll have to put my mind to it. I'll slip a housekeeping book into my suitcase. Philippe will do better than me as a factotum. He's always been practical. The main thing is that those jobs will get us into England, though of course we'll be dirt-poor. It's funny, but I don't think we'll mind much. It will be nice to live in peace. I can hardly imagine what that might be like – I'll work at my English; by the way, thank you for putting me in touch with Miss Winteringham. She says that I still speak with a German accent, despite all my efforts. The pronunciation's the devil. I'm aiming to do written translation work some day; that would suit me."

They reached the terrace and walked on for a second round.

"Sonia, I've brought you the Japanese ivory figurine, the laughing beggar. You've always liked it. It's in the little box on the hall table. We can't take it with us. Philippe and I want you to have it."

"Oh, Elise..." said Sonia. Her eyes filled with tears. "I love him. I'll look after him. But if you don't mind, I'll regard this as a loan. I'd like to think that I might return him to you one day."

Sonia sighed. "I cannot convince Walter that we must leave. If at least he'd allow the children to go... And there's Oma to think of. Fanny has applied to send Rudi to England on one of the children's transports. We have to wait another week before the selections are known. Walter wouldn't hear of sending Max or Helena, even though they're older. Tante Gusti used to say that all sanity is but a veneer over an abyss of irrationality, and I feel as if I'm staring into a seething pit. He believes he can keep us all safe, the children, his mother and me, that nothing can happen to him or to us. Such arrogance, combined with a complete refusal to face up to facts."

Sonia added in a low voice, "Truly Elise, at times I feel I'm going mad. I might run screaming out of the house, except... where to? No place is safe. I can't make him change his mind. His mother also tried. He walks out of the room if we bring up the subject."

"The community depends on him."

"So does his family."

"You're busy too, looking after people," said Elise.

"Endless organising of petty details. Someone has to do it. I can't get used to the speed of the degradation, from the moment people lose their livelihood. Once their savings are gone, they can't afford to go on living in their houses and they look for cheap lodgings, and then their shoes and the women's stockings wear out: they practically have to beg to eat. It's shocking. Walter quotes Ecclesiastes."

"Ecclesiastes?"

"You know – 'An unhappy business, that which God gave men to be concerned with'. Not that he believes in God."

"A great gloom."

They smiled at each other.

"You seem to cope."

"Work prevents me from thinking too much. I deal with what's happening from day to day."

"And Fanny and Otto?"

"They've been trying. It's almost impossible. Otto's too old to find employment overseas. She'd find work in Britain as a servant, if she applied, but she cannot abandon him. He's thinking of approaching the Christian organisations. They might help him as he's not a member of either Jewish community, but it doesn't look good. That's why it's so important Rudi should go."

They walked in silence until they reached the terrace again.

"I hope and pray that it won't be long before we meet again."

Sonia had never heard Elise mention prayer.

At the door, they hugged and kissed and then she watched Elise walk away, tears running down her face. Elise looked back and they waved; she was crying too. Then she disappeared round the corner and a breeze caressed Sonia's cheek, light and pleasant, almost optimistic.

She took the box from the hall table to her boudoir where she opened it carefully. The little Japanese figure laughed up at her, a friendly presence, witness to humanity's madness. She sobbed, her face in her hands.

When Helena first arrived home for the autumn holidays nothing seemed to have changed. Tante Fanny, Uncle Otto and a few friends joined the family to light the Chanukah candles, bringing their own candelabras. Looking at the collection of candelabras on display, she realised that their old silver one was missing. It had always been the centrepiece, taller than the others. Instead, a modest brass chanukiah stood among those brought by the visitors. Theirs also seemed less elaborate than in the past. One was even home-made, a branch stripped of its bark and varnished, the small coloured candles positioned at irregular intervals in clumsily carved indentations, leaning every which way, as if assembled by a child.

Her father said the blessings and she helped Rudi and the younger children light the eight candles in each candelabra, for it was the last day of the festival. All other lights were turned off, so that they could enjoy the little glowing forest of light on the table. As they sang the familiar Chanukah songs, her father put his arm around her. Helena had learnt the descant of *Maoz Tsur* at school and she confidently pitched her voice to her father's bass so that it felt right though contrasting, like an embroidery where threads of different hues intermingled. She would have liked the sound to continue, to hear again the flowing together and apart of the different layers, but the song was soon over. Her mother looked happy, for once.

Later, she asked about the brass candelabra; her mother said it was quite old and had been in the family for a long time.

"But where is the silver one?"

"Gone. The Nazis took it."

"They took it?"

"Helena, do stop asking questions, you're giving me a headache."

Helena's pleasure evaporated. She went looking for Max who said, "The Nazis made everyone bring their silver and jewellery to a warehouse in town."

"But how?"

"They passed a law which says we're not allowed to own any."

Helena had noticed her mother wasn't wearing her pearls. She thought of the other items she knew well: the big ring with the limpid stone, the brooch; also the necklace from the bank which she'd only seen her mother wear once, at Max's bar mitzvah. And the silver necklace with the links in the shape of leaves. She asked, "Are they gone for good?"

"It seems so. It happened a month ago. I was going to work at the publishers one morning and I saw Mama with a basket; it was on their bed and she was looking through it. Her pearls were on top of other stuff."

"Other stuff?"

"Jewellery and things. Also the Shabbat candlesticks and the chanukiah."

Max looked away and added, "I just happened to see her. No one had mentioned anything. She said she'd arranged the pearls on top because they looked nice." After a moment's pause, still looking away, he said, "The kiddush cup too."

The kiddush cup was silver, an ancient thing, battered and plain. Father had said the cup had come down through the generations from eldest son to eldest son.

"What did Father say?" asked Helena, her voice quavering despite her efforts.

Max said, "What he always says: that all things come and go, anything one owns can be mislaid, broken or lost, by theft, fire or flood." And she knew what he would have said next, that he would have peered at Max from under his bushy eyebrows and said, "It is who you are that matters, your character. Behave honourably, always, for no one can take that away from you."

"And Mama?"

"You saw for yourself; she won't talk about it."

TWENTY-ONE

The attack came in early November. The hammering started all at once, so loud that Sonia had to shout for the maid to hear. "Open up before they break that door!"

She stood in the middle of the hall, her right hand holding her left, the way she'd always stood when guests arrived.

For all the noise they made, they were only two men in ill-fitting SA uniforms, one tall and thin, the other short and rotund, a ridiculous pair, one with an axe, the other with a crowbar. As the door opened, they charged in but stopped, flinching as they met her gaze which she invested with all the contempt she could muster. She did not speak. Then the smaller one shouted a vulgar insult and they carried on, yelling in hoarse voices as they pushed past her to the drawing room. She watched as they slashed the upholstery, overturned the armchairs. Thank goodness the children and Walter were away.

A delicate round table was thrown over, kicked and smashed, the pieces strewn about; they attacked a large painting, a landscape she'd never liked much, pulling it down, the frame leaving a long scratch on the wallpaper, the glass shattering as it hit the floor. She thought of

Elise's ivory figurine which she'd left on her secretaire. She went quickly down the hall to her room, pausing in the doorway to look around: there seemed to be no place in which to hide the statuette. She picked it up, concealing it in her hands as best she could and stepped into the kitchen next door. Her apron was hanging on its hook by the window; she slipped it into its wide pocket. She returned to the hall; they were in the dining room, and she watched the polished table splinter under the blows of the axe. They were still yelling, the usual invective against Jews, foul Jews, the bane of Germany, who should be lined up and shot. She heard the curses as if from a great distance – irrelevant to her. She stood in the hall with her clasped hands, and witnessed the rampage through her home.

The maid was praying, facing the wall. If only Greta was here – but she'd left a few months earlier, had handed in her notice, collected the wages still due and said goodbye with a firm handshake, walking out with her suitcase without further ado. This elderly Jewish woman had replaced her.

The house was rapidly and thoroughly ransacked, the men charging from room to room. She heard the locks crack and break as they forced cupboards open, pulling out the linen, the glass, the china, smashing what was breakable, overturning the cutlery drawers onto the floor, the crashes deafening. In Walter's study they swept the books from the shelves, hurled them across the room. Papers, pens, pencils and the old carved blotter were pushed off the desk, ink was flung in long dark jets across the rug and the walls; the brandy decanter flew in a slow arc, shattering a windowpane. They tugged and yanked at the heavy winter curtains, wrenching the rods from the wall. Just as well Walter was away – he would have fought them, nothing good would have come of it. They were upstairs now; oh God, where was Oma? The larger of the two returned, and yelled at her, "Get your goddamned husband out from whatever goddamned hole he's hiding in!"

223

She despised him with all her being. "You're in luck, he's away! He's a real fighter, a veteran! He'd soon deal with you!" She spoke in dialect, as to a servant. He stepped back, shook his fist in her face. "We'll get him, we'll be back! *Heil Hitler!*"

They clattered out of the house, down the steps, suddenly gone, leaving the door wide open. Bitter cold blew in. She was shocked to see a crowd outside; besides the milling SA, ordinary people stood in the street and stared without shame, some triumphant, some with avid curiosity. They could see right in, for the house was lit up like a theatre set, the lights on in every room. She stared at them in anguish and fury; in the twilight she thought she recognised the butchers' twins who'd once played football with Max, and Kris, looking horrified; she saw the tobacconist, the baker, the woman who sold newspapers at the tram stop. Some faces were guarded. This was SA business – no one intervened. No police in sight. No help from Benno Martin. The words of the psalm occurred to her: "I shall raise my eyes to the hills..." No help from anywhere! Enraged, she closed the front door more violently than she'd intended. She stood listening to the chaotic sounds, the shouts, the slam of car doors, engines revving, shouted SA commands.

"Oh, Frau Mannheim, your lovely house," whimpered the maid.

Sonia ran up the stairs calling, "Oma!"

Some banisters were broken. Little white feathers covered every surface, billowing around her, floating gracefully in the stairwell. They must have slashed open the eiderdowns.

Oma appeared on the landing in her dressing gown, her hair loose, awry.

"Are you alright?"

"I was taking a nap, I heard them coming and hid behind the door. They didn't find me." She clung to Sonia. She was shaking. "They made a dreadful mess."

Sonia kissed her. "Come with me, will you? Let's see how bad it is."

They went down the stairs, hand in hand among the swirling feathers. "From order to anarchy in under half an hour!" said Sonia. She felt numb. In the boudoir, the chair's upholstery had been eviscerated and the secretaire tipped over. The photo with her parents and Fanny in its new wooden frame was intact, except for the broken glass. In the study, she unearthed the phone from the wreckage, piled up some of the books and placed it on top, dusting it with her sleeve.

She phoned the police station; the line was engaged. She held no hope that the police would help, but she was curious to know what they'd say when she reported what had happened, what was still happening in houses nearby. At the kitchen door, she and Oma stared at the devastation: egg yolks oozed slowly down the walls. The deep wooden drawers of flour and sugar had been pulled out and turned over onto the floor, creating a snowy landscape of mounds and valleys on the dark red tiles. They must have started there, for floury footprints were all over the floor. A shattered jug lay in a puddle of milk, shards of earthenware scattered around. Oil pulsed slowly out of the big metal oil can which had fallen on its side. Sonia picked it up – it contained a remnant of oil. She said to the maid, "We'll clean up the oil first."

The maid stared at her, at a loss.

"Use tea towels and throw them out," said Sonia. There was nothing to preserve; this was the end. Her apron was hanging where it had been before; she retrieved the ivory figurine from its hiding place.

Some pots and pans were still serviceable, but the crockery had been smashed. A sack of potatoes had been sliced open and the potatoes scattered; they would be edible, she thought – or might there be glass splinters? Too risky, they'd have to be thrown out. In the oven, the small roast for dinner was still cooking. She opened the door to the cellar – the smell of wine and vinegar was overpowering, the shattered glass on the floor dangerous. She retrieved the bottle of cooking wine from its place behind the baking tins and stepped back with care, closing the door behind her. Helena's cup had rolled under the kitchen table, unaccountably whole. The contents of the cutlery drawers were spread over the floor; she swept them into a pile and searched for a corkscrew. She rinsed the cup under the tap and divided out the port carefully, a small amount for each of them. They took turns to drink. Oma sat on the one chair which was whole. Cold night air came in through the broken windows.

The maid said, "Madam can't stay here."

"They've done what they came to do. They won't be back," said Sonia. "Not tonight. You may go if you wish."

Sonia paid her and she went. She would probably not return. It didn't matter, thought Sonia; they would have to leave the house soon. She swept what was on the kitchen floor into tidy piles. As she went round examining the damage, she switched off the lights. She found herself muttering *"El male rachamim, el male rachamim."* Why was she praying? She should be cursing. Among the devastation of her daughter's room she dropped to her knees, buried her face in one of the pillows on the floor and howled into it.

The phone rang in the study and she ran down.

Walter said, "Are you alright?"

"Yes, we are, your mother too, but they've ransacked the house. How did you know?"

"It's happening across the country."

Her heart seemed to stop. "The children."

"Ring Helena's school. I'll catch up with Max in Hamburg. I'll talk to you as soon as I know."

She tried the school, but the phone was constantly engaged.

They'd only broken one windowpane in the living room. She bundled a kitchen towel into the hole.

She and Oma agreed they should eat, despite their lack of appetite. It was an odd meal of crackers, roast and a single shared apple, during which they hardly spoke. They drank water, and later an infusion of chamomile – the Indian tea had been strewn over the floor.

Sonia phoned Helena's school. The line was still engaged. She forced herself to wait several minutes between attempts. In the living room she shored up the broken sofa with books and used the remains of an eiderdown as padding to cover the springs poking through the torn fabric. A small lamp retrieved from the floor cast a familiar light through its crooked shade. The little ivory figurine sat within arm's reach on a vacant bookshelf.

Oma fell asleep, wrapped in blankets, half lying in an armchair, her mouth open, shrunken and brittle as a bird. Nothing more could be done, for now.

At last Sonia spoke to Gertrud Feiertag, who said that all was calm at the school. She was aware of the raids, mainly in the big cities. They were prepared in case of an attack; Helena was well and so were Inge and Lore. Sonia spoke to Lore's mother; her house had also been ransacked. There was no answer from Inge's home. Sonia sipped chamomile tea from Helena's cup, staring into the shadows.

In Hamburg that afternoon, Max, his friend Karl, and Tante Nina's son Wilhelm had been dispatched to the large attic where they could make as much noise as they liked; they had settled on the floor with a new game called Monopoly, a gift for Wilhelm's recent birthday. At first, they'd argued about the rules, but by late afternoon the game was well under way and Max was winning, accumulating property on the Kurfürstendamm. Beyond the dormer window at one end of the long room, the roofs of neighbouring houses were silhouetted against the heavy November sky.

Tante Nina was related to his mother. She and Uncle Bruno had made Max welcome, inviting him to dinner a couple of times a month, a pleasant change from his spartan student hostel.

The dinner bell summoned them twice before they were willing to interrupt the game. In the dining room a lamp hung low over the big round table, enclosing it in a circle of light. Tante Nina ladled out soup from a steaming tureen.

As they began to eat, the phone rang in the hall and Uncle Bruno went to answer it. They heard him exclaim in surprise. The call seemed to end abruptly, and Uncle Bruno returned, but he did not sit down; he stood gripping the back of his chair. They waited for him to speak. His expression was strained and Max was surprised to realise he was upset. He'd never seen an adult so upset.

"What is it, my dear?" asked Tante Nina.

"A trustworthy source has informed me," said Uncle Bruno at last, "that Nazis are burning the synagogues. They are destroying Jewish shops and homes all over Hamburg. The boys should stay here tonight."

"The synagogue's on fire?" asked Wilhelm.

"Because of the murder in Paris," replied his father. The newspapers had reported in sensational terms that a young Polish Jew had shot a German embassy official, in protest against the deportation of his parents to Poland, where they had been abandoned in no man's land without shelter or food. "The rabble has taken to the streets, ransacking everything Jewish. They're out of control."

Wilhelm asked, "Won't the police stop them?"

His mother shook her head.

Max could remember a time when he too had trusted the police, had trusted they would keep people safe, even Jews.

Tante Nina went to the window and looked out. "All's quiet here."

Uncle Bruno said, "Maybe from the attic," and the boys pushed back their chairs and raced up the stairs. Crowding around the one window, they saw black smoke billowing in the distance, sparks and the glow of flames above the roofs. When Uncle Bruno and Tante Nina arrived, they stood back to let them see. Uncle Bruno put his arm around his wife.

Max felt very unsure. He had no idea what would happen next, what his role was in this horrifying, anarchic world which had abruptly supplanted what had been a familiar and predictable scene. What was he supposed to do? What would his father expect of him? Until this moment, the Nazis had appeared brutal and primitive, but not life-threatening, not to Max himself. His father had affirmed that law and order would prevail in due course, because the majority of Germans were decent folk. It had been some time since he'd heard his father say that.

Aunt Nina said, "Come downstairs, boys. Good food is getting cold."

They went down slowly and sat at the table.

The food seemed unappealing, or was it that he no longer felt hungry?

Nina put her hand on his shoulder and said, "You're safe here." They were not likely to be targeted because Uncle Bruno wasn't Jewish.

Karl wanted to pick up some clothes and books at the hostel, but Uncle Bruno said, "Best not go out now. It may not be safe. Who knows what may be happening over there."

There was silence after that. They all heard the knock at the door.

Nina snapped at the boys, "The attic! Go! Now!" as she gathered up their plates and cutlery from the table. They gaped at her. "Wilhelm, hide their glasses and napkins, quick, in the cupboard."

Bruno was peering through the curtains. "It's all right, Nina, no need."

The maid let the visitor in, a young woman carrying a baby, holding a small child by the hand. Her face was pale and her eyes huge. The child buried its face in her skirt.

Tante Nina put her arms around her.

"Leah, my dear," said Bruno.

Tante Nina led her away. Later, she told them what had happened. "A crowd came, and her husband was arrested by the SA. They broke down the front door and the windows. She was pushed around, but fortunately she's only bruised."

The phone rang again and again.

Aunt Nina called him. "Your father, Max."

His voice sounded the same as usual. He was in Stuttgart. He told Max that Oma and his mother were fine, and that she was investigating the situation at Helena's Landschule; nothing much would have happened there, as the riots were mainly in the towns. There was some damage to the house, according to his mother. He had not seen it himself. The Orthodox synagogue in Nuremberg had been burnt down. There was much to attend to and he had to go, but he would ring again soon with a plan for Max who was to stay at Aunt Nina's in the meantime, where he was safe. With that he said good bye and the call ended. Max put the receiver down, at a loss.

The three boys returned to the attic window. It was dark now. They could see a glow in the distance. The neighbourhood was very still, as if holding its breath. Uncle Bruno said, "If someone comes – which is unlikely – climb onto the roof and hide behind the chimney stack until we come for you. There's room for two. We'll get your coats up here so you don't catch cold." The roof looked steep, but Bruno showed them the narrow ridge they might walk on to get to the chimney. Max realised it was intended for chimney sweeps and for some reason felt reassured.

Beds were made up for him and for Karl on mattresses in the attic. He was given a pair of Bruno's pyjamas. Lying in the dark, he and Karl talked for a long time. They were both desperate to return home. Karl came from Düsseldorf and like him had registered with the authorities on arrival in Hamburg. Might the police search for them at the hostel? Would it be dangerous to go there? What had happened to the other boys? They wondered how long they should stay at Tante Nina's. Where else might they go? Was it safe on the streets? More and more questions, no answers. The adults didn't know what would happen next any more than they did; no one could know. They'd been told to stay put, but was it not up to them to make up their own minds?

TWENTY-TWO

The next morning, Tante Nina gave them towels, soap and toothpaste. It felt strange to have neither toothbrush nor a change of clothing. After a cursory wash, Max joined the others at breakfast.

Uncle Bruno had been out early to investigate; he'd seen the hostel. "Not in good shape," he said. There had been a fire and the windows of nearby shops had been smashed.

"Was anyone at the hostel?" asked Max.

"No," said Uncle Bruno. "No one could live there now."

Max pondered the statement as he ate. He wondered what had happened to the other students. He had trouble imagining the room where he'd studied and slept, burnt, destroyed. As the day passed, the extent of his loss dawned on him: books he'd brought from home, a pullover knitted by Oma, the expensive fountain pen he'd received on his bar mitzvah. What he wanted most was to rejoin his parents. He longed for his father to phone. The phone rang often, but not for him.

Uncle Bruno left for work saying he didn't expect to accomplish much, but hoped to gather more information about what was happening to Jews. Max and Karl spent the rest of the day indoors. Karl tried repeatedly to phone his parents, to no avail. Tante Nina wouldn't let them go near the windows or out to the garden, in case the neighbours saw them. They hadn't the heart to play Monopoly. They tried cards, but only Wilhelm was keen. The young woman stayed in a bedroom with her baby, only emerging for meals. Tante Nina brought the young child – a boy – into the living room to play with coloured wooden blocks. Wilhelm built towers which the boy knocked down. At meal times, they took turns feeding him: it was something to do; the mother smiled briefly as she looked after the baby. Tante Nina looked preoccupied. The phone would ring and murmured conversations would follow. People rang at the door, came and went. They listened to the radio on the hour, but there was nothing of relevance to them. Karl was worried – still no news from home. No one knew anything. They'd run out of things to talk about.

At long last, one of Karl's relatives rang. Karl's mother had been slightly hurt and was recovering at home. The whereabouts of Karl's father were unknown. Karl was told to stay with Tante Nina because Hamburg was safer. His mother sent her love. Karl disappeared up to the attic.

Max tried to read *Durch die Wüste*, a Karl May favourite he borrowed from Wilhelm, but gave up when he found himself reading a page over and over without remembering what he'd read. His thoughts kept returning to his father's voice over the phone, and to the rising smoke he had seen through the attic window. He asked Hans for writing paper and sat at the table. Words formed themselves into a poem about dark skies and columns of smoke, seen from a high window. In the afternoon, he worked at it, trying to find the right words, the right order. Tante Nina looked over his shoulder and made a little approving noise. Max was embarrassed because the poem was short, but he couldn't think of anything else to say. She asked him to read it aloud to everyone after dinner, and the young mother, who hardly spoke most of the time, said suddenly and firmly that it showed promise:

> Beyond sharp rooftops, flames
>
> stain the sombre day red.
>
> Black smoke rises, sparks melt
>
> into the dark clouds,
>
> erasing the horizon.

Wilhelm said he didn't know what to make of it and Max folded the paper away in his bag. The compliment he'd received felt sweet. He thought about the writing and how absorbed he'd been, how content.

After the Chanukah holidays, Helena returned to the school by the lake and the outside world fell away, ceasing to matter.

She shared a room with Lore in an old cottage in the grounds. The walls were white, the sheets and eiderdown a cheerful blue or red gingham, Bärchen occupying his customary place on her pillow. She studied English with Tante Sophie and engaged in research projects, besides singing in the choir and helping in the kitchen.

To her delight, Inge arrived one day, her position at the Nuremberg school having disappeared as the roll shrank. She told Helena that her father's zip factory had been sold in the prevailing unsatisfactory deal. Her parents were applying for visas at all the embassies. Helena thought about the teachers and children leaving the school, fleeing Germany in an exodus. They were bid farewell at assembly, and new children and teachers were welcomed, as she had once been.

As far as she knew, her own parents were not preparing to leave. Tante Trude had stated recently that she would keep the school open for as long as there were children who needed it, and unexpected tears had rolled down Helena's cheeks. She wasn't sure why she'd wept.

Otherwise life was calm, the routine unchanged. One November morning, she and Lore were on duty in the dining room, preparing the tables for lunch. They had the big hall to themselves, and Helena hummed as she gathered the cruet sets. She sat down to wipe them and top them up with salt. Beyond the great semi-circular window at the far end of the room, bare trees lined the drive. The middle-grade children had gathered a great pile of branches from the forest in front of the house for a bonfire that evening. Helena was looking forward to roasting sausages and potatoes.

"Let's get this over and done with," said Lore. "We've still got our beds to make, remember?"

The harsh shriek of the alarm bell shattered the quiet, the bell screaming urgency, going on and on. Helena clapped her hands over her ears; she stared through the window, transfixed. Something was terribly wrong; the black swastika and the red Nazi flag were coming up the drive, carried by unknown children. She recognised one of the adults, a villager who'd delivered supplies to the kitchen. Following them were people in brown SA uniforms, with poles, sticks and pitchforks, their faces distorted by rage, yelling. She couldn't hear them because of the bell's clamour. Lore had grabbed her arm and was shouting too. The frenetic scream of the bell was overpowering. Mesmerised, Helena stared at the approaching mob, people whooping and howling. She realised that some of the poles were rifles; a truck was bearing what looked like a long metal cylinder; that was the barrel of a gun. It swivelled and turned its black eye on her.

She yielded to Lore's frantic tugging and they ran to the door amid a deafening crash as the great window shattered behind them, the enormous sound of splintering, crashing glass briefly overriding the bell's continuous ringing. She was shrieking herself; she couldn't help it. She heard feet pounding the uncarpeted corridors and the wooden stairs. A woman screamed in the nearby kitchen. People shouted, an unknown male voice bellowed, the words unintelligible.

In the hallway, a teacher was directing the stream of terrified children out of the door with urgent gestures: Helena read the words on her lips: "Quickly! Go, go!" During emergency drill they'd been told to run to their rooms as soon as the bell rang, to run immediately, as fast as they could. "Don't stop for any reason: grab your suitcase, your coat, run to the gathering place. Don't waste a minute! Your leaders will tell you what to do!" The whole thing had been rehearsed, but in quiet, without that bell. They'd heard it once, briefly. They'd made a game of the exercise, timing themselves. The leaders had checked the contents of the suitcases: a coat, a change of clothes, paper and pencil, a tin cup, toothbrush, towel, soap, a comb and money.

Lore and Helena ran out with the other children. A girl tripped and fell, and Helena reached out to help her, but Tante Klara appeared, taking charge, waving Helena away, "Go, quickly, now!" Helena struggled to catch up with Lore, who grabbed her hand, pulling her along as they ran. Helena was already out of breath, afraid she might fall too. They reached their room. An alarm bell shrieked here, relentless.

Lore grabbed her suitcase and shouted, "Helena, come on! Hurry!"

Helena snatched Bärchen from the floor by the unmade bed, and reached into the cupboard for her small suitcase and her dark green Loden coat. She stuffed Bärchen and the coat into the suitcase with the other things, struggling to close it.

The case clicked shut and she ran out, following Lore up the slope. Her breath came in deep raspy gasps; her legs felt heavy. She caught a glimpse of the pregnant art teacher scuttling out of the main house's door, pulling a small girl by the hand. On the first floor, a man in a brown uniform was breaking the windowpanes with the butt of his rifle, one by one, methodically.

The alarm rang on, its shriek mitigated by distance as they ran through the vegetable garden and the orchard towards the forest, joining the others, everyone scrambling for the cover of the trees. Her suitcase banged against her shins.

They passed the row of pines which hid the school from view. She felt relieved and gasped, "They can't reach us now; they can't see us; they don't know where we are."

Lore bent over to catch her breath. "We never made our beds..."

"Just as well," said Helena and they laughed.

They were tiring and could only run in spurts. A stitch stabbed Helena's side. She could see Egon ahead, gesturing, urging them on. The ringing was faint now; she remembered the sound of the big window breaking and the crash of glass, and she shivered, nauseated.

She said, "They're destroying everything."

More children were arriving behind them.

"Come on! Move!" someone said.

Panting, they walked up the forest path with the others, relieved to be sheltered by the trees and to reach the large hut where they'd always gathered at the start of their walks. "They can't see us here," said Lore.

There were effusive greetings as friends embraced and held each other, though they kept their voices quiet; then they stood clustered around their suitcases. More children and teachers were coming up the path. Helena wondered where Tante Trude was. Egon was organising groups according to a list: seven children per adult. Inge was with Helena but Lore wasn't; no swapping was allowed. The leader of their group was a young woman called Eva, who had taught maths. Their group would make their way to the railway station in Potsdam, less than an hour's walk away. Others were aiming for a nearby village; each group followed a different route.

Then Tante Trude arrived with some older students, carrying a small child wrapped in a blanket. One of the students was weeping. "Come, children," said Tante Trude as she gave the child she was holding to another teacher. "Please listen to the instructions. We all need to keep calm."

Eva counted them all several times, pairing them up; she held the hands of seven-year-old twins, Rebecca and Sara. Helena was assigned Simon, a sturdy six-year-old. She took his hand and was surprised at its size and strength. Inge was to mind Klaus, nine-years-old and crying because his older sister, Karoline, was still missing. Someone went in search of Karoline; Inge embraced Klaus, talking in soothing tones.

Simon went to pee behind a tree; he kept looking back as if worried the group might leave without him. The twins clung to Eva, limpet-like, one on either side. "Coats on, children," said Eva. Helena helped Simon pull his jacket from his rucksack. His teeth were chattering. She buttoned up the jacket, aware of his gaze searching her face. She smiled at him; then she quickly buttoned her own coat and stood holding Simon's hand, not knowing what to do next. She watched the headmistress as she moved among the groups, saying a few words, kissing each child before they left. "We should go now," she thought. "This is taking too long."

The Nazis were just beyond the trees. The urge to turn and run became almost unbearable; she closed all the buttons on her coat, felt as if she were suffocating and opened them again. Where was Karoline?

Lore ran over in tears and said, "We're going now, goodbye Helena. I don't know what is happening, take care!"

They hugged tight, as tight as they could. When would they meet again?

Karoline arrived. "My finch," she panted, holding up a cardboard box. Everyone knew about Karolina's bird. She'd been caring for the fledgling since discovering it in the orchard grass a few days earlier.

"Is that all you brought?" asked Inge.

Karoline said, "I'm wearing my coat. I didn't think I could carry anything else." She added in a shocked voice, "They were throwing books out the windows!"

"We're off, Trude," said Eva, shouldering her rucksack.

The headmistress kissed them one after the other. "Helena, *mein Liebchen*. Be brave, be good, God bless!" She did not appear worried; her manner was as kind as usual.

They ran down the familiar path into the forest.

Helena glanced back. Tante Trude waved and she waved too. Where were the Nazis now? She hoped destroying the school would occupy them long enough for Tante Trude to get away with everyone else.

The little group walked fast, and the hut and Tante Trude disappeared behind a bend in the path. Helena held Simon's hand. Karoline was still chattering about the books, talking much too loud until Eva asked her to hush; she said they were safer now because no one knew where they were. Helena thought that the leafless trees did not provide much cover. The group was visible to anyone looking their way.

They walked for about an hour, following the pace of the little ones. No one spoke, no one complained.

Simon whispered, "Helena, where are we going?"

"To Potsdam railway station," answered Helena, whispering too. It was strange to be whispering outdoors. "We're half-way there already."

The further from the school the better. She kept turning over in her mind the sudden shocking change, from a serene orderly life, with meals and lessons at regular times, to wandering terrified through the forest, like modern Hansel and Gretels, not knowing where they would sleep that night. They would never return to the school, that part of their lives was over. She longed for her mother and father.

Simon trotted along beside her. "And then? Where do we go from the railway station?" he asked, gazing up at her, his brown eyes anxious.

"We'll probably take the train to Berlin. Don't worry, I'll look after you." She wasn't used to young children. To her surprise, her answer seemed to reassure him. She swapped sides with Simon so she could carry the suitcase in the other hand. She grasped his hand firmly. The track they were following was a familiar one.

The younger children were beginning to flag.

"We'll stop soon," announced Eva. "And I'll tell everyone what we're doing next."

The little ones whined, "Eva, I'm tired."

"Me too."

"When can we stop?"

"Hush now, just a little further," said Eva. "Please keep as quiet as you can."

Helena wondered what would happen if they weren't quiet enough, and someone heard them. The thought was linked to the memory of the Nazi flag in the drive and the angry villagers, their guns and pitchforks, and her mind replayed the sound of smashing glass as the huge window disintegrated; she was struck by another wave of nausea. They had fled to the forest for safety but the forest was unreliable, treacherous – someone might come looking for them, might perhaps find them...

They stopped, but only for five minutes. She was glad Simon was with her, glad to hold his hand while they walked, even though he was only six years old. Being with the group was reassuring. They walked for what seemed like a long time. Simon kept saying he was hungry. Helena thought of the lunch they'd missed: leek and potato soup, fresh brown bread and butter. Someone had reported that the Nazis had overturned the big cooking pots in the kitchen, poured the soup out over the kitchen floor. Food for more than a hundred people, wasted. She thought of the picnics they'd enjoyed on their walks, the large round loaves cut into thick wedges, spread with butter and passed round, with chunks of cheese and an apple each, washed down with water from a stream.

Helena could tell by the light shining through the trees that they were near the edge of the forest. Eva stopped by a big fir tree and they crowded round her. She reminded them to speak quietly. She took a big water bottle from her rucksack and poured water into everyone's cups. Helena shared hers with Karoline. Karoline opened the bird box for Helena and Simon to peek in. The little bird was struggling to stand up from the bed of dry moss he was lying on. Helena poured a little water into his drinking bowl.

"He's had to do without water, but only for a little while," said Karoline.

"Like us," said Simon.

They sat under the tree on the dry pine needles, their suitcases and rucksacks around them. Helena drank her water. Eva said, "Children, time to pee. We'll rest a little and then we'll walk to the railway station. It's quite near." They scattered through the trees, though no one went very far. When Helena returned, she found Simon huddling close to Eva.

TWENTY-THREE

Sitting on the ground under the pine tree, Helena felt the cold creep into her body. She rubbed her hands together and shivered. The sun had sunk behind the trees, creating long thin shadows, though it was only mid-afternoon. She watched Eva, who was absorbed in sorting the papers she had pulled from her rucksack – lists and addresses, a destination for each of them. Helena was to go to Tante Liesel.

"This running-away business is exhausting," she thought. She longed for an end to the nastiness and uncertainty. If only she could be home with her parents, safe and snug in her bed. She remembered summer evenings, falling asleep with her window open, listening to the beloved voices rising from the terrace. She thought of Tante Fanny, so serious since Rudi had left for England. Helena had endeavoured to make her laugh, tried to bring back the light into her eyes by hugging and kissing her, but she wasn't able to dispel the sadness. Alicia Klein was in England too. For the first time, Helena wondered why her parents had not sent her on a Kindertransport. She wondered how Rudi was coping. He was a bright, confident child and people liked him, though he could be a nuisance at times. Her mother said that the

English family he lived with were good to him; the father was a lawyer and there was a dog. Helena would have liked a dog.

She wondered what England was like. She didn't know very much about it except for stupid things: they drank their tea with milk, and it rained often. According to her father, the British were a force to be reckoned with, though they had not really won the Great War. He said the Americans had done that. Germany's honour called for revenge. A teacher had said so at the school in Nuremberg. Or maybe that was what the Nazis said, what Father called propaganda. She was becoming confused, drowsy in spite of the cold.

Her parents were not planning to leave. A thought came to her, insistent: "It's time to go!" She suddenly felt completely awake. She sat up straight, staring ahead; the thought was very strong, accompanied again by the image of Nazis coming up the school drive and the sound of the big window breaking. She pinched her hand hard to stop it. She felt an urge to get up and run, run somewhere, anywhere, that very minute, but of course that was nonsense – where would she go? She felt absolutely sure that they should all leave Germany: Father, Mama, Max, Oma and herself. The sooner the better, she thought. It had never occurred to her before that her parents might be wrong about such an important issue. She'd listened to the discussions around the dinner table, her father saying that they had to endure, that they belonged here and she'd believed him. She tried to sort out her reasoning. Her father was a clever man, a strong, capable person to whom people turned for advice. When he spoke, they listened. But she felt that she no longer wanted him to decide for her. She knew what she wanted, what her family should do now.

She whispered to Inge, "I think that all of us, all the Jews, should leave Germany."

Inge nodded, "Yes, so do I."

"What do your parents say?"

"Mama wanted to leave ages ago, but Father wouldn't leave the factory. Then the Nazis took over and wouldn't pay enough. They're searching for a country that will agree to have us even though we're poor."

"Most people want to leave."

"Except Tante Trude."

"Yes, she said she'd stay and keep the school going."

"Until there are no more Jewish children to teach."

"It's different now," said Helena.

"She can't go back, can she?"

"No."

The school had been destroyed. They knew it, but were reluctant to say so out loud.

Inge said, "Lucky Ilse is in Paris now." Ilse was Inge's cousin.

"Paris would be nice," said Helena. She had visited Paris with her parents, seen the chic Parisiennes on the Champs Elysées and climbed the Eiffel Tower. The food had been wonderful. "Some people think that Paris is not far enough." Uncle Fritz had said that after Uncle Robert's departure.

Eva had finished sorting through the papers. "Children, please listen. We're near the railway station; it's at the end of that road you can see there, through the trees. The bus station is next to it. We'll buy food there before you go."

She told each child their destination, reading out the names and addresses from her list. Karoline and Klaus had an aunt living near Potsdam; Inge, an old cousin in a village on the outskirts of Berlin; the twins were to stay with Eva in her Berlin flat until their parents fetched them. Inge hugged Rebecca who was on the verge of tears.

Eva turned to Simon, "Darling, you're going to your granny in Berlin, and you'll travel with Helena whose aunt lives nearby. Helena will look after you. You'll be there by the end of the afternoon."

Simon whined, "I'm hungry *now!*"

Eva hugged him. "There'll be food at the station, we're almost there."

Klaus whimpered, "I want to go home!"

Karoline said, "Kläuschen, once we're there, Mama and Papa will come as soon as they can."

Klaus buried his face in his sister's shoulder.

A light rain began to fall. Helena pulled up her hood. She found Simon's woolly hat in his rucksack.

Eva said, "When we reach the road, we turn right. There aren't many houses. We'll walk in small groups, no more than two or three, so as not to attract attention. If someone talks to you, say you've got a train to catch, apologise politely and keep going. Whatever you do, don't run."

"This is scary," said Karoline, a wobble in her voice. Under the dark curls, her brown eyes were fearful. She clutched her brother with one hand, the bird box with the other.

"Would you like to walk with me and Klaus?" asked Eva.

Karoline nodded.

"The twins will walk with Inge, and Simon with Helena. But before we start, we must look tidy."

Eva stood up and brushed the pine needles off her jacket and skirt with both hands. She asked Inge to brush her back. Then she attended to Klaus. She didn't appear in the least worried, whereas Helena felt more frightened than she'd ever been in her life. The thought of walking without Eva and the others was terrifying, even though it would only be for a short stretch and she would have Simon for company.

They polished their shoes as best they could, taking turns to spit on Eva's handkerchief and rubbing fiercely. They were wearing hats or hoods because of the rain, but someone produced a comb and they did their best with it. Helena tucked Simon's hair tidily under his cap. They brushed the pine needles and twigs off each other's clothes. The light was sinking fast under the trees, and they couldn't see very well. On the open road it was still daylight.

Eva doled out a large piece of chocolate to each of them, an unexpected treat. Helena and Simon gobbled down their portions. Helena realised that Eva had kept none for herself or for Inge. She felt half regretful and half glad; she'd been so hungry that it would have been hard to share, though they'd only missed lunch. She remembered fussing over food she didn't like, her mother nagging, saying poor people went hungry and she was lucky to have enough. She hadn't felt lucky at the time.

Inge and the twins left first. Helena and Simon waited until they reached the road before starting off, hand in hand: it was like a game, but it wasn't a game at all. When they reached the road, they looked back and saw Eva, Karoline and Klaus half-hidden among the trees behind them, waiting. Helena remembered the Bible story of Lot and his wife who looked back when she shouldn't have. Eva had said that people were more likely to notice them if they kept glancing back. Helena wished she could turn round one more time. Simon tugged her hand; the gap with Inge and the twins was growing larger. She forced a smile. "Here we go!"

Holding hands, they walked past fields and trees. "Lucky it's raining," said Helena. "No one's outside." A horse and cart clattered by, the driver's face invisible under his hood.

This walk was much shorter than the hike through the woods, but it felt interminable. A half-empty bus drove past; its sign said *Bahnhof*.

She could see a board ahead indicating the way to the station. She watched Inge and the twins follow that road and disappear round a bend. It seemed then as if she and Simon were altogether alone in hostile territory. She would have liked to walk faster but reminded herself to keep to the same pace. She hoped no one was watching. Simon walked trustingly beside her, holding her hand in a tight grip.

When they reached the turn-off, she caught sight of Inge and the twins as they disappeared through the station doors. Her heart was thumping in her chest. Simon asked, "Will there be any nasty people there?"

She smiled at him as best she could and said, "We'll be safe, Simon." She hoped it was true. She fixed her gaze on the doors. The station was busy with people coming and going.

Inside the familiar station hall, they became anonymous, two travellers among others. They passed a kiosk with a *Stürmer* display. "Don't look, Simon!" said Helena, catching sight of a headline celebrating attacks across the country. Her stomach churned; were her parents safe? And Max?

They made their way to the waiting room. It smelled of cold cigarette smoke and neglect. Deep wooden benches lined the walls; the high windows were obscured by wire netting and the few electric bulbs hanging from long wires provided little light. Inge and the twins were huddling in the gloom. Helena was so relieved to see them that she could have hugged them. Mindful of Eva's instructions, she sat down beside them, whispering to Simon to sit down too. The last time she'd been in this waiting room she'd been on her way home. She recognised the posters on the walls which advertised railway holidays for workers, courtesy of the Nazi Worker's Party. The workers looked sun-tanned and happy, but every poster featured a large black swastika. She shuddered. A nearby traveller was reading the *Völkischer Beobachter*. She tried to read its headlines from where she sat. They seemed to confirm there had been Nazi attacks elsewhere.

Then Eva, Karoline and Klaus arrived – a great relief, which made Helena realise again how frightened she'd been in their absence. She wondered about the paper: was it worth buying?

Inge left them to buy food. Helena thought how she might disappear, and no one would know what had happened to her. She wished there was something to do rather than waiting. Simon was kicking his heels. "Let's take another look at you," said Helena. She brushed him down again as best she could. There was mud on his coat and a button was missing. Her efforts made little difference; he still looked unkempt.

"What are you wearing underneath?"

Simon opened his coat: a pair of navy corduroy trousers and a blue pullover smeared with bright green paint.

"We had art this morning," he said. He was on the brink of tears.

Helena kissed him and did up the coat's existing buttons. "Never mind, darling."

Eva had slipped off her rucksack. She sat down next to Helena and took her hand. "Helena, my dear, your train leaves in fifteen minutes. I have your tickets." Helena sat dumbstruck. Not yet, she wanted to say, not yet, please. She wasn't ready. She stared at Eva, her thoughts racing. How could she leave everybody? How would she cope on her own? Eva said quietly, "Please Helena, you have to go, my dear – say goodbye now, be quick! Remember, Simon will follow your example. He relies on you."

Inge had returned with a paper bag full of apples. "A woman was selling them from a barrow." Between Potsdam station and the safety of Tante Liesel's Berlin apartment lay a treacherous journey, when anything might happen. The twins were agitating to go to the toilet and Inge was about to take them. Eva told her to polish their shoes again, with toilet paper to get rid of the mud. Helena's own shoes were not very clean, nor were Simon's, but there wasn't time. Eva gave Helena the tickets, one for Simon and one for her, and Inge gave them each an apple.

Eva said, "The journey takes less than an hour, no time at all. Inge, I won't be long, their train leaves in a few minutes."

Inge and Helena hugged and kissed. The others clustered around, despite Eva's warnings. They wanted to touch and hold each other. They were all in tears including Eva who said, "We must stop this, please children, we must! People are looking." Sniffing, Inge quickly told Helena her cousin's address which Helena repeated. She wouldn't forget. There was no time to write anything down.

"Keep in touch," said Inge, smiling, an arm around Karoline. So brave! thought Helena. Eva took her and Simon by the hand and they went to the platform. There were only minutes to go; the loudspeaker was announcing the train's imminent arrival.

Eva hugged them both. "Thank you for everything you did these last few hours," she said to Helena. She seemed grave. "You've been very brave, Helena, and Simon, you've been brave too, darling. Always do what Helena tells you. One day we'll meet again."

Helena's stomach lurched. Would they?

As the familiar red-and-cream train drew in, they stood close together on the platform. Helena and Simon hugged Eva one last time and stepped into the carriage. It wasn't full. The passengers seemed indifferent, absorbed in their own thoughts. Helena walked down the central aisle, her suitcase bumping her shins, Simon following close behind. No SA or SS men, no Hitler Youth, as far as she could see. She noticed an old lady who resembled Oma, and two vacant seats facing her; a good, safe place for them to sit. Simon ran to the window to wave to Eva; Helena lifted the suitcase and rucksack into the rack. Eva stood smiling up at them, but Helena could see that she wanted to cry. Simon clung to Helena as they waved. The train started and picked up speed, leaving a receding Eva waving on the platform. Then the train went under a bridge and she disappeared.

Helena closed the window as the train's din settled down to a regular rhythm. She sat down beside Simon and leant back. It was comfortable here. The grandmother was plump like Oma, but less well dressed. Then Helena noticed a tiny silver and enamel swastika on the lapel of her coat and her heart sank. She hoped Simon wouldn't notice, but then his hand crept into hers and held on tight, and she knew without looking at him that he had.

The lady scrutinised Helena and Simon, from their faces to their muddy shoes. "And where are you off to, children?"

Helena gulped and said, "To Berlin, to visit relatives."

"Was that your mother?"

"No, our aunt."

"Ah," she nodded, satisfied. "She looked too young to be your mother."

It was warm in the train. Helena was afraid the old lady might ask further questions, but she was reading a magazine. They ate their apples voraciously. Helena tried to slow herself down, to make it last; Simon finished his and gave her the apple core, which she dropped into the rubbish bin under the window. The train stopped at a station in the countryside. More people got on, but no one came near them. Simon fell asleep. So much had happened since the morning; it felt as if several days had gone by. Helena felt her own eyes close.

She woke to a smell of food, a wonderful smell. Beside her, Simon shifted. She saw the old lady eating a roll with a sausage in it. Simon sat up and stared at it. He looked at Helena and then back at the sandwich. His mouth opened a little. They both watched intently as the lady ate. She felt their gaze and smiled at them.

"Very good sausage, the best," she said. "My son's a butcher; he makes them himself." She sounded pleased with herself.

Helena thought, she doesn't know we're hungry; she mustn't know.

The ticket collector arrived, a tall man with a jovial air and a large brown moustache with waxed tips. He punched the lady's ticket first. Simon shrank back. Helena could tell the conductor was having thoughts about them. He examined the tickets carefully and clipped them. She could hardly breathe. What if he asked for her name or Simon's? That would give the game away: her family name wasn't obviously Jewish, but Simon's was Levy and they hadn't prepared him to lie. The conductor put away his ticket clipper and said briefly, "Next stop Wannsee." He went on to the next car; she could hear his voice asking for the tickets there.

By now she was very hungry. She tried to distract herself by looking out of the window.

"I want to go to the toilet," Simon whispered.

They stood up and the lady looked them up and down again.

"We'll be back soon," said Helena politely and guided Simon to the end of the carriage.

"I don't like that lady," whispered Simon as he went in to the toilet. "She's wearing a swastika."

"Ssh!" said Helena.

The conductor came by and stopped. "You're on your own, aren't you?" he asked.

Helena nodded.

"These are difficult days. All kinds of things happen on the train, even when I'm around, so stay by that old lady, she should help keep you safe. I can't be everywhere and trouble doesn't need much time.

A young girl shouldn't travel on her own these days, and that's a fact. I wouldn't let my own daughter travel like that."

They returned to their seats. The old lady dozed, her mouth open, snoring occasionally. Simon sat by the window looking out, occasionally whispering to Helena that he was hungry. They could see another roll peeping out of the paper bag in the lady's basket, its smell tantalising. Helena briefly entertained the fantasy of stealing it. She looked at her watch; another ten minutes and they'd reach Westkreuz, where they had to change trains.

The loudspeaker blared the announcement, waking the old lady. They were about to arrive. Helena helped Simon slip on his rucksack, picked up the suitcase and said goodbye. How could she have thought the woman looked like Oma?

They stepped out of the train, straight into a milling crowd of excited young people in uniform, Hitler Youth and League of German Girls, shouting in high-pitched voices about their plans for the day. One of the girls near Helena screamed, "Sigi says we might even see the Führer!"

TWENTY-FOUR

Tante Nina called Max to the phone, "Your mother!"

His mother's voice was quiet. She asked him how he was and when he said he was well, she continued in a sharper tone, "Your sister is at Tante Liesel's in Berlin. You are to catch a train to Berlin as soon as Bruno can organise it and bring her home to Nuremberg."

He was taken aback by the way she spoke, but he wasn't inclined to argue; after the long wait, the thought of action, any action, was invigorating. He wanted to start right away. He felt excited rather than frightened. If his mother wanted him to go, the journey was probably safe enough. She'd not said why his sister was in Berlin rather than at school, but he assumed there had been disturbances there too.

***

Tante Nina forced him to eat an abundant meal before he left; she hovered over him, plying him with unnecessary advice, to avoid Nazis and Hitler Youth, to look as if he knew where he was going, to sneak away if someone else got into trouble, not to get involved in any way. "No heroics!" she admonished him. He nodded, his mouth full. "Remember," she said, "no matter what happens, your only goal is to bring your sister home, safely!" Karl wanted to leave too, but they wouldn't let him. Max felt sorry for him. It occurred to him that Karl might leave anyway, that he might slip out when no one was looking.

Uncle Bruno said that travelling in the evening was best, because people were tired and less alert at the end of the day. He and Tante Nina wanted him to wear *Lederhosen* and a shirt like the Hitler Youth, but they couldn't find any to fit him, so to his relief they let him wear his own clothes. Tante Nina worried about the cold and forced a knitted scarf and a woollen ski cap onto him, which he pushed into his bag. He wished they would let him be and just let him go. Uncle Bruno was to accompany him to the station and buy his ticket. They'd made up a lame story, of a family funeral in Hamburg. He was to say that he was going to Berlin because his father had recently been transferred there from Nuremberg. That would account for his accent, slight but detectable. Hopefully no one would ask to see his papers. Max found the fuss rather silly. Why would anyone bother him? He'd be an ordinary passenger.

Tante Nina gave him more money – "Keep it hidden" – plus an apple, two boiled eggs, bread and cheese and a bottle of apple juice. They crowded into the hall to see him off, hugged him and wished him luck. Tante Nina kissed him. Their worry was infectious. He didn't know what the situation would be like outside. He was glad of Uncle Bruno's company, for the start at least. It was dark by now, the weather cold and clear.

Uncle Bruno said, "Ready?"

The carriage was full and the fat woman sitting beside Max talked continuously to her husband in the local dialect; Max understood only some of it. It had to do with being too cold or too hot, windows being open or shut, and how a relative's health had suffered in a similar situation. Her husband nodded from time to time without saying a word. Max couldn't concentrate on his book. He was still shocked by what he'd seen on the way to the station: shattered shop windows, glass on the pavement, broken furniture scattered on the street. Mayhem. He'd been confronted with a reality where nothing was safe. The other passengers appeared not to care. They dozed or looked out of the window; no one spoke to him. He tried to attract as little attention as possible. The woman's voice droned on beside him, too close for comfort.

He left the compartment to escape her monologue. He stood in the corridor, his forehead against the window, watching the moonlit landscape go by. The train would arrive in Berlin at 8:00 p.m. He'd seen a group of SA at the railway station, but there were none in this part of the train; some Wehrmacht soldiers were clustered at the far end of the corridor. A middle-aged man stood nearby smoking. He relaxed a little, enjoying the freedom and a mild sense of adventure.

Someone stopped beside him. Looking round he first saw the black uniform. An SS officer, the silver runes, pips and stripes of a *Hauptsturmführer* on his collar. He was lighting his cigarette with an elegant silver lighter, embossed with a swastika. He nodded to Max and proffered the cigarette packet.

"I don't smoke, thank you."

The man inhaled deeply. "First drag, the best." He was about thirty, a bit paunchy. "Travelling to Berlin?"

How to get out of this situation? How to get rid of this man? "Yes."

"Business or pleasure?"

"I'm fetching my sister from Berlin. My mother doesn't want her travelling on her own."

"Very wise. Meanwhile, you yourself get to travel around on your own, fancy free." He leered.

Max produced a grin. "Not that free. I'm expected."

"At the station?"

No one would be at the station, so he said, "At my uncle's, tonight." Out of the question to mention that Tante Liesel, a mere woman, was his guardian.

"Gives you some leeway, doesn't it. A man needs freedom of action, after all."

He didn't know what to say.

"How about a little fun on the way?"

"I beg your pardon?"

"I've a first-class compartment and some schnapps."

He'd have to string him along. "I'm not a great schnapps drinker."

"Prefer beer, do you? I'll get you some! Come along now."

Impossible to refuse. Max followed as the officer pushed through several crowded carriages until they reached the first-class wagon. The compartment was empty. The officer took a bottle of schnapps out of a leather bag, uncorked it and offered it to Max.

"No, thank you."

"You did say you were a beer man. Sit down, sit down!"

The officer rang for service and a waiter arrived. "A beer for my friend!"

"You've finished school, haven't you? What are your plans?"

Max hesitated and then said, "The police, I'll join the police force." He had no idea why he'd said that. The words had popped into his head.

The man seemed interested, "Why is that?"

"My father is with the police in Nuremberg."

"With the police in Nuremberg?"

A waiter appeared with the beer. Max took a sip. He'd give it all he had. "Yes, he's the Commissioner for Police. His name is Benno Martin." He'd better not drink much after this.

The leer disappeared, "I've heard of him."

Oh God, thought Max, he's going to find me out.

But no, the Nazi was keen to impress the son of Nuremberg's Police Commissioner. He talked and as he talked, he leant forward, his gaze pinning Max down. He explained in detail how he had risen through the ranks to be an officer in the SS, how he'd personally met Hitler several times, gesturing with the schnapps bottle for emphasis. Max listened in genuine fascination, doing his best to hide his discomfort, sipping the beer. What would his father do, coming face to face with such a man, who knew Hitler personally, who loved him, who wanted to get rid of the Jews, the communists, the Gypsies? "A scourge, to be wiped out," said the *Hauptsturmführer* with a sweeping gesture. He'd now embarked on a rant about the brilliant future of the great German *Volk,* of their Third Reich.

There was a brisk knock on the door and another officer came in. Max was introduced, "The son of Polizei Präsident Martin, you know, Nuremberg's police president." This man too was interested, wanting to know more.

"Martin," said Max, clicking his heels. He realised this was his opportunity. He turned to his host and said, "Will you please excuse me. Thank you for your kind hospitality."

They tried to keep him, but there was no need to worry about turning them down. He had higher status and they dared not offend. They had to let him go. He almost laughed out loud, though once he was in the corridor on his way back to his compartment, his legs shook badly.

Emerging from the train into the high vault of the Lehrter Station, Max paused to look around. He remembered arriving at this station when he was younger – a palace among stations, Berlin's pride and joy. He remembered how overwhelmed he'd been by all the colours, the sounds, the movement of people and machines, the throng: tall Uhlan soldiers in blue-and-red tunics, sober dark-suited men, elegant women in big hats followed by maids and by uniformed porters carrying suitcases and boxes. Only inches from the quay, a monstrous black locomotive had drawn away in a cacophony of shrieking, groaning metal, accompanied by clouds of steam, exerting a power beyond belief, followed by a noisy succession of lumbering wagons. And dominating the crowds and the enormous machines was a voice which echoed up and down the huge space, imperative, commanding, like the voice of an all-knowing god. Nowadays, in 1938, the voice was still the same, announcing in authoritative tones the arrival and departure times of trains, coupled with the names of the great cities whose names studded Germany's history, names he'd once loved. The station was as busy as he remembered, but everything seemed smaller, the uniforms duller, the colours muted, except for the enormous red flag draped above the concourse, with the menacing swastika.

Hoisting the strap of his bag onto his shoulder, he hurried to join the flow of people leaving the station, fearful of running into the SS officers again. As he stepped into the night, he inhaled the fresh air with pleasure. A tangy smell rose from the Spree River. He could see barges being unloaded under the harsh electric light of projectors. Despite the late hour, the area teemed with activity, car headlights moving in a continuous file on the bridge near the station; further along the embankment he could see the outline of Humboldt Harbour's cranes. Feeling less conspicuous in the crowd, he made his way to the suburban railway station where he caught the S-Bahn to Charlottenburg without a hitch. So far, so good.

Charlottenburg station was near Tante Liesel's. The streets were busy, the shop windows still illuminated despite the late hour. Swastikas were everywhere, fanions arranged in shop displays, hanging from lamp posts and trees, flags draped on buildings – no different from Hamburg or Nuremberg. As he drew closer to his destination, he passed the smashed windows of a large shop: shards of broken china and glass littered the pavement – no one was sweeping them up or removing them. It was unlike anything he'd ever witnessed – chaos reigning unchecked, unmitigated. He came across another devastated shop, and yet another. Antisemitic graffiti were scrawled on their walls. He thought of Bruno's description of the hostel in Hamburg, of the burning synagogues. Now he was terrified: his heart racing, his chest tight, his hands sweaty. Was there any safety in Tante Liesel's apartment, or at his parents' house in Nuremberg? They were no more than bolt holes, provisional sanctuaries.

When he reached a residential area, the streets appeared intact, at first. Then glass crunched underfoot, scattered over a wide area. On the pavement, in the gutter or among the bushes in a garden there would be debris: an upholstered chair on its side, with a broken leg; a cutlery drawer lined in green felt like the ones at home, smashed, twisted out of shape; fluttering material which turned out to be curtains or someone's clothes, or books and sheets of handwritten paper, shocking artifacts of private worlds, exposed – like walking in on someone naked. Looking up at the tall buildings, he could see the smashed windows. Disorderly, violent, utterly un-German. Criminal.

Destruction was evident on Tante Liesel's street too. He walked fast through a little park, emerging opposite her building. Windows on the third floor were shattered. It occurred to him for the first time to worry – had they attacked Liesel, hurt her? Helena? He tore across the street and into the house. Panting, he told the surly concierge Tante Liesel's name and was let in. Rather than wait for the lift, he ran up the steps in big strides, two at a time. The heavy door to the flat was shut, its surface battered, deeply gouged. His heartbeat hard in his chest. He rang the bell, and when no one answered he hammered on the door for good measure.

After a moment, Tante Liesel's voice commanded, "Stop that immediately! We're opening the door."

She stood tall in the doorway. The grim look on her face reminded him of his father. They were cousins and the likeness appeared at odd moments, both of them large, both ungainly. Liesel's stern expression dissolved as soon as she saw him.

"Oh, Max, how wonderful!" she said, reaching for him and pulling him in. She closed the door, kissed him on both cheeks and examined him closely. "So wonderful to see you!" she said again. "For a moment I thought they'd come back." She led him into the living room. "Helena!" she called. The room was a shambles. He looked around, bewildered. She'd covered the broken windowpanes with various objects: a tray, a painting, elsewhere a cushion stuffed into the hole. She didn't mention the destruction. "So lucky the heating's working, have you noticed? The main thing is that you're here and so is Helena. Helena!" she cried. "Where is the child?"

Helena appeared in the doorway. She looked different. Her face was pale and under her eyes were dark circles. She stood stiffly for a moment and then walked over to Max and put her arms round him, her head against his chest and held him tight. She didn't speak. She closed her eyes. He put his arms around her and kissed the top of her head and smelled her familiar smell. He wasn't used to holding her.

"Helena is very tired," said Tante Liesel. "She hasn't felt much like talking since she got here. She ate a lot at first and then she had a bath. Since then she's been keeping me company. What can we do for you? When did you last eat?"

"Tante Nina force-fed me before I left, but that was several hours ago."

"How are they?"

"They're fine. No one came. Hamburg's synagogues were burnt down."

Liesel nodded, "Here too. And they attacked Helena's school."

"And my hostel. I was at Tante Nina's, luckily. What happened, Helena?"

Helena shook her head and looked away.

Liesel said, "You're both well, which is the most important thing. You must be hungry, Max, and I've no edible food left in the house. They trampled over the food that was here; Helena and I ate what they'd missed. I'll get some good fresh food and we'll celebrate. I won't be long."

Not a single chair had been left whole. No tables either. He couldn't believe what he was seeing. Tante Liesel was matter of fact. "They were very energetic," she admitted. "That sofa is ruined, they used an axe on it; it's not safe to sit on. See if you can find cushions that are not too ripped and make yourself comfortable on the floor. Pile up the rugs. They missed some quilts in the bedroom, and my linen cupboard too."

As she left, she said, "Look after each other. I'll be back soon."

Max wandered through the apartment. In the kitchen, broken crockery had been swept into tidy piles on the floor, leaving clear areas near the sink and the cupboards. The spoiled food must have been removed. The damage continued to amaze him. He lifted what was now rubble off the rugs in several rooms, helped Helena shake off the dust and bring them into the living room. They created a pile of several layers, and Helena fetched some blankets. One was stained – ink or wine – but the spots had dried.

They arranged the rugs on the floor, and Helena brought pillows and lay down. She covered herself with two blankets. She didn't speak.

He sat down beside her. "Mama rang this morning to say that I'm to fetch you home."

Helena nodded. She reached out, took hold of his hand and closed her eyes. She appeared to fall asleep quickly; her breathing became regular. Asleep, she looked more like her old self.

He disengaged his hand gently and made himself comfortable beside her. He considered reading the book in his bag, but there was too much to think about.

When he heard the front door open, he woke up in alarm, but it was only Tante Liesel. She stood in the doorway smiling at them. She was carrying two bulging shopping bags. He stood up quietly so as not to wake his sister and followed Liesel down the corridor. She busied herself unwrapping the parcels. He said, "Helena isn't talking."

"No, my dear, not yet. She's had a shock and she will need you to look after her during your trip home. Your father's in Berlin; did you know?"

"I thought he was in Stuttgart?"

"Someone drove him here for a meeting. He hid under a blanket, lying in the back of the car. Can't have been very comfortable. The train would have been too risky – he might have been recognised. He wants to see you before you leave."

"Where is he?"

"Not far from here. You're going there tonight. You know they've arrested all the Jewish men they could find? They came looking for

Ernst yesterday. The blessed stupidity, arresting the men and not the women – as if we were of no account. I know, we should be grateful," she said and she kissed him lightly on the cheek.

He thought of the pale young woman at Tante Nina's. "I knew there had been some arrests."

"Everyone's been taken to Dachau."

"When will Uncle Ernst be back from England?"

"Coming back? Max, he's not coming back." Liesel's son David was also in Britain, studying electrical engineering at Manchester University.

It felt like an abandonment.

"But what about you?"

"I'll join him and David there."

Helena's voice said, "We must go too."

They turned.

She stood in the doorway. She wasn't wearing shoes and her feet looked child-like, vulnerable in dirty white socks. The hem of her skirt hung loose.

"Father says–" he started to speak.

"Father is wrong," she said. "We must go."

He didn't argue.

Together they helped Liesel prepare the meal. They struggled with a great starched damask tablecloth, folding it to a smaller size and placing it on the rugs, where it lay like a strange stiff object, a vessel of some kind. They each had a starched damask napkin but no plates. Liesel arranged the food artfully on two wooden trays. She had found disparate spoons and forks, the odd knife. The silver cutlery was gone; Liesel said it had been thrown out of the window. Other things had been stolen outright. They sat on the floor, close to each other, eating voraciously, mostly with their fingers. The food was extravagant, wonderful, better than any food he'd eaten for a long time; out-of-season vegetables: a tomato salad with creamy mayonnaise, his favourite; a cucumber salad with lettuce and a vinegary dressing; also a potato salad – more mayonnaise. Liesel had brought Helena's favourite for her, Frankfurter sausages. There was also finely sliced beef fillet with capers and liver pâté. He ate the meat to please her.

"What the Scandinavians call a smörgåsbord," said Liesel. "With the best of everything."

"How did you find all this?"

"Darling, everything is available at a price."

She opened a bottle of red wine and another of sparkling white Rhine wine and she and Max drank straight from the bottles because there were no glasses. Helena didn't want alcohol and disappeared to the kitchen to drink water from the tap. Max and Liesel talked, an incongruous kind of witty nonsense, laughing uproariously. Helena sat between them, smiling at their jokes.

They finished with Black Forest gateau and cream and lounged on the floor, licking their fingers, replete. Liesel collected the leftovers, and Max put the corks back in the bottles and took them to the larder off the kitchen. They folded the tablecloth away. Helena lay down under the blankets again. Max took his book out of his bag and propped himself up on cushions beside her. Helena reached out and put her hand on his arm. She soon fell asleep. Liesel was kneeling, writing on the wooden tray resting on a tower of encyclopedias. "To-do lists," she told Max.

TWENTY-FIVE

The discreet knock on the door sounded like a signal.

"It's alright," said Liesel, and went to open the door. Max could hear a man talking in a low voice. Liesel returned and said, "Your father has sent for you."

"What about Helena?"

"He's seen Helena."

"Will you tell her I'll be back soon?" It seemed wrong to leave her, but Liesel hurried him out.

The elderly man in the hall looked him up and down and said with a little bow, "Honoured to meet the son of Rechtsanwalt Mannheim."

Max bowed back, embarrassed.

They left the house and walked through the streets, their pace leisurely. The man asked him about his trip from Hamburg and his experiences as a student. He seemed genuinely interested and Max forgot there was anything to worry about and was talking animatedly as they reached the gate to the garden of a big house. They rang the bell. Someone opened the door and they were shown down a corridor and through several rooms and suddenly they were out in the garden again, at the back of the house this time. From there they entered an adjacent garden and another house, another corridor. In a large wood-panelled room, men were lounging around a big table covered in papers, in a haze of cigarette smoke, talking. It looked as if they'd been there a while; among the papers were coffee cups, wine glasses, platters with scraps of food and overflowing ashtrays. Some noticed them as they came in, and then he recognised his father's silhouette and gait as he made his way through the crowded room towards him. The familiar awkwardness brought a sudden lump to Max's throat. His father embraced him and turned to the room with his arm around him. The hubbub died down.

"My son, Max," he said.

Max clicked his heels and made a short bow. There was a general buzz of acknowledgement and his father took him into yet another room. It was like going through a maze.

They were now in what looked like a living room.

His father turned an armchair to face another, and they sat down, their knees almost touching. "Your trip from Hamburg went well?" His father's gaze was keen: he felt like an insect under a microscope.

"Yes, Father."

"Your task is to bring Helena home."

"Yes."

"When you get to Nuremberg, you are to do exactly what your mother tells you. Is that clear?"

"Yes."

Ordering him about, as usual.

His father paused and said, "No one knows what may happen. Always do the honourable thing, so that you may always hold your head up high."

He paused. "You're a good boy. I'm proud of you."

The lump returned. Max blinked.

His father stood up and he rose too. A quick hug and they left the room; the old man was waiting in the corridor. His father left them and they walked back to Liesel's flat in silence. When he came in, Helena was still asleep.

He ate some of the leftovers.

Tante Liesel sat on the floor, leaning against the wall with her stocking-clad legs stretched out, and watched him eat. "Young people have wonderful appetites."

"Would you like some?"

"No, thank you."

"Who were those people with Father?"

"From all over Germany, to discuss what to do since the attacks."

"Ah, the Central Association?"

"Yes."

"What can they do?"

"Nothing much, I fear. Your father was always stubborn. I do hope he'll see sense and leave the country soon."

"He thinks he should look after others. Also he can't imagine living anywhere else."

"Nevertheless, he may have to do so," said Liesel.

The next morning, Helena and Max took the train to Nuremberg. She was still not talking much, though she acknowledged what he said with nods. Tante Liesel had sewn the hem of her skirt, but she looked a little odd because she wore a jacket Liesel had given her which was too big and more suited to an older woman. She'd lost her coat somewhere.

"Look tidy," Liesel had said. "It's important. You do understand, don't you?"

He had food and drink for them in his bag and Liesel had given him money, more money. He'd tried to refuse but she said one never knew, it might come in useful; money seemed to flow freely from adults these days. She called a taxi and accompanied them to the railway station. She gave them each a big hug before they got on the train and he was surprised to see tears in her eyes. She waved and he waved back until she'd disappeared from view.

The journey was peaceful. No one seemed to think there was anything special about them. No one bothered them. He saw a family who could have been Jewish, judging by their air of desperation. The father wandered up and down the corridor searching for places for them to sit. Max and Helena's compartment was full, and Max was ashamed to feel thankful that they could not come in. He did not want to be associated with them; they might attract attention, danger. In the end, there was apparently no place for the family to sit together; he could see the father standing on his own in the corridor.

He'd seen SA on the train, but they didn't concern themselves with anyone else. Max had never given the Hitler salute, but he thought that this time he would do so, if necessary. The most important thing was to pass for an ordinary person, not a Jew. Helena sat like a statue. When he tried to talk, she listened but didn't say a word in response. It was almost as if she were holding her breath. Whenever someone entered the compartment, he could feel her shrink into his shoulder.

At Nuremberg, their mother was waiting on the platform, dressed entirely in black. Max noticed she wasn't wearing her pearls and then remembered why. As the taxi drove into their street, he experienced intense relief at being back where he belonged. Then he saw the broken windows and realised he would have to face the damage wreaked upon his own home. He felt a pang of physical pain in his chest. Helena's expression was frozen.

Oma opened the door, looking smaller than he remembered, and they all hugged. The hall was tidy, nothing missing except a large landscape, a lake at sunrise he'd never paid much attention to. He missed it now. He noticed great cracks in the mirror. His mother put an arm around Helena and took her into the living room. Max followed. The room seemed larger than before, and he realised there was a space above the fireplace where a painting had hung; glass panes were missing in the doors to the lounge and in the grandfather clock. The room was empty except for the big couch and a single armchair, covered in eiderdowns and pillows. It looked messy.

His mother explained, "We threw out what was broken and padded what was torn."

She sat beside Helena, holding her. Oma kissed him and patted his cheek, her hand reassuring, dry and warm; she turned to Helena and kissed her too. He watched her cup Helena's face in her hands and gaze at her. Then she sat down, taking one of Helena's hands between her own.

"It's all right darling, you're home now," she said.

Helena smiled at her.

The older women sat on either side of Helena, entwined with her, and he felt a painful rush of love for them all. He crossed his arms tight. His sister's pale face was grave, her expression remote, her eyes dark. His mother glanced at him, questioning, how was he? He nodded; he was fine. They reminded him of a charcoal sketch he'd seen somewhere of a mother striving to protect her children.

He'd expected to feel better at home, but he didn't. The sight of the devastation upset him; he felt restless, angry. He missed his father. He stood up. "I'll go to my room."

His mother called after him, "We've tidied a little."

The wallpaper in the stairwell had been splashed with something dark; a few banisters were broken. His room looked almost normal, except for the lopsided curtain rail and the tiny white feathers scattered over the carpet. His clothes and clothes hangers were jumbled at the bottom of the cupboard. The room seemed larger. Gradually, he realised what was missing, what had been removed – his chair and the lamp on his desk; a framed map of the world from the wall. Through the cracked windowpane, the view of the garden was the same it had always been, as if nothing had happened. The cherry tree and the chestnut trees were bare, but unchanged.

He toured the house, checking every room. The ravage in his father's study stopped him in his tracks. The leather upholstery of the armchairs gaped where it had been slashed, springs and horsehair coiling out through the gashes. He paused in front of the scarred desk and examined the bookshelves. The books had been put back any old way, upside down or stacked flat. The encyclopaedias, the ancient Bibles and the history books with the old leather bindings weren't in their usual places. Papers were piled on the desk. He went to the door and shut it, wanting to be on his own.

Later, he returned to the living room. "Where's Greta?"

"She left," said his mother. "Some months ago. I've some vegetable soup for you." She brought him the soup in a bowl which looked unfamiliar. "Take care, it's very hot. The bowl is from Frieda's house, she's gone to stay with her cousin."

He noticed that Helena's soup was served to her in her old childhood mug, the one with the cow.

When she'd finished drinking, Helena said, "We must leave Germany soon."

"Yes, my love," said their mother.

"What about Father?" asked Max.

"We'll talk about it later."

"Mama, we're not small children!"

She sighed. "The two of you will leave Germany as soon as it can be arranged. Father, Oma and I shall join you later."

"You can't stay behind," said Helena. Her voice rose and became shrill. "You must come with us. You must!" Their mother held her and Helena cried desperately into her shoulder, deep harsh sobs, her body shaking.

Tears came to Max's eyes. He watched his mother rock Helena, stroking her hair. Oma gave Helena her handkerchief. He saw her exchange a look with his mother over Helena's head. Oma took Helena's mug and went away. A few minutes later she returned and presented the cup to Helena, saying gently, "This is sweet wine, darling, it'll help you feel better." They coaxed her and she took a sip and made a face, and then had some more and then all of it. She gradually stopped crying.

"It's all been too much, hasn't it, *Liebling*," said her mother.

Max had the sense that the women were following a protocol he didn't know.

Helena put her head on Sonia's shoulder and murmured something. She started crying again.

"What is it?" asked his mother. She hadn't understood.

"I've lost Bärchen," gasped Helena. "I don't know where."

That night his father returned from Berlin: afterwards Max was no longer sure of the exact order of subsequent events. The situation was unstable, changing abruptly from one moment to the next.

The door to the master bedroom had been hacked off its hinges. With Max's help, Sonia moved it aside; it now leant awkwardly against the wall. They covered the doorway with a sheet, nailing it roughly into the architrave. Makeshift would do – the house no longer functioned as their home; they would be leaving soon. The vandals had managed to fracture the frame of the big double bed and the eviscerated eiderdown had released the tiny white feathers, settled prettily like snowflakes over every surface. The mattress was serviceable in spite of its ripped cover. Amid billowing clouds of down, Sonia had tugged it clear of the debris and onto the floor, where she slept under a huddle of blankets.

She woke when the light came on in the stairwell. She could hear steps on the stairs. They sounded like Walter's – he was never able to move quietly – but she wasn't sure. She'd locked up the house before going to bed, but someone could have entered through one of the broken windows. Her heart hammering in her chest, she crept towards the hanging sheet. Crouching low, she lifted a corner of the material to see who was there. Unmistakeably, those were Walter's shoes.

As they embraced, he asked, "The children?" Her head rested on his shoulder; she could feel his breath on her cheek, smell his familiar smell. She experienced immense contentment mixed with anxious foreboding.

"They're here; they're all right, your mother too. They're sleeping in the living room. They feel safer together." He looked haggard and a little wild. She kissed him again and pushed him towards the stairs. "Go and see your mother. She's probably awake – she's hardly slept these three nights. I'll get you something to eat." She found a pullover which she tugged over her nightgown and a pair of hiking socks to keep her feet warm.

She'd managed to buy food and some items of cheap crockery the day before. She put the onion soup on to heat, and fried some sausages and potatoes. Walter and Oma arrived as she sliced the bread. She put a small pat of butter on a saucer. He sat down at the table and looked around, studying the devastation.

"Mother said there were only two of them?" he asked.

"Only two, a tall one and a short one. As you can see, they took the destruction to heart." She placed the steaming bowl in front of him.

Oma sat on a stool from the garden shed, her hands crossed in her lap. Outside, the night was still.

Between spoonfuls he said, "The situation is bad everywhere. Thousands rounded up."

Sonia nodded. "Dachau. Walter, they came for you; they were searching for you. You're not safe here, not safe anywhere in Germany. This time you must go, I beg you. We must all leave." A court hearing was coming up in Holland; she knew that the travel documents were ready.

Oma said nothing.

"How can I leave now? People need help more than ever." The flow of supplicants had been unceasing, the phone ringing, despairing women at the door, wanting his advice. "You and Oma can go with the children. I've work to do here."

"I won't leave without you. The children must go. Helena's not quite well; something happened to her during the school evacuation."

He looked up in alarm. "She wouldn't speak when I saw her in Berlin."

"She speaks from time to time."

"Have you found anyone who might help?"

"A nurse who checked Helena. Physically, she's all right. She has trouble sleeping, she wakes up with nightmares. I've given her half a sleeping pill."

"Max?"

"He's fine."

TWENTY-SIX

In the morning the SA came for Walter.

Sonia noticed the van when it stopped outside the house; she saw the SA at the gate. She called Walter and he joined her in the hall as the deafening uproar began, the door shuddering under the blows, accompanied by shouts and curses. Walter opened the door and they were immediately swamped in commotion. One of them shouted his name, and the men grabbed him. He confirmed he was who they wanted. He didn't resist; he was taller, but there were more of them, and they were younger, fitter. She snatched his coat from the rack, bundled it in her arms and ran after them as they marched him down the path. They shoved him into the back of the van. She saw him trip as he climbed in and fall under the punches and kicks, the swearing and screaming continuous. She managed to thrust the coat into the van before the doors were slammed shut. She hoped he'd manage to retain it. He was no longer young and the weather was cold. What would conditions be like in prison, or at Dachau?

Once the van had disappeared down the street, she turned back to the house. Her body felt leaden, drained of strength. Climbing the few steps to the porch was an effort. Oma and the children were in the hall, Max with his arm around Helena, his face set.

Sonia knew very well what she needed to do. Whenever Walter had been away, she'd assisted the women who came for advice; how to support and help a son, a husband or a father under arrest; she'd explained many times what could be done even before the case came to court.

Her first task would be to establish where he was held. She would enquire at the prisons herself. Having located him, the begging would begin: for permission to bring him proper food, warm clothes, clean bedding, to see to his washing, to provide needed medication, writing materials and books, but above all begging for permission to visit the prisoner.

They screamed obscenities and hit him as they pushed and punched him into the van. He stumbled, tripping on the step and falling onto his hands and knees. The blows continued on his back, his buttocks, his legs. Enraged, he kicked back, but his foot missed and he almost fell flat on his face. There were people inside the van, hands tugging at him, trying to help. He heard Sonia's voice, a bundle was thrown in. The van was dark; someone spoke, but he couldn't see them. The doors slammed shut, the van took off with a lurch and he almost fell again. He fumbled his way to a seat – there was some kind of bench along the side. Someone gave him the bundle and he clutched it. Two small oval windows in the doors let in a glaucous light. His hands were unpleasantly wet from the gritty mud on the floor – his trousers would be muddy too; he tried to dry them on his handkerchief, aware that he was probably smearing more mud onto himself. A man beside him said his name and Walter shook hands with him awkwardly, a bizarre formality under the circumstances. Another man was a shadow on the opposite side of the van. As the van rumbled on, they introduced themselves.

"It's outrageous," said Walter.

"Shameful," said the other.

The words were too weak, thought Walter. He tried again. "No respect," he said, the words sounding infantile as soon as he said them. He reminded himself that every man under arrest would have experienced the same brutality. Indignation was a facile emotion, a hindrance. He tried to calm down, to think rationally. "Where are they taking us?" he asked.

"No idea," said the other.

The van came to a halt, voices bawling outside. "Three more bloody Jews!"

Someone dealt the van a powerful blow. It reverberated like a gigantic metal drum and they cringed and covered their ears.

The doors were wrenched open. "Out! You scumbags, out!"

They were hauled into the daylight; half-blind, he almost fell, hampered by his bundle, ducking blows; there was no point in fighting, but he did so anyway and was satisfied to land someone a punch on the jaw. Three came at him together then, hanging onto his arms, holding him, hitting and kicking. One of them stank, unwashed. He struggled, attempted to protect himself. He caught a glimpse of his fellow captives: dishevelled, frightened, pathetic.

They twisted his arm behind his back; he was threatened with a truncheon, but someone shouted, "Not yet!" His legs shook; he could hardly stand. He gave in, allowed himself to be led. As they frogmarched him into the building, he recognised the place: the German Labour Party's headquarters, on the corner of Essenweinstrasse. A few houses away, whisps of smoke wafted from the ruins of the Orthodox synagogue.

His captors delivered him into a low-ceilinged waiting room crowded with people who sat on benches or stood in silence, as immobile as wax figures. The air was warm, rancid. An SA with a truncheon stood by the door; a very young man was posted by the window, armed with what looked like a broomstick. The benches were packed; he was sent with the other two to join a line of men standing against the back wall, under a row of identical posters of Hitler, messianic with imperial eagle and swastika. The line shuffled and contracted to accommodate the newcomers.

Walter recognised many people. They were the well-to-do. You could see their wealth, the good shoes, well-tailored clothes, smart haircuts. The women and older people – some seemed very old – sat on the benches. Here and there an acquaintance acknowledged him with a look or a blink. In a tentative challenge, he began to tidy himself, smoothing back his hair, brushing himself down with his hands. The guard roared at him in dialect, "You fat bastard at the back, stop that! Still, you stand still, asshole! Don't move a finger or I'll bash you to hell and back!"

Another SA entered the room and the Jews rose to their feet, the men in line stiffening to attention. The older SA yelled, "Stand, you scum, you stand when an Aryan enters the room!" He shouted at an elderly woman, "Get your sorry ass moving, you old sow! Faster!" He slapped her and there was a collective gasp.

"Shut up, assholes!" screamed the SA in charge. An older man protested and was punched and thrown to the ground; the SA walked away as soon as he fell. Walter wondered whether they had been ordered to moderate their violence, to avoid serious harm? He watched in silent sympathy as the man slowly pulled himself up and resumed his seat; Walter could see his hands shaking.

Why had they been brought here? For what purpose? Walter watched as people were summoned and taken away one by one. They did not return; this was an organised job. Did Benno know, did he condone whatever they were up to? First the women and then the men were taken in small groups to the toilet, brought back unharmed; when his turn came, he managed to drink some water from a tap and relieve his thirst. Some sort of processing was taking place, but what for? Time went by and standing became uncomfortable. A slow throb developed in his thigh, where a piece of shrapnel had been lodged since the war. His feet ached. He was thirsty again, and hungry. He thought of Sonia who had watched as they dragged him away. He thought of his children and his mother. Where might he end up? Stop that, he told himself. The future will be what it will be; no point in worrying. Taking care not to move his lips, he began reciting Faust's monologue to himself, over and over, a practice he'd found helpful during tense periods in the trenches. The SA guards were replaced. Still they stood. One of the women was weeping, sniffing at intervals. Now and then new people were brought in, as bewildered as he'd been. The harassment was mild in comparison with yesterday's attacks. He thought of the many men dragged away in the previous day's raids, incarcerated in Dachau – thousands, apparently – and forced himself to change his train of thought.

Finally, he was called. "Move!" yelled the SA guard, prodding him with his baton as they left the room. Walter could hear indistinct shouting. The SA opened a door and they descended a rough staircase. The haranguing gained volume as they entered a vast cellar where a number of SA men screamed abuse at people standing in rows, men and women, each apart from the others. The air here was chilly and damp, smelling of mould. He caught a reek of shit as he passed the prisoners – someone had soiled himself. They parked him on his own in a far corner, facing a dilapidated brick wall.

"Eyes ahead! No looking round!" punctuated by a punch to the kidneys. "Arms up!"

He was terribly thirsty; his arms soon ached. He could hear the young men shouting, "Stand on one leg, assholes! Don't move! You over there, shitface, no moving, d'you hear!" He heard the thump of blows, cries, more blows, whimpers. He experimented, peered sideways, even turned round once quickly. They were beating a man with a baton. Later, it occurred to them to make people beat each other: much hilarity from the audience; hoarse groans from the victims.

A young SA caught him peeking and punched him. "Face the wall, you!" Walter recognised him: the pub-owner's son, barely Max's age. He saw the recognition reflected in the young face.

"Heinrich!" said Walter.

The youth's mouth tightened and he kicked Walter, though not very hard. "Stinking Jew!" A truncheon hit him painfully on the upper arm. "Knee bends, get going!"

They were kept at it for what seemed like a long time; he panted, increasingly breathless, hot and sweating, his knees on fire from the unusual exercise, his thighs aching. He was too old, too fat... He hoped he wouldn't die. A guard struck the back of his knees with his truncheon, shouting, "Lower, fatso! Squat lower, lower!"

His legs collapsed; he fell and they were onto him immediately, snarling, shouting, "Up, asshole, up! Fancy a little rest, hey? Not likely, not with us!" They hauled him up and he stood on unsteady legs.

He noticed that they punched people's arms and torsos, kicked their legs. They're avoiding the head, he thought. The yelling was unremitting. In the midst of the hullabaloo his name was called and he was hustled towards a guard with a clipboard, a SA sergeant who marched him down a corridor into a separate room and stationed him in front of a young man in an ill-fitting three-piece suit with the swastika armband, sitting at a small table. A bureaucrat, thought Walter. The youth asked his name, found it on a list and ticked it with a flourish before picking up some sheets of printed paper, which he began to read aloud. "Irrevocable power of attorney..."

Power of attorney? Alarmed, Walter forced himself to concentrate.

"Who're you?" he interrupted.

"Adolf Wirtz, Notary," announced the young man, smoothing his moustache. His demeanour reminded Walter of one of his less reliable subalterns.

He had to know. "Who's the agent?"

"Karl Holz."

Streicher's second in command. "Why?"

A blow to the kidneys. "No talking!" yelled the sergeant.

Wirtz handed him a pen, "Sign here!" He put the pen down.

"What's it for?"

"A property..." Wirtz searched through the document for the address "...on Pierckheimerstrasse."

"Not on your life!" said Walter.

He was kneed in the belly; doubled over, he heard the sergeant summon men and was dragged out of the room into a tiled place which echoed. A washroom.

The beating was systematic; there was nothing much he could do. He tried to protect himself, lost his balance, fell onto the concrete floor. They wore boots, and he screamed when they kicked him in the back and legs. The beating continued until an order was shouted. He lay curled up, his body shaking, his breathing ragged. He hoped they'd given up and lay without moving; the pause lengthened. His attackers were still there, waiting. For what? Were they checking whether he was dead? Driven by thirst, he crawled to the nearest basin. On his knees he slurped water from the tap, while they watched. The respite was brief; they pulled him to his feet, and returned him to the basement, where he endured more taunting and torment, shivering with shock. How long since his arrest, he wondered. It must be getting on for a day.

The guards yelled, "Stand still, perfectly still, filthy swine!" They walked round the room, hitting and punching those who wavered.

He stood at attention, considering the process of company aryanisation and the loss of property. They wanted the house.

A new batch of guards arrived, wanting their fun, making the prisoners shout antisemitic slogans. He was beaten for failing to display the required enthusiasm. He focussed his attention on a crack in the wall, to absent himself from what was done to him, to not feel the pain. It got through to him anyway. The guards turned their sights on a woman who was obese, mountainous. They'd have to be careful not to damage her if they wanted her to sign, he thought, she wasn't strong; one of their tormentors had the sadistic idea of removing her clothes, one by one, forcing everyone to watch as the guards jeered and she shook and wept. He was glad to be summoned and taken to the room with the table and the power of attorney, a different guy this time. He refused to sign and suffered another beating in the bathroom, curling himself up, less noisy this time except for the grunting, both his and theirs. He was aware of his age, his lack of fitness – how long could he endure? There was a problem with one of his eyes. He couldn't remember the blow which had caused it. When he touched his face, it was sticky; there was blood on his fingers. The attackers were many, young and working in relays. He'd die of a heart attack sooner or later; what would happen to Sonia and the children? He couldn't bring himself to sign the house away.

Nevertheless, after several more rounds, he came to care less about the house and more about surviving, and in the end, half blind and spitting blood, he knew that no property was worth dying for.

When they dragged him in front of the table, Wirtz was back, freshly shaven and smug. Walter stood on shaking legs in front of him. He leant on the table. The guard was onto him, snarling, "Stand up! Hands off the table!"

He managed to stand despite the pain in his back. Wirtz got the file and opened it. He was given a fountain pen which he dropped, his fingers too bruised and swollen to hold it. The guard made to hit him, but Wirtz said, "Bring that chair."

Sitting was a great relief. He leaned forward and covered his face with his hands. Pain throbbed behind his left eye. He could feel a swelling and crusted blood on his forehead and cheek.

"Don't hit him, he's ready," said Wirtz. "It'll only take longer."

"Water," said Walter. He was given a glassful which he gulped down.

Wirtz stood beside Walter, took his right hand and placed it on the table. He inserted the pen between Walter's fingers and held it there for him. "Sign!" he said.

Walter scrawled his name.

Then he vomited over Wirtz's shoes and was beaten again.

Three days after Walter's arrest, Sonia answered the phone. The voice was male and plebeian, with a marked local accent.

"Frau Mannheim, please."

She recognised the inflection of officialdom – news about Walter, at last. Fearing the worst, she knelt on the floor, clutching the receiver. She'd not been allowed to see him or to bring anything for him to the prison.

"Frau Mannheim speaking," she said as calmly as she was able. She must not cry.

"Hold the line," commanded the voice. A faint buzzing sound followed.

She waited.

"Sonia, it's me," said Walter. "We've got three minutes. Sonia? How are you, how is Mother, the children?"

He sounded his usual self.

"Sonia?" he said.

She took a deep breath. "Yes, yes, Walter my love... We're all well, very well. And you?"

"I'm all right, occasionally uncomfortable, but that will pass. No need to worry, please tell Mother, definitely no need to worry. They moved me to the police prison this morning. Sonia, please listen carefully." He spoke now with a slow, deliberate cadence, "Make the necessary arrangements for emigration for us all. I'd suggest Robert and Hilde. Can they take the children? Maybe someone else we know? I've been given to understand that there's no alternative. Please repeat what I've said, so I can be sure there's no misunderstanding. Oh, and I'm allowed books; please bring me Goethe, *The Apprenticeship* and that English grammar."

The following morning, she dressed in the dark suit which she usually wore to funerals. She ate breakfast with Oma, Helena and Max. Oma said, "Take something to eat, you never know," and gave her an apple and a cheese sandwich wrapped in a tea-towel. She put them in Walter's briefcase, which also contained the books he'd requested and a large manila envelope with the family's documents and passports. Max's papers weren't included; they would have to be signed by the authorities in Hamburg, his official place of residence. Sonia went to the hall, put on her black hat and waited for the taxi.

She gave the driver the address of the police prison. "After that, the police headquarters on Jakobsplatz." By getting Walter transferred to the police prison, Benno Martin had extracted him from the SA's grip, protected him from their brutality, possibly from death. The family now needed his help to get out of Germany. She'd attempted to see him several times already, in vain.

On arrival at the police headquarters reception, she asked for Chief Commissioner Oberführer Dr Martin. "Please inform him that Dr Walter Mannheim's wife is here."

A messenger boy was sent. He returned promptly and she was told, "The Police Commissioner sends his apologies."

"I'll wait," she said. "Please let him know."

She was courteously shown to the waiting room where she sat, a supplicant among many. The crowd was disparate and fluctuating, people from all walks of life, some recognisably foreign. She watched the functionaries passing in the corridor beyond the open doors. No sign of Benno Martin.

Mid-morning, a woman with ginger hair in an unfashionable style came into the waiting room and called out her name. "I'm Oberführer Dr Martin's secretary," she said. "He will not be able to see you." Her expression was neutral, neither condemning nor sympathising.

He won't be able to see me tomorrow either, thought Sonia. "Please be so kind as to give him these documents as soon as possible," she said, handing over the precious envelope into the secretary's freckled hands. They were thin hands, work-worn, the nails trim and unvarnished. Sonia looked into her eyes. "I shall wait," she said. The woman's face remained impassive.

He would know what needed to be done. At midday she ate the cheese sandwich and the apple. She sat on the bench for the rest of the day; the woman did not reappear and no one spoke to her. She saw a senior officer go by whom she'd once known, who'd been a guest at her house years ago – was it seven? Or ten? She saw him look away in haste, avoiding her gaze. She watched the erratic movement of dust motes in the shafts of light from the tall windows. Determination held her emotions in check – the anger, fear and doubt. Towards the end of the afternoon, as the crowd ebbed and darkness fell, she sat in dim electric light surrounded by silence and shadows. When the clerks went home, one of them came over and politely asked her to leave. In a daze, she caught a taxi home.

They were hoping for news. She said there was none yet, and they sat together in the ruined kitchen while she drank a cup of tea and ate a boiled egg and a bowl of soup. The odd feeling of detachment persisted. Half an hour later the doorbell rang. A young man in dark civilian clothes shoved the familiar brown envelope into her hands and ran away – or so it seemed to her. She watched him disappear into the night, pedalling hard on his bicycle. She closed the door and went to her boudoir. She closed the door. Taking a deep breath, she opened the envelope.

The documents had been stamped and signed. They could go. There was a handwritten note that said: "I can do this only once." No signature.

She sat down and closed her eyes. "Thank God!"

TWENTY-SEVEN

Sonia woke from an unsatisfactory sleep, her body stiff from sitting, her mouth dry. She heard the tail-end of an announcement on the train's public address system. They were arriving in Paris, rumbling at a slow pace through a canyon of tall grey buildings. Around her, passengers were pulling their luggage from the racks; a queue formed in the corridor.

The train stopped and people surged towards the exit. The corner of someone's suitcase dug into her thigh. Still drowsy, she shuffled forward. She climbed down the three steep steps to the platform, clinging to the handle. In the morning's cold sharp air, she felt more awake. Loudspeaker announcements echoed through the high space, the French clipped, dense. She hurried through the crowds to the toilets, queued, paid for a clean towel and washed her face and hands. The mask staring at her in the mirror was shocking – she looked haggard. She tidied herself automatically, lipstick and comb; left a tip in the saucer for the shrew guarding the place. She drank a cup of tea at the *buffet de la gare* and found a taxi, summoning her schoolgirl French to direct the driver. He was proud to answer in German, explaining he was from the Alsace, near the border. She shrank from his cheeriness. He noticed her reluctance and stopped talking, let her be. It was a long drive.

She climbed the stairs to the seventh floor, resting at intervals, pulling herself up on the handrail. A note was pinned on the door, the name Loewenthal in elegant cursive, contrasting with the rickety door. She couldn't find a bell, so she knocked.

Hilde opened the door almost immediately. "Sonia!" They embraced, holding each other tight. Hilde drew her in, closing the door. "Wonderful to see you! How is everyone, we've been terribly worried! Such awful news... Robert has gone for his morning walk. He'll be back soon."

Hilde had written that the place was small, a maid's apartment, only two rooms, a tiny kitchen – that must be the alcove – no bathroom, and a shared toilet down the hall. Paris was packed with refugees; the rent was astronomical. Sonia looked around – two long narrow windows overlooked rooftops, an unmistakeably Parisian view, which she would have enjoyed under ordinary circumstances. The *Blue Horse* hung above the sofa; she recognised the ormulu clock on a shelf.

"Come and sit down, have some breakfast, a cup of tea?"

"Tea would be nice. I ate something on the train." A lie, but she couldn't face food. "They're holding Walter at the police prison; Benno Martin had him transferred, out of the SA's clutches. They allowed him to phone, and at last he agreed that the children might leave. The paperwork is done."

At the French consulate, the person she'd seen had pleaded with her, "Madame, you should *all* depart *now*! Right now! Please, do not delay!"

Hilde said, "Max can stay with us. We'll find something for Helena, don't worry. I so wish you didn't have to go back to Nuremberg.

Robert will be here in less than an hour. How much time do you have?"

"Just today," said Sonia, "I'll take the night train home."

The tea arrived in a fine Rosenthal cup. "I brought this one good cup to cheer me up, plus a few other bits and pieces. The rest is in storage – what we were able to take with us." Hilde sat down. "We're a bit crowded when everyone's home, but the evenings are cosy. During the day Robert is mostly out, looking for work, and Emil's at university. On the weekends we go for long walks; I'll show you the other room presently, where Robert and I sleep; Emil sleeps here." The mattress was propped up against the wall, concealed behind the sofa. Laid flat, it would take up most of the available space. "We'll get another mattress for Max."

Sonia wanted to say, "Not for long, I hope," but in truth she had no idea how long Max would have to stay. They'd applied to emigrate at all the embassies. The tea was hot and strong. She felt better.

"And for Helena? Who were you thinking of?"

"Here's my list," said Sonia. She had five names, five addresses, old friends or relatives.

Hilde pointed to the first name. "His brother has just arrived from Austria and is living with them; you couldn't fit a pin in there, it's that tight." She read through the list, pointed to another name, shaking her head. "They're in a bad way. There's a lot of tension. He may be violent at times – not right for Helena. The other three should be possible. You'll have to hurry if you want to see them all in a day; it takes a long time to cross the city. What about Julia and Rolf? You've forgotten them."

"I didn't think they were suitable," said Sonia, taking back the list.

"Sonia, I know what's stopping you, and you must get over it. Despite everything, Julia is one of the nicest women I know."

"Too nice by far," snapped Sonia as she tucked the paper away in her big leather handbag, avoiding Hilde's eyes.

"She's the one woman I'd trust to look after a daughter, if I had one," said Hilde. "Unfailingly kind."

She crossed the room to the table, wrote down the address and pushed the note into Sonia's hand. "You may have no choice."

Later that afternoon, Sonia sat in a café in front of another cup of tea. She hunted through her bag for aspirin against an imminent headache.

The first family she'd visited was the one she favoured, but the mother, a childhood friend, had just discovered she was pregnant: at her age, in times like these, when they already had three children! How would they find a doctor for an abortion, and the cost... They were eager for news of everyone back home. She saw their desperation and said nothing about Helena, though they probably guessed why she'd come.

The next people were distant relatives, an elderly couple, childless. They'd left Nuremberg at the first sign of trouble, even before the Nazis' ascent. Their apartment was spacious and beautiful. They wanted to know how everyone was after this terrible time, and they agreed to take Helena, "Of course", they said after exchanging a brief glance. The wife thought they might put a stretcher bed in the storeroom.

They climbed three floors to the storeroom, under the roof. An attic; no bathroom. They weren't able to put her in the guest room, they said, because they had frequent visitors. Sonia would understand it was essential for them to keep in touch with everyone – where would they put them otherwise? Young people were adaptable, weren't they? Sonia thanked them. She said she feared her daughter might inconvenience them and took her leave.

At the last address, a stranger opened the door. No, he didn't know about the family she was looking for; he'd been living there for a week. She stood on the landing outside the closed door, at a loss. It was four o'clock in the afternoon, and the train to Germany departed at eight that evening.

She would have to ask Julia.

Julia was kind and beautiful, in a willowy sort of way. They'd once been close friends, Julia and Rolf, Walter and Sonia.

When Rolf discovered the liaison, he'd phoned Sonia. "Julia has promised to put an end to it. It's best we don't meet."

Sonia had confronted Walter who refused to discuss anything. Sonia moved out of their bedroom. He'd not protested, but after a few weeks she felt stupid and lonely. Walter had opened his arms and held her close, as if he were not the one responsible for her misery. She didn't know if he'd stopped seeing Julia, and Rolf did not ring again. She knew people gossiped. She sometimes saw Julia at large parties, a wedding or a bar mitzvah, but they did not speak.

Julia opened the door and took her to Rolf, who embraced her and kissed her.

After they'd exchanged the news about Walter and everyone's health and whereabouts, he said, "So Hilde suggested that Helena might come here?"

"Can you take her?"

Rolf turned to Julia. "Can we?"

Julia said, "Of course." Their two daughters were younger than Helena; the three of them could share a room.

"Her visa will be ready tomorrow and we shall come on the first available train. I'm very grateful," said Sonia. Julia showed her the room and the spare bed which was on casters and rolled under one of the other beds. Sonia accepted yet another cup of tea. She hadn't eaten much during the day.

Rolf asked, "But what about you and Walter?" She knew what he was thinking; time was running out.

"I can't leave Walter," she said. "Or Oma, for that matter. She'd never leave without him."

Rolf accompanied her to the railway station and saw her onto the train.

Walter came home two days later. Sonia opened the door and gasped. He saw himself in the cracked hall mirror, thinner, his face bruised, his suit rumpled and torn. He told her he'd lost the sight in his left eye. "From the arrest, when they beat me up," he said. "Benno got me out of their clutches. One of the doctors jailed with me examined me as best he could. He said the loss was probably permanent; there's nothing to be done. It throbs a little. The other eye is good, the rest of me healthy enough. I've a cracked rib. But I'm here, I'm alive."

He told her about the house. He almost wept.

She leaned over and kissed him. "Darling, you had no choice."

"They'll throw us out soon," he said. "I'm amazed they haven't done so already. The power of attorney gives that scoundrel Holz the right to conclude a contract of sale on our behalf. There was something fishy going on; I saw him in a huddle with people who had no business there; I suspect they're acolytes wanting their share of the action. I don't know how they'll make the registration in the land register stick – probably by corrupting the magistrate. We're entitled to ten percent of the price, but by the time they've finished with us, nothing will remain – additional charges, taxes, you know their routine. They'll take everything."

Sonia said, "People are leaving in droves. Apartments are available; we can live somewhere else."

He wasn't listening. "Of course, Streicher is behind Holz, getting him to do the dirty work. They're diddling the Nazi Party, not that I care; but it may be possible to prove that Streicher is behind this, and the Nazis won't stand for it. I told Benno I had the bill of sale as proof. I'm sure he'll take it further. If he doesn't, he runs the risk of coming under suspicion himself."

"Why should you care, Walter? They're one as bad as the other."

He turned his battered face towards her. "This could spell the end for Streicher; he's responsible for what Holz is doing. In principle, the Nazi Party is entitled to the revenue from the sale of our properties, but from what I saw they're being flogged off to people who can't possibly afford to pay what they're worth."

"Still obsessed with Streicher!"

"He *must* be stopped. Benno will report what Streicher's up to; it'll end his career. Himmler won't stand for it."

Sonia said, "What we need now is a doctor for you. The pogrom has uprooted everyone, we're all nomads, it's difficult to find the people one needs." Fritz and Frieda had left for America. "I'll find someone before Helena and I leave for Paris."

When Max was about to leave for Hamburg, his mother kissed him and said, "I'll be with you in two days' time, my son."

She didn't usually speak that way. Everything was strange. She'd written a list of all the documents he was to gather – permissions and certificates from six agencies, including the police. She warned him it would not be easy, and gave him money. People were always giving him money. "Take good care, Max," she said in a tone of warning. "I'll be in Hamburg as soon as Helena is settled in Paris." When the paperwork was done, he would fly to Paris, his first experience in an aeroplane. Something to look forward to.

Max travelled back to Hamburg and Tante Nina, who welcomed him as usual. Wilhelm was at home with nothing to do, restless and dissatisfied. His father was looking for work for him 'in the meantime'. Karl had left – for Argentina, the only address a *poste restante* in Buenos Aires.

The following morning, Max took the tram to the income tax office, for a certificate proving he owed the state no money. The waiting room was crowded, the officials contemptuous and slow. Over and over, as people were summoned from the waiting lines, Max witnessed the latest humiliation the regime had foisted upon them: "The Jew Wilhelm Israel Rosenblum", "The Jew Kurt Israel Orenstein." All Jewish men now bore the name Israel in addition to the one their parents had given them. He was called "The Jew Maximilian Israel Mannheim". A Nazi gimmick, taking an honourable Hebrew name and turning it into a slight. The name Sara had been inflicted on the women.

Many of those waiting were elderly. Had the younger ones been arrested, or had they already left the country? He wondered again about his friends at the language school. He had no way of finding out what had happened to them.

The next day, he managed to complete the police procedure by mid-afternoon, steadfastly ignoring the rudeness. A woman had what seemed like a break-down, weeping deep sobs, hiding her face. People watched out of the corner of their eyes without moving their heads. Another woman led her away.

When he'd finished with the police, he returned to Tante Nina's and went straight to bed, only getting up for dinner. He needed to visit four more offices, to obtain four more permissions. He knew that harassment was the only purpose of these bureaucratic barriers; his father said that from a legal standpoint, a valid passport with a visa should suffice.

The next day, his willpower flagged and he got up late. Tante Nina was concerned and asked if he was well. He said he was, but in the end he didn't leave the house. His mother arrived the next morning. When she found how little he'd achieved, she was icy with rage, terrifying. "Get those papers this instant; we leave the house in fifteen minutes! We've not a moment to lose!"

He tagged along in her wake. They stood in queues with other Jews. They did not talk. Confronted with official disdain she remained polite and unswerving. She did not falter. She repeated requests until they were met. He watched her and thought how single-minded and strong she was.

After two long, wearisome days, the task was done. They bought his ticket to Paris that day. She never stopped; he couldn't have done it without her. She had made him take his suitcase that morning, and they caught a taxi to the airport. She was kinder now, patted his hand and talked about Uncle Robert and Tante Hilde in Paris. He couldn't visualise the future. He kept thinking, "I'm leaving Germany forever." He had no wish to remember any of it. He tried not to think about his parents staying behind. His mother said they would come as soon as they were able to. At least Helena was in Paris. He knew he was living through momentous upheaval yet everything he did seemed trivial.

At passport control, she kissed him goodbye and gave him a little push. He picked up his suitcase and walked to the queue. When he got through, he turned round and waved. She gave a discreet wave of her gloved hand. The customs officer stood behind a low table. Max could see his mother smiling at him.

He put his suitcase on the table. The man looked at Max's passport with the big red J stamped across the page, and ordered him to open the suitcase. The officer then turned it over and shook it, tipping Max's clothes and belongings onto the table, where they lay in a heap. Max gaped.

Staring at Max as if daring him to protest, the customs officer pushed everything from the table onto the floor. Max watched in disbelief as the tip of a polished boot nudged at his clothes and books on the floor and withdrew. He looked up at the officer who continued to watch him, saw the satisfaction in the red-lipped mouth under the moustache.

"Pick up your shit, Jew-boy, and fast!"

The retort left Max's mouth before he could think, his voice sharp, "You threw it down – clear it up yourself!"

The man slapped him.

Later, much later, his mother would tell him that this was the worst moment of her life.

Max crouched down by the pile of his belongings and stuffed them into his suitcase as fast as he could. When he was allowed to go, he glanced at his mother – she was holding her gloved hand to her cheek as if she'd been hit herself. He would retain no memory of the flight to Paris.

TWENTY-EIGHT

In London, a middle-aged man called Reg sat in his shirtsleeves at a table in his restaurant, under a framed print of the Crystal Palace. The greyish light from the street did not reach this far back and the bracket lamps were lit. It was eleven o'clock in the morning. The big room was pleasant and warm; the tables covered in white tablecloths were set for lunch and he was enjoying a break, finishing a cup of tea after the morning parley with his wife Agnes and the cook.

He'd married Agnes straight from school. Then came the Great War and he'd lost a foot in Flanders. He reckoned it saved his life; he was honourably discharged, out of trouble. The prosthesis didn't get in the way of anything he wanted to do. His father let him manage the restaurant and he was able to expand the business, buying up the butchers' premises next door, enlarging the dining room. He now had twenty tables and a staff of twelve, if you included Agnes.

Agnes's sister had given birth two days ago and Agnes had gone to help. She'd be away for a week. The skivvy had handed in her notice because she'd found herself a job in a factory – war-work which paid better. That left a vacancy for someone to wash the big pots and pans and the floors at night. Last week a regular customer, Mr. Magid, had asked whether he'd consider employing a foreigner, a refugee from Germany. He said that he'd employed two of them at his workshop for the past month and found them good workers, punctual and reliable. Mr. Magid knew of other refugees who were also looking for work. Reg had decided to try one out, under the circumstances. He'd heard that Mr. Magid was a Jew; he surmised these refugees were Jews too.

The door opened and a woman came in. From the style of her clothes, she was well-to-do and probably foreign. Unsure why she was there, he stood up to greet her. "Good morning, ma'am."

"Good morning." A pleasant voice, the accent confirming she was foreign.

"Can I help you?"

She looked down at a piece of paper she was holding. "Mr. Burrows?"

"Yes." He thought she looked tired.

"The man at Bloomsbury House said I must come here at eleven o'clock. You want someone to work in the kitchen?"

"Yes."

"I would like this job, please." She pronounced it *tchop*.

"You're a refugee?"

She nodded, "My name is Sonia Mannheim. I am a refugee from Germany." She seemed to understand his difficulty. She indicated her clothes and added with a smile, "Not for work."

He hesitated. People like her didn't work in kitchens, they didn't work at all, as far as he knew. Her hands were long and fine, the fingernails oval and regular. The skivvy had to clean the toilets, the one for customers and the one at the back for the staff.

"The work is hard."

"Yes," she said. "Floors? Cooking pots?" She nodded and smiled as if to encourage him.

There was no mistake, but he hesitated.

"Mr. Burrows, my husband and I, we have no work, no money, no English." She smiled again briefly. "Kitchen work I know. Please. Please. I beg you."

Embarrassed by her pleading, he suggested a trial period of one week and after he'd explained with some difficulty what the word trial meant, she agreed. She seemed confident. With a feeling of unease, he agreed she would start on Tuesday. The wages were apparently what she'd been told to expect. She was satisfied. Still, she seemed more like a customer than an employee.

It felt wrong at first, but it turned out all right. When she arrived the next day, she was wearing English clothes, the kind a cleaner would wear. He realised she did her hair differently from English women and moved differently. She was elegant, so she still looked out of place. But she was punctual and reliable, just as Mr. Magid had said. He only needed to show her things once and she did them thoroughly. She seemed tired at the end of the first day, but she turned up promptly the next. She was pleasant and the other staff seemed not to mind her being German. She didn't stop work when his back was turned or waste time chattering and she took her break when it was due. She didn't complain; on the contrary, she thanked him for employing her and when the week was up, he agreed to keep her on.

Sonia rummaged through the various piles of women's clothing in the Red Cross charity shop; it was her first day off and she needed workaday clothes. Her sensible clothes from Germany were too good for kitchen work. She'd tried on one of Liesel's work skirts, but was swamped in it. Besides, she suspected Liesel needed it herself. During her first week, she'd worn clothes borrowed from another refugee, a friend of Liesel's, someone nearer her own size.

They had managed to escape Nuremberg when she'd almost given up hope. Walter maintained his equanimity no matter the circumstances, but she was made of weaker stuff. A mysterious list had surfaced; twenty-five people from Nuremberg were to be sponsored by a rich man called Willi Neumeyer who had emigrated years earlier and was now a British subject. Walter, Sonia and Oma were among those rescued by this unexpected act of generosity.

As Sonia searched through the piles of clothing, her thoughts returned to Helena and Max. What could she have done differently? How had she allowed a situation to arise in which both children were far from her, exposed to grave danger, while she and Walter were safe? She could not forgive herself or Walter for that matter. She was consumed by the fear that something awful, something irremediable would happen to one of them or to both.

She tried to keep everybody in mind – Helena and Max in France, Fanny and everyone else in Germany, including dear Frau Koslovski. Not doing so felt like a betrayal. It seemed the only contribution she could make to their welfare. The tension exhausted her, but she felt compelled to keep up the practice, however irrational it might be. She found a dark-coloured skirt and after a search in a different pile, two blouses which might fit her. She took them to the cashier.

At times, the longing for her children and her sister, and her terror that they would suffer harm were unbearably painful, particularly when she had nothing to distract her – as she waited for the bus, or sat on the Tube. She might see a girl Helena's age, or someone resembling Fanny, the same hair colour, or a similar gait. She would feel an icy grip in her chest, as if her heart were about to stop. She felt better since starting work; it distracted her some of the time.

During the first week, the difference between English and German working-class people had penetrated the shell of anguish enclosing her. Mr. Burrows was polite, not only to her but to all his staff. In fact, by German standards, everyone was polite to everyone else. People were asked to do things, rarely told. No one shouted orders. It wasn't only a question of speech, it was deeper, an attitude. Reg was unmistakably the boss and the staff knew their place, yet there was something else going on which didn't happen in Germany. She would have to think about it.

She had dreaded the communal mealtimes, but found that no one burped or ate with their mouth open. They waited without impatience for their turn to be served and asked politely for the salt. They used napkins and did not blow their noses in them. Occasionally someone might put their elbows on the table. She had not expected to be impressed.

The cutlery was strange, different; the shape of the soup spoons was round, not elongated like Continental ones. They ate their dessert with both fork and spoon. They rarely brewed coffee, and when they did, it was too weak. You could see the bottom of the cup, taste the water. She watched how they cooked and what they served. British cooking had a bad reputation. She could understand why – overboiled vegetables, little use of cream, no wine in the sauces. The occasional bay leaf, but few other herbs; the vegetable water was sometimes discarded, a waste. Fish in parsley sauce, mint with lamb – these were new to her and tasted good, but hardly rated as haute cuisine. The meat was the usual, minced beef and lamb, or chops and sausages, roasts. From time to time, when it was her turn – fairness seemed the rule – she was given a share of leftovers to take home. That was a boon.

After living with hostility for so many years, she expected discrimination and was vigilant. She didn't understand everything they said over lunch or during the tea breaks; it was safest to keep quiet. There was no sign of antagonism or contempt; she almost felt as if something were missing. She realised they were indifferent to her identity. She discussed it with the others at home; these English people didn't understand German antisemitism. They were going to war against the Germans. They weren't concerned with the Jews, which was strange – her Jewishness had always been the most salient aspect of her identity and had caused her much suffering. Now she lived among people for whom it seemed a matter of indifference. No one enquired about her life before she'd arrived in England. They didn't talk much about themselves either; they were reserved and possibly not interested.

A few months later, someone left and there was a shifting of positions in the kitchen: she was offered the job of peeling the vegetables, work less grinding which paid a little better. The promotion cheered her up. Her English was improving though she had to be careful because some terms used by the kitchen staff were deemed vulgar, unsuitable for a lady, despite Agnes's fierce monitoring.

There were two armchairs and a small couch in the living room Walter and Sonia shared with Liesel and Ernst. Walter sat in one of the armchairs, writing letters on a board lying across his lap. It was the door of a bedside table Ernst had removed from its hinges. They all needed to write, and the other three crowded round the small dining table. Everything here was tight: the beds and doors narrow, the handles set low. The kitchen and bathroom were minuscule. Sonia and Walter occupied one bedroom, Liesel and Ernst the other. An additional room had space for a narrow cupboard and a single bed. David slept there when he was home from university. There was no room at all for Oma, who had gone to live with other Nuremberg refugees, distant relatives. Over the generations, they were all related.

Sonia wrote to the children, to relatives and to friends like Elise and Philippe, who were also in England but whom they could not visit because they lived too far away. Walter's letters were sent to people he knew as well as to some he hardly knew at all, asking for a moment's consideration, pleading for good will, for help – how in God's name to get the children out of jeopardy and into England. The problem was not money, though he had none; the obstacle was British immigration law which dictated the conditions of entry. Positions were needed for Max and for Helena, though at sixteen she was officially still a child; he wished his English were better, so that he might research legal options himself, find regulations which might allow his children into the country.

In the evenings, after they'd eaten, the women tidied up and they listened to the evening news and other programmes in English on the radio, Ernst translating as best he could. When the news was encouraging, they'd discuss the implications. The four of them talked and talked – the limited information rehashed, the conversation circling, going nowhere. He reflected on his state of mind and on Sonia's; despite an appearance of calm, they were both in utter despair. He never saw Sonia cry. In the evenings he watched her knit, which she did with a degree of fierceness, her mouth a thin line. She had unravelled a brown pullover from the charity shop and washed the wool in the bath with Liesel's assistance. They had hung it to dry in long strands above the bath. She was knitting a pullover for Max.

Searching for distraction, Walter had examined Ernst's books. He and Ernst had selected many of the same classics – Goethe, Schiller and Heine – so the choice was limited. Sonia had bought a murder mystery at the charity shop, *The Murder of Roger Ackroyd,* by Agatha Christie. Lacking other options, Walter decided to try reading it. He'd heard from other refugees that Christie's books were easy to read, a good way to improve one's knowledge of the language. He read this one slowly, the dictionary by his side, learning about the British way of life as well as improving his English. He thought he might come to enjoy English books, in time.

When the letters were done, and after he'd read as much English as he could cope with, Walter would open a ruled notebook and record the events of the day in German, describing his efforts to rescue the children and his attempts to find work. Writing it all down helped him sleep at night.

He was a supplicant during the day, one of the many refugees who trudged from agency to agency, crowding the bleak waiting rooms, defeating British attempts to shape them into an orderly queue, desperate to speak to someone in authority who might help. When he was interviewed, he would extract the bundle of tired documents from his leather attaché case and plead on behalf of his children in deplorable English; it happened once to his relief that the man across the desk spoke German and he was able to manifest for a few moments the effective personality he'd once been, fluent and forceful. He knew he appeared well-to-do in his expensive overcoat. At times that was helpful; at others, not. He looked up the English word for his real status: he was a "pauper" and he pondered his loss of wealth and standing, which eroded his ability to persuade people to listen to him, to save his children.

He walked for miles, despite Sonia's entreaties to spare his shoes. His wanderings took him to the Heath; in open spaces, among trees and ponds, he felt less estranged. Once a week he took the Tube to Bloomsbury House on Russell Square, where he encountered a crowd of displaced people like himself and scrutinised the German-language noticeboards for opportunities, hoping to find a new conduit into Britain for the children. He also looked for work. He'd felt confident Sonia would find employment easily and it had not taken her long. For himself, he was less sure. He was too clumsy to work in a restaurant like Ernst. Now and then he ran into someone he knew; sometimes there was good news in the midst of the chaos, friends who'd managed to emigrate and reach the relative safety of Britain, or who'd found work, or who told of families reunited despite the difficulties. When he told them about the children, he avoided their gaze. "A way will be found," he'd say. One must never give up hope. He could not afford to doubt.

On his walk one day, he passed a toy shop and stopped to look at the array in the window. He was often surprised by the differences between Germany and England in even the smallest things. Here on display was a strange looking miniature locomotive mounted on equally miniature railway tracks. It had apparently been constructed out of bright red metal pieces pierced with multiple holes, screwed together with tiny nuts and bolts. A flat red box containing the neatly organised elements for construction was open beside the train. Red boxes in decreasing sizes were stacked one upon another in a tempting pyramid. At the top the smallest box contained just enough pieces to put together a simple car, including four black rubber wheels with red hubs. The arrangement brought his friend Gerhard to mind; he would have approved. Gerhard's business had exported toys from Nuremberg to the entire world. The business had been sold in the usual manner, at a loss, and Gerhard had departed for the US with his family. Sonia might know how to reach them. He'd known Gerhard since childhood, been in the same bar mitzvah class. He'd not thought of him before, but Gerhard might know someone making toys here or in America or somewhere else who would be willing to employ Max, Max who was so young, so completely untrained in any practical skill. Someone in refugee circles was bound to know how to reach him. In the meantime he would visit the labour exchange – something might come up. He met refugees from all over Germany. He avoided those whose stories emphasised injustice and loss; they were all in the same boat, and he carefully protected his positive outlook from possible erosion; he needed to cling to hope against all odds.

The competition for employment was overwhelming, foreigners flooding the country from all over Europe. People were straining bone and sinew to escape – the image of a despairing multitude often sprang to mind, people massed along the French coast, among them his own children, crying out for succour. He'd shake his head and try to think of something else.

Rescuing both children would take a miracle. Miracles did happen; just consider how he and Sonia had left Germany. The opportunity had arisen all of a sudden, forcing them to act fast. Sonia had dealt with the unavoidable bureaucracy and they'd escaped. But since arriving in England, he felt untethered as if he were a ghost drifting unnoticed through a crowd. No one here knew or cared who he was or where he'd come from or what he'd done with his life. Back home, he'd belonged, however uncomfortably. Within the community he'd been trusted and respected. Beyond the community, people may have refused to greet him in the street, but they knew perfectly well who he was and what he stood for; they knew he was a decorated veteran of the Great War, and a respected Jewish lawyer from an established Nuremberg law firm.

These days, Sonia and he would wake before daybreak, before Liesel and Ernst. Sonia would make them a cup of tea. They all missed coffee; he hoped the craving would fade soon. Sonia rarely talked to him. He surmised that she held him responsible for their dilemma; after all he was the one who had prevented her from acting sooner. Left to her own devices, she would have saved the children, from him and from the Nazis. It had occurred to him that she might hate him now. In bed, she kept away, not that it mattered – he had no desire.

During the day he was mostly on his own. Liesel and Ernst were at work – she as a maid and he in a pub, originally as a waiter, by now the owner's right-hand man and trusted adviser. Sonia left home early for her job at the restaurant, returning in the late afternoon. When he had nowhere to go, he'd sit at the table by the living room window and study the previous day's English newspaper with the help of the dictionary. If the language penetrated his thick German skull at all, it did not seem willing to remain there. Languages had never been his forte, not like Max.

Max's letters were irregular, but Helena wrote once a week. He was the first to read them, several times over. When she got home, Sonia would take the letter to the bedroom and read it in private before giving it to Liesel and Ernst. After they'd read it, the pages would be returned to the envelope and the envelope added to the bundle of previous missives, two packets, each bound by a red elastic band and kept in a red metal Oxo box on the bedroom dresser, between Elise's ivory beggar and the framed studio photograph of the family taken the day before Helena's departure – Max handsome and reluctant in a suit, Helena wearing her best dress. They looked intelligent, polished, lively. In the photo, he and Sonia stood between their children, unsmiling, as if in mourning, Sonia gazing straight at the camera, her hands clasped in front of her, her beautiful face grave, serene despite the impending separation. That had been six months ago – a different country, a different era.

On a recent Sunday morning he'd slept longer than usual. He found her seated on one of the straight-backed chairs at the table in the living room, in her dressing gown, a cup of tea by her side, with the letters. She stopped what she was doing when he came in and went to make his tea. While she was away, he touched her cup: still full, quite cold.

She'd been reading Helena's letters, one by one, from the beginning. Max's letters were in the box, facing away. She must have already read those.

She brought him the tea and gathered up the letters, their envelopes and the box, and left the room. He heard the door to their bedroom click shut. The cold tea was still on the table. He went to the window. The dreary street was empty under the prevailing Sunday torpor. He realised he was wringing his hands and made himself stop; he must not become a dotard. Sitting by the table he sipped the tea. He couldn't remember when he'd last cried; he must have been in short pants.

A quarter of an hour later, she emerged to prepare the usual spartan breakfast; toast, a few fried potatoes and an egg each. More tea. Then they went out. They endeavoured to stay away on Sundays to give Liesel and Ernst more room. Sometimes they visited other refugees, old friends from Germany, bringing their own frugal lunch so as not to impose.

Sonia would wedge a thermos of hot tea upright between the sandwiches, apples and a metal mug in the old brown rucksack. They always began by visiting Oma who had aged considerably since leaving Germany. When the weather was good enough, they'd walk to a nearby park with her and sit on a bench. When it rained, they took refuge in one of the local libraries or a church.

The British Jews had done their best, helping them settle in, making sure they could afford to eat and were warm and dry. The contact was somewhat uncomfortable; only twenty years had passed since they'd fought on opposing sides of the great slaughter. Meeting Englishmen of his generation, Walter wondered where and when they'd fought. He suspected they wondered, too.

That afternoon, when Max returned from the Préfecture to the little apartment, he told Robert and Hilde, that they wouldn't renew his *permis*, and fled to the other room, a private space until Emil came home. Emil would want to study there after dinner. He studied every spare moment; there were no obstacles in his way, whereas Max who would have loved to study like him couldn't even obtain permission to stay in France, let alone study at the Sorbonne. The best he could do was read books in French, buying the literary classics in second-hand shops if they were cheap enough, selling them back for a pittance when he was done.

Without a *permis*, he'd be obliged to return to Germany. Uncle Robert said there were about 3,000 Jews still trapped in Nuremberg. Three thousand people, including Tante Fanny and Uncle Otto.

His mother had given him plane tickets to London and Lisbon, but they were useless without a job offer, and no opportunities had materialised in Britain or in Portugal, despite his parents' efforts. It seemed that the net had been cast as wide as it would go.

Were he to return to Germany, he'd end up in a concentration camp, most probably to die; every refugee knew that. Remaining in Paris was imperative, a matter of life and death. Hundreds like him queued from early morning at the Paris Préfecture. He'd prevailed over the interminable process twice before. But today the clerk had refused to renew the *permis* and pushed the papers back at him, peering past Max to the next person, who'd stepped forward eagerly, disconnecting Max from the line, ejecting him. He was unwanted, *unerwünscht* again. He'd have to return to Nuremberg. He thought he'd go mad. A matter of life and death, the words churned in his mind. He'd heard of someone who'd killed himself rather than go back. That would be better than letting the Germans do it. He wondered how one could kill oneself without causing trouble.

There was a knock at the door and Uncle Robert came in. "We'll go to the Préfecture tomorrow morning. I'll come with you."

"But the man said..."

"He's a state employee, overworked and underpaid. He's probably realised there's money to be made. We'll pay him."

Uncle Robert patted Max's shoulder. "Come and have dinner."

After the meal, Max excused himself. He felt too agitated to sit and read. "I'll go for a walk."

His aunt looked up from her book. He could see she was about to protest, but Uncle Robert said, "See you in the morning, Max. Try not to worry too much."

Tante Hilde caught his hand. "Take care, Max darling."

He breathed in the crisp night air. At this late hour in mid-week, the *quartier* kept to itself: drapes pulled across windows, no lights showing. Here and there, a bar was open. The city was quiet, the moon shining on empty cobbled streets. He hardly looked where he was going, striding ahead, teeth clenched, fists tight in his pockets. He walked for a long time.

When he reached the Seine embankment, he stood on the quay staring at the flickering lights reflected in the black water, which flowed and flowed endlessly like time itself, until someone approached him and suggested something to him in a soft voice, something disgusting. He fled. Reaching an empty square, he sat on a bench and wept. He felt utterly alone. Then he resumed walking.

Towards the morning he found himself in Montmartre: he thought of the day about to begin, of the trial which lay ahead and he felt nauseous. He went up to the Sacré Coeur and climbed the steps. At this early hour he had the place to himself. Reaching the top, he turned to look at the city spread out below; the sun was rising, touching the roofs and the crests of trees with gold, against a clear blue sky. For the first time, he remembered how his father had told him never to give up hope, and sat on the steps a while longer, looking out at the beauty of a new day.

He realised he ought to get back home and walked down to the houses below. An old man sweeping the pavement in front of a shop told him the way to the Metro. He caught a warm smell of baking bread and followed it to the bakery. They weren't actually open yet, said the pretty girl behind the counter, but she smiled and sold him a *pain au chocolat* anyway, fresh from the oven. Another two hours before the Préfecture opened. On the Metro, he dozed all the way back. Uncle Robert was waiting for him at the flat.

Uncle Robert inserted bank notes among Max's papers. French notes, a huge amount of money. When the time came, he handed the bundle over to the clerk, who slipped the notes out of sight in a practiced movement without looking up. He stamped the documents and handed them back. "Next!"

As they left the Préfecture, Max cleared his throat. "Thank you."

He searched for other words, but Uncle Robert shook his head and gave him a pat on the back; they travelled home in silence. A few months later, Uncle Robert paid again.

Then suddenly everything was resolved.

Through a friend of his parents in America, a job was found for Max in England, in Nottingham, at a toy factory owned by a Quaker. The Quakers did not fail to help; Max wondered how it was that they understood a situation the rest of the world refused to acknowledge. He was apparently to be an assistant of some kind. The unbelievable invitation arrived and Max obtained a visa within a week. He took the Metro across Paris to see Helena and say goodbye.

She had no trouble with her *permis de séjour*. She said she was well, but he felt uneasy about her. She looked heavier and a bit messy, pimples on her face, her hair untidy, too long. Her clothes didn't fit properly. She'd be sixteen in two weeks – Tante Hilde had reminded him, as had his mother in her recent letter – and he gave her one of his old Karl May books as a birthday present. She seemed pleased. At least it was in German – her French was still poor. He wished he could do more for her, look after her, though he wasn't sure what needed to be done. He had no spare money to give her and it wasn't as if they could swap places. Nevertheless, he felt like a traitor, leaving her behind while he headed for safety. There was nothing he could do. Germany was breathing down France's neck; what might happen if the Germans reached Paris? He didn't speak of his fears and hugged her tight when the time came to leave. She looked at him brightly and stroked his cheek the way their mother used to, as if she knew what he was thinking.

A way had to be found for Helena to enter Britain, he thought. He clung to the hope that one day they'd be together or at least in the same country. He'd be far from his parents; he'd checked the distance between Nottingham and London in an atlas in a bookshop. Travel was likely to be expensive. He'd be on his own. He flew out of Paris the next day, into the unknown.

TWENTY-NINE

1939 was drawing to a close. During her first months in Paris, the thought of her parents marooned in Nuremberg had weighed a great deal upon Helena. She'd been reluctant to go to bed, afraid of falling asleep, because of the nightmares. Tante Julia's sleeping pills made her head feel heavy in the morning. Then her parents managed to get out. There was no question of their travelling via Paris, though they were desperate to be together for even a short time. Her mother wrote that it was simply impossible. The German authorities allowed them to fly to London and to London only. That was almost eight months ago.

During the first six months, she'd seen Max no more than three or four times because the distance was too great to walk and the cost of travel prohibitive. Then he left suddenly, when a job offer came through. Max went to the British Consulate where his papers were stamped. He came to say goodbye; they found it difficult to talk. He said something about it being her turn now, and then he was gone. Of course he had to go if he could. She hadn't cried.

She tried to talk herself out of feeling abandoned. She wasn't sure she'd be able to do what was required to immigrate to England. Her mother wrote about her father's efforts to find a way, and she told herself that she had to trust that he would succeed soon, though she did feel that time was running out.

Eight months was too long for her, too long for everyone in the crowded household. Tante Julia and her husband were kind, but they could not disguise the fact that her presence was inconvenient. The apartment was cramped and there was no maid. Tante Julia did the washing and ironing and was often tired, sometimes irritable. Helena helped where she could. She noticed that Tante Julia wasn't as organised as her own mother; she might forget that a certain shop was shut on Wednesdays and they'd run out of an essential item, like milk or bread. Helena thought she once heard her crying. She knew her mother had given money to Tante Julia to cover her keep, but she worried it might not be enough; Tante Julia never said a word.

She had to get herself to England, to her parents and Max, though Paris was safer than Germany. She thought that war was imminent. She'd seen men in uniform in the streets and on the Metro, and one morning, on her way to buy bread, she saw military trucks rumbling by in convoy, transporting large bulky objects covered in tarpaulins. If a war was to occur, she feared that the Germans would win, because they were ruthless. She knew that. She'd seen German soldiers marching in Nuremberg; in comparison, French soldiers seemed unkempt and lacking determination.

Life was easier here, more pleasant than in Nuremberg; people were polite and kind in a way Germans were not. No Nazi flags, no signs warning people not to trust Jews. Nothing about or against the Jews anywhere. She could be like everyone else, as long as she didn't speak. Her French was bad, though her accent was the real problem. People didn't like *les Boches*. They didn't like her in Germany because she was Jewish and in France because she was *Boche*. Tante

Julia and her husband spoke German at home, but the girls attended the local primary school and seemed to have picked up French easily.

She and her mother wrote every week, but the letters didn't arrive with any regularity. The postal service was unreliable because the men had been called up. Women were helping wherever possible. She'd even seen a woman driving a tram.

Her mother wrote letters of encouragement. She said many of their Nuremberg friends were in England by now. Oma, Tante Liesel and Uncle Ernst were concerned about her and sent their love. She wrote how she and her father thought about Helena all the time and would not rest until she was with them. Her father worked tirelessly, canvassing one organisation after another to arrange sponsorship for her. He had not succeeded yet; they hoped it would not be long now. Her mother was working in a restaurant, uncomplicated work, she wrote. Helena had a vivid dream one night: she was with Mama and Father in the garden in Nuremberg, the wisteria was blooming over the terrace and they were happy. There were no Nazis. She woke feeling peaceful.

Helena applied to a variety of organisations which might help her emigrate. She visited the British Embassy repeatedly. Overwhelmed with refugees, they had no suggestions beyond telling her that she needed a sponsor in Britain, someone who would put up the money for her or declare that they wanted to employ her; she was only sixteen years old, with no experience of any kind. Her parents had not found anything. Not yet. Today she was returning to the headquarters of the Red Cross. Tante Julia had given her money for the tram and the Metro and a chunk of baguette with slices of sausage wrapped in paper, and the usual apple. She carried her documents and her passport in a satchel which she wore with the strap diagonally across her chest. In one of her bad dreams, someone stole it, leaving her stranded without papers. Carrying them around was risky, but there was no other way.

She left the apartment at dawn. The queues were huge at any time, but arriving early increased one's chance of success. Some people tried spending the night there to be first in the morning, but the police would not allow it and sent them away.

Tante Julia and Uncle Rolf were pursuing an exit visa themselves. They were trying to organise papers for Argentina. That was refugee parlance: "to organise". The term covered all the comings and goings, the waiting and advocating, the stamps to be bought, and the officials to be seen, lobbied and persuaded.

She knew her mother would disapprove of her appearance. She'd put on weight, her bra was too small, and she had trouble closing her skirt. She'd fought with the buttons, the hooks and the eyes, but at the end they'd given way and now the safety pin from her sewing kit kept her skirt up. She tugged her pullover down to cover the untidiness. She had polished her shoes. They let the water in when it rained, which was unsurprising considering how worn they were; she walked as much as she could to save on fares. She didn't like to return to the flat any sooner than she had to. One time, she passed the nice hotel where she'd stayed with her parents. She'd stood in front of it remembering how much fun it had been until the doorman asked her to move on.

She wondered where Lore was. She was supposed to have gone to Palestine. Helena had no address to write to. And how were Tante Fanny and Uncle Otto? And Inge? It was as if a giant door had swung shut on Germany, stifling every sound within. Her own life nowadays consisted of wandering the streets and talking briefly to officials who were busy, sometimes impatient, mostly uninterested. In the spring she'd passed by a garden where lilac was flowering and the smell had reminded her of the garden and her hiding place in the lilac bushes. She walked past that garden whenever she could, until the blossom was gone.

She met other refugees. When she ran into them for the second or third time, they would engage in a desultory conversation. "No luck yet?" they asked. They weren't all Germans; there were people from Poland and Russia and other unfamiliar places, mostly Jews, crowds of them. Some were desperate and that was why they pushed and shoved the way they did whenever an official appeared. She'd seen adults in tears more than once. A man who looked like one of her relatives, tall and well-dressed, had stood with his face buried in his hands, his shoulders shaking. She tried not to cry herself.

She had a list of all the organisations which might help her get into England and she had worked her way down it once already. She was trying for the second time. Her mother sent her further suggestions. She was registered with the local Jewish welfare organisations. The woman she'd seen at the Alliance Israélite was busy and anxious. She spoke French or Yiddish and, in Helena's opinion, was too agitated to accomplish much. She didn't listen and sent Helena to the wrong place. Helena wasted a week following her advice. It was as if that lady's mission was to move people on and out of her office, rather than help them properly. Maybe she just didn't know what to do. They were so many, how could they all be helped? On rainy days, her queuing finished, she would sit in a cheap café not far from Tante Julia's apartment. People came and went, and no one noticed her. She knew she looked untidy; she combed her hair whenever she remembered during the day. It had grown long and was hard to control. Then she heard the waitress make a comment about her – something derogatory, she didn't understand exactly. She had not liked the tone and stopped going there.

Occasionally she went to a café where French newspapers were available to customers. She'd buy a cup of tea and try to make sense of the headlines, but she couldn't judge how serious things were; they so often seemed alarming, whereas nothing appeared to change very much in what Helena thought of as the real world. She listened to the conversations between Tante Julia and Uncle Rolf after the evening news on the radio. They censured what they said in front of their daughters, so Helena's yearning to understand the implications of what she read and heard often went unsatisfied. German newspapers were sold in a bookshop nearby and at the railway station and she could read the visible half of the front page without buying the paper; the triumphant headlines frightened her. At least there was no *Stürmer* here.

At the Red Cross, she waited in the queue with everyone else and had time to wonder how it was that the building itself felt different from a German one. It was French in some essential way and she tried to prevent her thoughts from drifting into anxiety by working out what that was. Things were less orderly here, messier, more fallible. Opulence and neglect, both. Before arriving in the packed waiting room, she'd stood among the throng on the marble staircase. She'd noticed that the statue of the half-naked young woman on a pedestal in the entrance hall was coated with a layer of grey dust on its head and shoulders. Once, as she walked into a grand old building, a cleaner was scrubbing the floor in the foyer, singing an aria from an opera she knew; an unexpected delight that made her homesick for her childhood and for Nuremberg, which no longer was home. She could understand why one would want to sing in this hall, the ceiling was high and his voice rang out and filled the space in a lovely way. It occurred to her that in Germany, some official would have appeared and forbidden the singing. She imagined how he would have put a stop to it – with indignation and sharpness, as being some kind of *lèse majesté*. The French did not seem to mind. They didn't mind that people talked loudly, that they ate whole picnics as they waited. She'd been offered food more than once and even some wine. Those people had been Italians, she thought. The French officials were less stiff, less frightening than Germans. They could be brusque and rude, because they were harassed, but they were also capable of smiling or even of cracking a joke. That had happened once and she'd been so unprepared for levity that it had passed her by at first; it took her several minutes to work out what the man had meant and then she'd laughed all by herself as she walked down the stairs.

She was clutching her number and waiting her turn. She was among the first fifty or so. She'd been firm with a young man who had wanted to push past. Firmness was the best way – not getting excited and shouting.

Finally, her turn came. She went in and closed the door behind her. The man behind the desk was grey and wrinkled, with the shadow of a beard. There wasn't very much of him, except for his sharp little eyes. He took her papers in a brisk movement, read them quickly and looked up at her again and asked, "So, and you are wanting?"

She said she wanted to go to England. "My parents are there." For a moment she had a lump in her throat.

He looked back at the page, marked something with his finger and looked up at her again. He reminded her of a clever bird. "How old are you?"

"I shall be seventeen in February."

"So you are *mineure*, a minor."

She didn't understand.

"You are a child still, therefore you belong with your parents."

Of course she belonged with her parents. What did he mean?

He took out a printed form and started to fill it out. He was copying from her papers and she didn't know what he was doing. She was aware of her heart thumping in her chest. She must know, she must find out. She asked him as carefully as she could. It was not the right formula, but how else to say it? She pointed to the form and said, "*S'il vous plait, qu'est-ce-que c'est?*"

He stopped writing and said a little impatiently, "*Ça, Mademoiselle, c'est une demande pour un laissez-passer pour l'Angleterre.*"

It is a request for permission to pass to England.

She stared at him and he nodded and said it again.

From the powerful, mighty, blessed Red Cross.

The British Embassy would bow to this, she knew as much; they would let her through, and she would be with her mother and her father and Max again. She held her hands tight together in her lap and stared down at her fingers; she dug her nails into her palms, trying to hold on and not make a sound. Why was she feeling pain now? Why was this so hard?

She whimpered a little, despite her efforts and sobbed as quietly as she could until he had finished. She had no handkerchief and had to sniff. When he gave her the paper, she wanted to kiss him or kiss his hand, but she knew that it was wrong too, so she did her best German curtsy, as deep as she could go and said with as much gratitude as she could express in only two words, "*Merci, Monsieur.*" He waved her away grumpily, shaking his head.

Back in the crowded corridor, she wiped her nose quickly on the sleeve of her coat. The form was in her bag, which she held in a tight grip. He had told her she still needed a stamp of approval from another person at the Red Cross, "a formality". It would entail waiting and queuing; she would not allow herself to believe in the miracle until that task was completed. Then she had to clear the hurdle of the British Embassy. She was stern with herself, but beneath her discipline a song sang in her like a small stream running under the winter ice, a promise of spring – she was going to be free at last, she was going home.

THIRTY

She was on her way within two days. The situation had worsened recently and when she went to the British Embassy to collect her *laissez-passer* with its precious stamp, the people queuing seemed more desperate and hopeless than ever. She wanted to weep for them. She and Tante Julia went to the post office and sent an expensive telegram to her parents announcing her arrival in London. She would take a train to Dunkerque, a boat across the Channel and another train to London. A train to London! She imagined her parents standing on the station platform, waiting for her, her mother standing straight and elegant. Max wouldn't be there, he was far away and couldn't come home often, probably not until Christmas. She realised she was thinking of home without knowing where that was. Being with her parents anywhere would be home.

The night before her departure she was unable to settle, unable to sleep for a long time. She couldn't wait for morning to come, to get on the train, leave Paris and be on her way to England. The train left at nine in the morning from the Gare du Nord.

That morning, she wore her satchel across her chest as usual. She had worried about her documents. Where would they be safest and which ones would she need for the trip? Tante Julia said to keep her passport and her tickets for the train and the boat in the satchel, together with the money she'd given her. It seemed like a lot of money. Tante Julia said it belonged to Helena. She had French money in one purse, English money in another. The English had a complicated counting system, not in tens like other countries. Uncle Rolf had written it out for her on a piece of paper, which she kept with the money. The other documents – the German papers saying she was allowed to leave the Third Reich and the copy of the request for a *laissez-passer* from the Red Cross – they could be tucked away in the suitcase, which wasn't very big. When Helena was leaving Nuremberg, her mother had packed it and had told Helena not to pack any more than she could carry. She remembered her mother's words, for when they got to the Gare du Nord, there were no porters; Tante Julia said that most of them had been called up to the army. "Just as well," she said. "We couldn't afford the tip!" and they laughed. Helena knew that Tante Julia was worried about the future and the prospect of war. They were both pleased she was going. Helena tried to hide her exaltation, but it was difficult.

Tante Julia translated what the railway employee told them at the information desk, which wasn't really necessary, but Helena didn't mind. It increased her confidence: when she got to Dunkerque, after going through customs, she'd be able to walk from the train straight onto the boat. The train journey would be long, about six hours. There usually was a restaurant car, and refreshments sold on the way, but the lady was not sure that would be the case today because of the situation. She meant the war. It didn't matter, as Helena and Tante Julia had packed food. She had the usual baguette with cheese and charcuterie, wrapped in paper, two apples and a bottle of water. They went to the platform where a sign confirmed that the train to Dunkerque was departing at 9 a.m. No one else was there. Tante

Julia looked for someone to confirm this was the right train and at the last moment someone in a uniform and a cap came by, looked fleetingly at Helena's ticket and nodded, saying, "*Oui, c'est ça,*" and walked away. That was all the corroboration they got. The ticket was for a seat with a number and a letter. Helena identified the carriage and climbed aboard; she found her seat and put her suitcase in the string luggage carrier above it. The carriage had a central aisle and all the seats had white doilies on the head rests, which Helena thought of as French style. The smell was the familiar railway one, a machine smell mixed with old cigarette smoke and dust. The seat was high and well-sprung.

There were still five minutes to go, so she went onto the platform again to say goodbye and to thank Tante Julia properly, giving her a big kiss. She'd been unpredictable at times, but she was a dear. Helena climbed back up onto the train, found her seat and wound the window down. Tante Julia was waiting for the train to leave. Helena wanted the train to leave too, for her life in Paris to be over, so that the next part could start, the part where she was reunited with her parents. Finally, the train drew out of the station with the usual screeching and bumping and after a last wave to Tante Julia, she was able to sit down and watch the morning light reveal the Paris suburbs as they slipped by. It was mid-November and most of the trees were bare. She thought again about the Frenchness of the city. In Germany, there were many houses with beams and steep red-tiled roofs. In Paris, the houses were tall and grey, more like boxes, she decided. The further they moved from the centre, the smaller the houses. She could see suburban back gardens which weren't pretty, used mainly to grow vegetables or store miscellaneous objects.

She'd taken Max's book for the journey. A boy's book, about Indians and cowboys; she didn't like it much and returned it to the satchel. She looked at her watch and then out of the window. She felt bored.

She must have fallen asleep. When she woke, it was eleven o'clock and they were in the countryside. It was flat and empty, fields upon fields, brown earth without furrows. Clouds hung low, with a faint white glow where the sun was hiding. From time to time the train's whistle shrieked and they crossed a road in a flash. If one leant out of the window and looked forward and backward, the train seemed the only thing moving in the landscape, as if all of life had been swept up into it, a dark low line moving steadily ahead, its plume of white smoke extending backwards. On the other side of the carriage, the view was identical. She walked slowly up and down the central aisle. There really was no one else in the entire carriage. There was nothing to read except for a piece of newspaper she discovered on one of the seats. She tried reading it, but it was not interesting, all about a book someone had written. The notice on the black-and-white enamel plaque under the windows warned not to lean out while the train was in motion. She counted the seats and straightened the doilies, going right to the back of the train to check that they all lined up. At either end of the carriage was a door onto a little ante-room with the exit doors on either side and a door with a glass panel which led outside, onto a narrow metal bridge to the next wagon, with a thin railing on either side. She wouldn't be able to walk on that bridge as the train thundered along – too frightening. It would be best to wait for the train to stop. There was also a toilet. She opened the door and closed it quickly: smelly and dirty, no different from the toilets on German trains.

From time to time, they flashed through tiny railway stations without stopping, with just the whistle's shriek of acknowledgement. She washed her hands gingerly in the toilet and went back to her seat. It was time for lunch and she ate her cheese sandwich and the one with the charcuterie. She wished a controller would come and check her ticket. She thought it was time, but no one came. She drank from her water bottle and ate an apple. Surely she wasn't the only person on the train? She thought about that. Would they have told the controller not to bother going on the train, if there was only one passenger? Maybe there were passengers elsewhere, all of them together with the controller and she had been put on her own in this wagon, because of her *Boche* name when the seat was reserved for her. She shook herself. They only knew her name and it didn't mean anything to the French, it was simply a name. She had noticed that during her months in France. Maybe the controller simply didn't like those frail bridges either. Maybe he would come when they stopped somewhere.

About ten minutes later, the train slowed to a halt. There was nothing on her side of the train, no buildings, no station, just the endless fields, and nothing on the other side either. The train stood still and the silence grew deeper. She went into the ante-room at the end of the carriage and tried the door onto the little bridge. She couldn't open it. She went to the other end and tried there, to no avail. For a moment she felt imprisoned and breathless, and then she realised that she could open the exit doors if she wanted to. She hesitated. What if the train started again and she couldn't close it? What was the point of opening it if she wasn't going to get out? She didn't want to get out because the train might leave without her. The thought of being left behind overwhelmed her with panic and she returned to her seat, to sit down. When she felt better, she wound down the window and peered out. There was no movement anywhere. Had the train run out of coal? Was something about to happen?

The train started up again with a jolt and she lost her balance and sat down with a bump, much relieved. It didn't regain its original speed. After about half an hour it stopped at a little country station. There were some bare flowerbeds encircled by round stones painted white, and a white picket fence. She looked for the name of the place. There was a board with a name, but someone had painted over it, in white again, and it was impossible to read. She had no idea where she was. She stuck her head out, just in time to see a little dark figure climb into the train's locomotive. No one else was around. She didn't know why they'd stopped and there was no one to ask. The train started again. She was worried. Why was no one else on this train?

Maybe this was not the right train after all, a frightening thought. She was alone and no one knew where she was. She realised for the first time that this had not happened before; there had always been other people with her when she'd travelled. Even little Simon had been a reassuring presence. Max had brought her home to Nuremberg and her mother had taken her to Paris. Max was tall and people thought that he was older than his age. He was practically an adult anyway. She wished he was with her.

The train stopped again in the countryside, this time for twenty minutes. Helena checked the time on her watch. She wondered where she would end up. She hoped she hadn't taken a train to Germany by mistake. She looked out of the window and saw no one. She said a prayer out loud to God, "Please help me, I'm afraid and I'm lost." Then she cried a little. The whimpering sounded lonely, there was no other sound.

The train started off again and stopped at another anonymous empty station. And so it carried on, in fits and starts. She couldn't think why it was that way. Once she saw a rabbit in a field or maybe a hare, and another time two black crows. The light was diminishing. She seemed to have been under way for a long, long time. She had eaten all her food. She stood in the central aisle and looked at the rows of doilies: they seemed to stretch ahead forever. She was afraid of falling asleep in case she missed the station at Dunkerque, or in case something happened she should know about, act upon. She took her suitcase down from the luggage rack and held it on the seat beside her. She put her satchel on again, so as to be ready.

Darkness was falling by the time the train pulled in to what seemed to be the final station. Looking out, she saw the name there on the board, black on white: Dunkerque! At last! She could stop worrying; her journey was going according to plan. She felt greatly relieved and stood up. Her body was stiff after all the hours in the train. She grasped her suitcase, touched the briefcase. She walked a few steps and turned round to check that she hadn't left anything behind. She felt very strange, as if she herself were not quite present, as she made her way between the rows of seats to the little ante-room and tried to open the exit door. A man came from the other side and opened it for her. He was wearing a uniform and a cap. He looked friendly enough and she asked him, "*Dunkerque?*"

"*Oui, oui, Mademoiselle, tout le monde descend ici.*"

She got off the train with her suitcase and satchel and walked towards the exit, where she found a sign indicating the way to "Douane/Customs". She knew what those words meant, but everything else was unknown. The station was empty. She really had been the only passenger. She reassured herself that at least she was in the right place.

The customs officers examined her papers and requested she open her suitcase. She watched them rummage through her clothes, then shut it as if defeated. They stared at her and asked questions. They spoke with a different accent from people in Paris and she had some trouble understanding what they said. By and large, the French spoke only French, she knew that. She asked them to please speak slowly. They muttered to each other and stared at her again, scowled at her papers and finally produced a form for her to fill in. They gave her a pencil. She had to write down who she was, where she was going, how much money she had and the currency.

When they looked at the form, they muttered again and asked her to follow them. They opened the door into a room which was an office with a desk and some chairs. On a table was a typewriter covered with a cloth, she could tell by its shape. They asked that she wait. She sat down with her suitcase by her feet and her satchel on her lap. They both left the room. Then she heard the key turn in the lock.

Her heart seemed to stop. She thought of her mother and father and how no one knew where she was. She sat very still, scarcely breathing.

After what seemed like a very long time, someone unlocked the door and came in, a tall man in a shabby civilian suit. He sat down opposite her with his legs stretched out and looked at her. She gazed back at him and thought that he had a nice face. He looked as if he needed a rest. He introduced himself, but she did not take in what he said. She looked at what he held in his hand – the form she had filled in earlier. He read out her name in a quiet voice – Helena Sara Mannheim – and raised his eyebrows at her questioningly, so she said "*Oui,*" and then he asked if he might please see her money. She opened her satchel, took out the two purses, opened them and showed him. He took them from her and counted the money quickly.

Then he said, "*C'est tout?*"

"*Oui*" again. That was all there was. He put back his head and laughed and laughed. It was so unexpected, it occurred to her that she hadn't heard anyone laugh this freely for a long time. She laughed a little with him – she couldn't help it; but she didn't know why. When he had recovered a little, she asked, "*Pourquoi?*"

He looked puzzled and showed her the form. He pointed to the number she had written down for the French money. He said to her in slow French, making sure she could follow him, "You wrote the wrong amount. This is exactly one hundred times more than what you've got. They thought you must be *une espionne* – a spy." He laughed again.

He accompanied her through the customs area and passport control and led her to a narrow gangway on to a boat rocking gently beside the quay. He shook her hand and then he left. She felt she'd lost a friend. On the boat, a thin woman emerged from below and said something welcoming in English. Helena stepped with caution onto the rickety gangway which moved a little with the boat, and from there onto the boat. She offered her ticket and the woman seemed satisfied, indicating that Helena should follow her. The stairs down into the boat were almost vertical and Helena hesitated – how to manage her suitcase and hold on at the same time? The woman reached up for the suitcase. Helena hesitated, not wanting to let it go, but then reminded herself that after all they were both on the same boat, so she let her take it and followed her along a narrow corridor. She was shown into a tiny cabin with a round window and two bunks, one above the other. The woman put the suitcase down. Helena picked it up immediately; she felt better holding onto it. The woman was talking in English again, about departure and arrival times.

Helena said in French that she would like something to eat. The woman showed her the way to a small room with benches along the wall, a couple of tables fixed to the floor and a hatch into a kitchen where a man was cooking. Through the portholes one could see lights on the deserted quay. She sat down, keeping her suitcase close to her body so that she could feel it was there, with the satchel on her other side. The cook told her in French that he would serve food as soon as the boat was on its way. Some ten minutes later, she felt the vibration of the engines through the floor and the walls. Then the quay moved away from the portholes. At last, leaving France! A bowl of tomato soup, some toast and butter and a cup of milky tea were put down in front of her. Two men came in and sat at the other table, speaking English. She could hear their conversation but couldn't understand what they said. They too were served the soup and toast with tea. She thought it a strange combination but ate it anyway.

Being among people again felt good, as did the knowledge that her journey was running its course. No one talked to her, and she didn't mind. She was very tired. The butter turned out to be margarine, which surprised her. The soup was followed by a greasy fried egg, bacon and potatoes. Drowsiness crept upon her in the warmth. She returned to her cabin, making sure to take the suitcase and satchel. The boat developed a smooth upward swing followed by a downward lurch, over and over, which made her queasy. She wished her stomach would adapt to it. The queasiness turned to nausea. Might lying down lessen the impact of the swing and lurch? She put the suitcase between the pillow and the wall, the satchel under the pillow, satisfied that no one could remove anything without her noticing. The nausea was threatening to overwhelm her. The thin woman knocked on the door and looked in. She went away, returning a moment later with a white enamel basin for Helena. Then she went away. Helena lay on the bunk clutching it, feeling worse and worse. Finally, she was sick. The colour alarmed her until she realised it was the tomato soup. She washed out her mouth with water from the tap – a notice said not to drink it – and cleaned the bowl. Her head on the pillow, with the satchel under it, she covered herself with a blanket, thought with great longing of her mother and father, and fell asleep.

She was woken up by the thin lady and a cup of tea. From what she said, Helena understood that they were about to arrive; the boat was still moving. Helena washed quickly and combed her hair. She tried smoothing down her clothes but they seemed irremediably crumpled. It was time to leave the cabin and she climbed the steep stairs with some difficulty because of the suitcase. She stepped out on to the deck; it was still dark, but the air smelled fresh and sharp; there was a mild breeze. Her benefactress was there. Helena fumbled for her purse and searched among the coins. Which would be the right one? She fished out a large copper coin, the biggest there was and gave it to her with thanks. The woman took the coin and turned away abruptly without a word. Helena was surprised. It would be another week before she understood to her great shame that she had rewarded the kind woman with the lowest denomination in British currency.

In the light of dawn she could see warehouses lining the shore, large squat buildings without windows. Between the shore and the boat, the dark sea heaved quietly. The boat drew near to the quay and a man standing there called out. A sailor threw him a rope. Helena watched as the man pulled at it until he could grasp the hawser. The boat bumped gently against the pilings. She had seen the same manoeuvre carried out on small boats on the lake in Caputh. The man looped the hawser round a bollard. The procedure was repeated further along the boat until it was secure. Then the gangway was put in place and she walked over it, into England.

THIRTY-ONE

A light shone on the sign above a non-descript door, "Immigration/Customs/Douane". Despite her fear and excitement, she noticed the lettering; less ornate than the French, and different again from German Gothic. The letters were simple, rounded, easy to read, almost childish. She knocked on the door. No one answered. When she tried it, it opened onto a featureless corridor. An arrow indicated the way which led to an office, where two gentlemen sat by a desk, both in uniform. She could tell the older one was a high-ranking officer by the number of pips on his shoulders. He stood up when she came in as if he were about to make a speech, pulling at his jacket which was a little tight. He looked pleasant, like someone's grandfather. She took her passport from her satchel and proffered it open at the page with the stamp that said she could enter the United Kingdom.

The officer examined her passport and gave it to the other official. With a slight bow, he said in flawless German, "Welcome to England, Fräulein Mannheim. You are safe now. I hope you will be very happy in our country."

She was kissed on both cheeks and warmly embraced. He smelled of cigar, like Father. The kindness and warmth were her undoing and she began to cry.

He didn't seem disturbed and held her until she calmed down.

He took her to a canteen, where the only other person was a lady in a frilly apron who made them each a cup of tea. They sat at a table and he enquired in a polite way about her trip. Helena found herself too overwhelmed to talk about it, even in German. He did not seem to mind. He explained about the rest of her trip, by train to London. When this train was about to leave, he would take her to the platform and put her on it. He said that he had all the time in the world; he was not a soldier on active duty, he was in retirement, but due to the situation he thought he might make himself useful to refugees, since he spoke German. He told her his name but she forgot it completely. She only remembered that he was a colonel. She would always retain a great fondness for England from that first encounter.

The day turned out blue and clear. The train made the comfortable rhythmical sound that all trains make. The people in the carriage looked unlike German or French people. The colour, material and design of their clothes were unmistakeably different; so were their faces and hairstyles. She became aware again of her own bedraggled appearance. There was nothing she could do about it. Contemplating the countryside, she wanted to remember everything she saw so that she would know it, recognise it in the future; this would be her home from now on. She would let go of France and Germany and develop feelings about this country. She wanted everything about it to become familiar, so that she could resume belonging somewhere as soon as possible.

The colonel had described Waterloo Station as very big. She imagined it huge, cavernous. He'd told her it was the last stop, so she couldn't miss it. He had seen her off and she had hugged him before getting onto the train. He had stayed to wave as the train left.

By now she'd been travelling for an hour; it was mid-morning and a trolley came round with sandwiches. She didn't know how to ask for one, so she pointed. It turned out to be very thin, limp white bread with a slice of bland rubbery cheese. She also bought a cup of tea, which was served in a thick white cup. That was good, strong and hot. There was no coffee on offer. She counted the number of cups of tea she had drunk since leaving France. It was exactly as they'd said at school: the English drank tea all the time, with milk.

She was exhausted as well as exhilarated at the thought of seeing her parents. Only an hour or so left to wait! Her yearning for them had become intense. It would be a relief to be together, to be an ordinary family again, though the thought of the meeting, the idea of seeing them and talking to them, hugging them after almost a year apart, during which no one had known whether they would ever be reunited seemed more exciting than any celebration she had ever experienced. She could hardly sit still and kept looking at her watch. The announcements were unintelligible, but she reminded herself of what the colonel had said, that she was to get off the train at the last station. The train stopped at intermediate stations: some people got off; others got on. The carriage was filling up. We're all going to London, she thought, but no one can be as happy as I am.

The train was suddenly wrapped in mist. Nothing could be seen outside. It wasn't like the morning mist in the mountains, it was more yellow than white. A bit of it seeped into the carriage and people coughed. The train itself didn't seem to be affected; it carried on at the same speed. People seemed unperturbed. She felt anxious because she could not see out, could not see where they were. A man noticed her agitation and spoke to her in English; he spoke in a reassuring way and she understood. He asked whether she needed help. She asked hopefully, "Waterloo?" A funny name for a station, to do with water. Water was water in English as well as in German.

She wondered about the loo bit, what it meant. She'd forgotten the little English she'd learnt in Caputh with Tante Sophie, having to live and speak in French these past months. The man nodded and showed her his watch and all his ten fingers, something to do with ten. They would arrive in ten minutes? She looked at her watch. In ten minutes.

He pointed outside and said, "Pea-souper."[1]

She knew he'd made some kind of joke. She smiled back and he nodded back, satisfied, but she had no idea what he'd meant.

They were arriving. The train was going through tunnels and it was suddenly dark. The lights dimmed and then they emerged into daylight again, the train slowing down gradually, wisps of fog trailing. People got their luggage from the racks. She took her suitcase down and held it tight. The man was nodding at her, repeating "Waterloo, Waterloo." Everyone was preparing to leave the carriage – this was it! Her heart was beating hard. She peered through the windows, but she couldn't see them yet.

She couldn't wait to get out, but she restrained herself, standing in line obediently like everyone else; they were disciplined, quiet, almost subdued, different from the vivacious French. She tried to see outside, and she finally stepped out, looking expectantly for her mother, waiting for a beloved voice to call her name. She looked for them up and down the platform. Many people were milling around, so she walked slowly along the platform carrying her little suitcase, her satchel strapped safely across her chest. Her father would tower above everyone else. Once or twice, she thought she saw them, but was mistaken. The crowd dispersed, the people disappeared and she was the only one left. She walked towards the main hall and when she reached it, she stopped, confused. She looked back, but the platform was deserted. Her legs started to shake and she wanted to sit down. Where were they? Where could they be? Tears came to her eyes. This wouldn't do. She talked to herself sternly; she was in

London, in the same country, in the same city as her parents, she must not panic. They must be close by; maybe they had gone to the wrong train, the wrong platform? They were probably looking for her frantically at this very minute. She chose a bench to sit on from which she could see most of the concourse, and she waited. She had their address and she knew where to find them; it was only a matter of time till they were together. Tante Liesel and Uncle Ernst were living there too; they would know where her parents were. It occurred to her that if all else failed, she could take a taxi.

She waited, scanning the tide of people flowing past her, coming and going, filling the station with movement and sound, then receding, leaving the hall almost empty. The loudspeakers broadcast announcements she only partly understood, but the voice sounded well-intentioned. She saw men and women in military uniform. She watched the clock and after more than a full hour had gone by, she admitted to herself that if her mother and father were in the station, they would have found her by now. She couldn't imagine why no one was there to greet her. Only force majeure would have prevented them from meeting her, she knew that. What if something had happened to them? Might one of them be ill or injured in some way?

It was time to ask for help. She had read all the notices and advertisements while she waited; one of them said "Information", the same word as in German and French, with a black arrow pointing to a window. The woman who sat there wore a uniform. The thought of approaching her was frightening; who knew what might happen? She might decide something was wrong with Helena, trouble might ensue, they might arrest her, or lock her up as had happened in Dunkerque, or worse, send her back to Germany... No, she had to be brave. She went to the window and stood in line. She took her address book out of her bag, and when her turn came, she showed the lady her parents' address, saying "Please, please." All the English she'd ever learnt had evaporated.

The lady read the address and nodded. She seemed to understand. They had a funny, friendly conversation, using words in both French and English. The woman seemed happy to help her; she wasn't interested in seeing Helena's *laissez passer* or her passport, though Helena offered them.

Other people waited in the queue, without pushing or grumbling. The lady pointed to an exit, said the word "taxi" and wrote down a number on a piece of paper, with the L symbol that represented pounds. That was what it should cost, approximately. She looked apologetic, which meant that it was a lot of money, though cost was irrelevant to Helena. She knew she had enough money and what she wanted was to find her parents as quickly as she could. She didn't think that she could last much longer. She needed to get home or she would cry and fall to pieces. She was also hungry.

Before going to the taxi, she returned to the platform to check whether anyone she knew had arrived in the meantime and was looking for her, but no. No one was there. Might she have missed them somehow? Or had the message in the telegram been garbled during the dispatch? They might be worrying about her at this very moment. Before going to the taxi, she sat down and wrote her parents' address in large capital letters on a page she tore out of her address book.

The shape of the taxi surprised her – square boxes on wheels, black and shiny. Again, an obedient queue, waiting. Crossing the street to reach them she was nearly run over; she'd forgotten that the English drive on the left. When her turn came, she couldn't find the door to the cab until someone opened it for her. The driver was on the wrong side of the car. Despite her anxiety, she was amused by her confusion: she truly was in England! The driver slid open the dividing partition and asked a question, probably where she wanted to go. She handed over her piece of paper.

"No English?"

"No English," she confirmed.

He said something else, probably asking her where she was from, but she didn't want to say Germany or lie and say France. Best not to talk. She smiled at him. The car started with a dreadful rattle and they moved out of the station. The pace was slow, for the city's buildings, shops, trees – everything was more or less concealed by the fog, a swirling blankness like a soft creamy wall just beyond the cab's windows. She suddenly remembered learning about London's famous fog.

She was glad to be on the move again. She was progressing towards her goal, albeit blindly. The driver seemed to know where he was going. She sat back, insulated by the partition, and found it easy to trust him. Despite the shock of her parents' absence and the fruitless delay at the railway station, she felt safe here, safer than in France, much safer than in Nuremberg. It was an unusual sensation. She leant back on the padded black leather seat, her handbag on one side, her suitcase on the other. She thought of the colonel's welcome, of the kindness of the man on the train, the calm voice of the announcer on the station's loudspeakers, of the woman at the information desk who had done her best to help her, and the waitress on the boat who had brought her the white enamel bowl.

They drove for a long slow spell. Once, the driver stopped the car, signalling she was to remain seated. He shone a big black torch along a wall. She realised that he was looking for the street's name. She couldn't see anything herself. He returned to the cab, said something in a reassuring voice and drove on. A little later, he repeated the exercise. Then he found someone to ask and that seemed to help. They drove for almost an hour.

The taxi stopped and he said something in a tone of finality. This must be it. She couldn't see anything except the pavement outside. She got out with her suitcase and satchel, and closed the door. She went round to his window and gave him a banknote. He said it was not enough. She gave him another and he nodded, but it still wasn't enough. She poured out the coins from the little bag into his hand and let him choose. She wanted him to wait – what if this were not the right place? What should she do? She didn't know how to say it. His departure happened quickly; he returned some of the coins, and the taxi was gone. Stranded in the fog, she looked around. Stone steps led up to a house. The right number was on the wall. She went up, rang the doorbell and after a moment someone opened the door.

Tante Liesel stood staring at Helena as if her eyes would pop out of her head and then she pulled her in, held her tight, calling out in a croaky voice between kisses, "Sonia, Walter, Helena's here! It's Helena!"

There was a sound, a cry and her mother rushed into the hall, followed by her father. "Helena!" She embraced Helena and hugged her till Helena could hardly breathe. She was weeping. Her father put his hand on Helena's head. They all looked and looked at her and she stared back at them: they were the same as always, but also different, thinner, greyer.

Her mother wiped her tears. Father kissed her and rumpled her hair. They crowded into the little living room; Tante Liesel made everyone a cup of tea.

"No coffee," said her mother apologetically. "Beyond our means."

At first everyone talked at once, asking about her trip, telling her about Max. Her mother sat next to Helena, patting her every now and then. They brought her food and she ate. They watched her as if she were an animal in the zoo; she wished they wouldn't. They exclaimed how much she'd grown, how tall she was, and they said again and again, "When Max comes, we'll be together again, the whole family, we're so lucky." They had not known she was coming – the telegram had not arrived.

When she'd finished eating, her mother said, "You're very tired, my darling. How about a rest?" She had a quick wash in the very small bathroom. In a narrow room was a bed which Tante Liesel had made up for her. She undressed and slipped under the German eiderdown and her mother came and kissed her goodnight.

But after she left, Helena could not sleep; she felt icy cold, and she lay awake for a long time, shivering and trembling as if she would never be warm again.

THIRTY-TWO

The Levys had advised Bloomsbury House that a small basement flat in their house was available for refugees, suitable for a family of three. They also mentioned that prospective tenants should be honest, willing to work and able to keep calm if and when bombardments occurred.

According to Mrs Jacobs, the lady from the British Refugee Committee, the Mannheims fitted the bill exactly. In halting Yiddish, she explained that Herbert Levy was a lawyer – she did not know what kind of lawyer – and so was his wife. The wife was very active helping refugees. She said more, but Yiddish is not German and they could not understand.

Despite Walter's reluctance, she insisted he accompany Sonia to the initial meeting with this landlady. They were to be appraised. That did not worry him – if they were not acceptable, who would be? – but in Sonia's mind the meeting loomed, threatening. They might fail to pass muster for some unaccountable English reason. On the other hand, she was eager to see this flat, which had its own front door and offered complete privacy. The proximity with Liesel and Ernst had become almost unbearable for them all. There were no quarrels or even raised voices, but great self-control and forbearance had been required.

On a cold grey day, Sonia and Walter followed Mrs Jacobs off the bus through broad quiet streets lined with terraced houses painted a uniform cream. The front doors were different colours, often navy or black, with an occasional whimsical red. Wrought-iron railings were painted a glossy black. The design of these railings seemed unusual to Sonia, different from German railings. As she considered this novelty, the world around her which until then had seemed ordinary, suddenly veered and changed, becoming unfriendly, swollen with ill intent: the buildings, the street signs, the grey clouded sky itself, everything seemed oppressive, inimical. For an instant she felt lost, an insignificant exile without a foothold. She grasped Walter's arm as they walked behind Mrs Jacobs. He patted her gloved hand as if he understood. In the park at the end of the street, the trees with their great canopies seemed threatening too.

"Here we are!" said Mrs Jacobs.

They followed her up the wide stone steps and she rang the bell.

Sonia took a deep breath. She noticed the silver mezuzah on the doorpost – a good omen. The green door opened. Lucia was a slender woman with sharp grey eyes and short hair. Well cut, shiny hair. Sonia washed her hair with ordinary soap these days, shampoo being a luxury. She had tucked it under her hat, which she would have to remove when they went in. She had pinned the wayward strands into a tidy chignon, though it did not become her. It couldn't be helped: a hairdresser was beyond their means. She had carefully considered how they should dress for the occasion – not that they had much choice. Walter wore his well-tailored winter coat and looked his usual self, a successful lawyer. She wore her warm green loden coat and matching hat, a style common in Germany. After almost a year in England, she knew that it singled her out as a foreigner.

"Hello," said Lucia, smiling. Sonia had pulled off her glove and extended her hand, which Lucia shook a little awkwardly. Walter clicked his heels and bowed, removing his hat. He had been told that Englishmen didn't click their heels, but the habits of a lifetime were hard to erase. Mrs Jacobs made the introductions.

"I'll take you to see the flat now. Then we'll have a cup of tea upstairs." Without waiting for a reply, Lucia ran lightly down the steps to the street and through a little gate in the railings, down narrow steps to a little box of a yard. She opened the basement door and invited them in. It led directly into a square living room. "This was Nanny's flat, but the girls are older now, at boarding school," said Lucia.

The one large window gave onto the yard – a view of grey concrete, surmounted by the black railing and the pavement. Sonia noticed that the chintz curtains were a little faded; the furnishings seemed haphazard. A serviceable brown armchair stood in a corner, a plain standard lamp and a small bookcase nearby; there was also a large couch. "It unfolds to a bed", said Lucia, bending over it. There seemed to be some trick to opening it and she struggled until Mrs Jacobs went to help her. Max will have to sleep there when he gets to London, thought Sonia; it may be a little short for him.

"This is the main bedroom, and this," opening an adjacent door, "is the second one." That would be Helena's room. A small window left the room rather dark. On the single bed was a pile of sheets, pillows and blankets. No eiderdowns. The bathroom was small too. The kitchen was roomier, containing the flat's only full-size table. The window was high up, framing the grey sky. There were a few pots and pans, bits of crockery and cutlery. The door handles were the now-familiar English shoulder height, the narrow doors opening the wrong way into the room, towards the wall.

Sonia paused to remind herself how lucky she was. She must not compare what was here to what she had been used to in Germany. All that was over, finished. She told herself how lucky they were to be alive, and felt the familiar flash of fear – please dear God, take care of Fanny and Otto.

She forced herself to pay attention. In the living room the only decoration was an etching of a medieval town – not a European town – in a thin black frame; in the bedroom a large romantic print of a woman with long hair, a clinging gown and a soulful look in her great eyes hung above the bed. That would have to go, thought Sonia. Lucia was saying that the heater worked well and that the flat was warm and dry even in winter, Mrs Jacobs occasionally adding her own explanations. Lucia showed Sonia a cupboard which seemed to be special in some way. She called it an "airing" cupboard; Mrs Jacobs looked on, nodding her approval. Sonia was perplexed, but she smiled in what she hoped was an agreeable manner. She would work out what that cupboard was about later.

She noticed that Walter had returned to the living room after a cursory glance at the bedrooms. She saw him standing by the window; he was examining a book he must have taken from the shelves. She thought, he's not interested, he's leaving this to me. He relies on my judgement. Looking around, she knew she'd be able to look after the family here. It would be tight, particularly when Max came home, limited space for two big men, but they would manage.

She counted her blessings: this was much better than staying with Liesel and Ernst. A place of their own, with their daughter, in a nice house, in a good neighbourhood, with educated people. It would be wonderful. Sonia turned to Lucia and enunciated the sentence she'd prepared with Liesel's help: "When you will have us, we will be most happy to stay here. My husband and I are very grateful to you."

They moved in the next day. Lucia was there to greet them. "Is that all?" she asked in dismay, staring at their small suitcases. Sonia smiled at her. They had more than many others. They were lucky, their family was whole, they were healthy and ready to start a new life in this country where Jews were treated like everyone else. She would make a home for them here and they would be able to cope with whatever might happen next.

THIRTY-THREE

She'd been listening for a taxi stopping on the street, but she must have missed it. She heard his key turn in the door. She tugged at the ties of her apron, pulling it off and throwing it onto the kitchen chair, smoothing her hair as she emerged from the kitchen, appearing as calm as she could: "Walter!"

He handed her his hat as he always did, and she hung it on the hatstand. They kissed and she stood back to take a better look at him.

"How was it?"

"With me, all is well," he said, "but Nuremberg... you would not believe what has become of Nuremberg."

He followed her into the living room.

"I feel as if I've been away for much longer than a week," he said.

She had made sure the house was tidy. Everything was in its place, the books, the photos of Max graduating, Helena with her husband and baby on the mantelpiece, a small vase with flowers, a week's worth of *Daily Telegraphs* in a tidy pile, next to the Langenscheidt dictionary. Ten years here, versus a life-time in Nuremberg, but this was home. The small round table stood by his armchair. She'd bought that armchair at auction some months ago, shabby but good quality.

She poured him a brandy; for herself the usual puddle at the bottom of the glass. She sat down opposite him. "Prost!" they said, raising their glasses.

"It's as if the city has died. No, not the house," he hastened to add, reading her alarm. "The house is exactly as we left it, as far as I could see. But the old city," he shook his head again, "Within the city walls, everything is in ruins, worse than here; so much destruction, house after house, street after street. Everything gone, well not literally gone, but you don't know where you are any more," he tried to explain. "The landmarks have disappeared, I don't mean monuments, I mean ordinary recognizable features like the tobacconist shops, the cafés, the post office. Where there were houses there's only devastation. No trees left, nothing but piles of rubble, or bald patches where the rubble used to be, lots of blank spaces; one struggles to remember what used to be there. It's amazing; I lost my way a couple of times. There's so much of it, jagged walls reaching up, no roof, where there once stood medieval houses; it looks like the photos of Coventry, except of course for the churches, *they* still stand."

He sipped his brandy. "What amazed me most of all was that when I saw this destruction of the town I was born in, I felt absolutely nothing," he said. He had continued to experience surprise at this absence: no satisfaction, no hatred, no compassion, no sadness; just a blankness.

He'd had business to sort out, people to see, links with the past. In due course, he would tell her everything. She asked,

"You saw him?" She clasped her hands in her lap.

"I met him in a little café on our street, not a place you'd know, it wasn't there before. Not what you would have considered a proper café before the war; the old places are gone, mostly." The tables were a jumble of different styles, the chairs didn't match, but whoever they had in the kitchen at the back could turn out decent sauerkraut and sausages; not much meat in them, but satisfying enough; the ersatz mustard was on the table, an echo of the old days. They'd drunk beer, expensively. He'd been wearing one of his good German suits; he'd lost weight during the war and it didn't fit too badly. They'd each sized the other up.

"And?"

"He's aged a lot." With his height and demeanour, Dr. Benno Martin still managed to project ease and power, though one couldn't say he looked well. He was thin, almost gaunt, with a pasty skin, deep circles under the eyes.

He'd rarely seen him in civvies, as the English called them; a baggy grey suit, ill-fitting over the shoulders, narrow lapels, the trousers and sleeves too short; since the demobilization badly dressed men were everywhere, it was the same in England. As they talked, he'd warmed to him again, despite everything. Ten years since they'd met... 1939 to 1949 – though one couldn't call what took place in '39 a meeting, really, they'd spoken for only a few minutes that night in the prison.

"His son died in the last months of the war, defending Vienna from the Russians. His wife killed herself after he was arrested. He was detained for a long time before the trial – almost four years."

Sonia nodded. Many years ago, she'd seen Benno's wife in the street; had the situation been different, they would probably have been on friendly terms. They only had one son, she knew that. "Was he not too young to be called up?"

"He was called up anyway; they were desperate. Lambs to the slaughter."

Sonia looked down at her hands. How many times had she heard news like this, over the years? During the blitz, the victims had been local and mostly English. Some of their own had escaped Germany only to die here, or had enlisted and been killed in action. During the war, what was happening on the continent was hidden, the reports too vague to carry much meaning; one knew nothing except what got past the censors; sometimes a cry or a whisper, a letter, a Red Cross postcard or an anecdote from a soldier on leave. But since the war had ended, they were flooded with people's stories. What had happened to them, where, how... As time passed, they got news from further and further afield. Someone was deemed missing, disappeared in the turmoil; a child was killed somewhere, in a concentration camp or outside the house they lived in; was it a murder or an accident? Or against all expectation, someone survived, married again, moved to a distant, exotic country, or amazingly, lived here in London just a street away. Or again, they'd died despite previous rumours that they'd survived and no one could find out where they were buried. Stories told in a single sentence, sometimes barely comprehensible, about the evolution of people's lives.

Martin had organized the transport which deported Fanny and Otto in March 1942. That was known for a fact. It had been one of the accusations at the trial and he had not denied it. The transport had been destined for Lodz, in the East. One thousand souls crammed into cattle trucks, no water, food or protection against heat or cold, abandoned on sidings, none to survive.

We are chaff, she thought. Three hundred years of documented history in one place, an illusion of stability and self-determination. The truth, she said to herself, is that people are chaff, blown here and there by the elements.

Their own children were both alive and well. She still had trouble believing their luck. She didn't like to connect the names of the quick and the dead. The children's survival was not connected to Fanny and Otto's death. She corrected herself; what had happened to them was not simply 'death'; the right word was murder. She shouldn't hesitate to use that word, but she did because even though it was the truth, it sounded as if she was dramatizing.

She would mull over what Walter told her later on, she would think it through, examine it carefully and consider the ripples initiated by these events, and what these ripples meant. That boy had been a few years younger than Max, barely an adolescent. Her lips remained tight, her hands clasped.

"He hasn't much money, I think. I paid for our lunch, such as it was, and he didn't protest."

"Our people won't be pleased that you sat down to a meal with him."

They weren't pleased that he'd testified in Martin's defence.

He nodded and said, "We owe him." The testimony had been argued over many times, between them and with their friends; they both believed that it had to be done, that it was their duty. There had been furious opposition, she'd even gone secretly to a rabbi, to hear what he would say, she the un-believer. The rabbi had said they owed him.

"He shouldn't have got off," said Sonia. "That's what I feel now. You needed to testify; I wanted you to; but he shouldn't have walked free. He shouldn't have got away with what he did."

The dead have no voice, thought Sonia. They cannot testify.

SELECTED BIBLIOGRAPHY

Arendt, Hannah *The Origins of Totalitarianism*, Meridian Books, The World Publishing Company, Cleveland and New York, 1962

Baker, Leon *Days of Sorrow and Pain; Leo Baeck and the Berlin Jews*, Oxford University Press, 1978

Berlin, L.C. *Dr Giora Josephthal*, http://www.rijo.homepage.t-online.de/en_nu_index.html rijo research, 2002

Berlin, L.C. *Dr Walter Berlin*, http://www.rijo.homepage.t-online.de/en_nu_index.html rijo research, 2000

Berlin, L.C. *Fritz Josephthal* , http://www.rijo.homepage.t-online.de/en_nu_index.html, rijo research, 2001

Berlin, L.C. *Memories of Hitler's Nuremberg*, http://www.rijo.homepage.t-online.de/en_nu_index.html, rijo research, 1961

Feidel-Mertz, Hildegard und Paetz Andreas *Das Jüdische Kinder- und Landschulheim Caputh (1931–1938); ein verlorenes Paradies*, Reformpädagogik im Exil, Neue Folge der Schriftenreihe 'Pädagogische Beispiele', Verlag Julius Klinkhardt, 2009

Gerzon-Berlin, Ann *Bits and Pieces: a Jewish teenager's recollections of the pogrom of November 9/10, 1938 in Caputh and Nuremberg* http://www.rijo.homepage.t-online.de/en_nu_index.html

Grieser, Utho *Himmlers Mann in Nurnberg. Der Fall Benno Martin: eine Studie zur Struktur des Dritten Reiches in der 'Stadt der Reichsparteitage'*, Schriftenreihe des Stadtarchivs Nürnberg, Band 13 [Himmlers' man in Nuremberg; the case of Benno Martin, a study of the structure of the Third Reich in the city of the Reich Rallies] 1974

Kaplan, Marion A. *Between Dignity and Despair; Jewish life in Nazi Germany*, Oxford University Press, 1998

Klemperer Victor *I Shall Bear Witness; the diaries of Victor Klemperer, 1933–1941*, translated by M. Chalmers, Phoenix, 1995

Kolb, Bernhard *The Jews of Nuremberg, 1839–1945*, translated by N. Clemerson, Fanceridge Publishers, 2016

Kohl, Christiane *The Maiden and the Jew; the story of a fatal friendship in Nazi Germany*, Steerforth Press, 1997

Schneider, Wolf-Kristian *Der Arisierungsskandal in Nürnberg und Fürth* [The Aryanisation scandal in Nuremberg] *Freie wissenschaftlihe Arbeit zur Erlangung des akademischen Grades 'Diplom-Kaufman'* an der Wirtschafts- und Socialwissenschaftichen Fakultät der Friedrich-Alexander-Universität Erlangen-Nürnberg, unpublished, Nuremberg City Archive, 1969

Rutsch, H.-D. *Ein verlorenes Paradies: das jüdische Kinder- und Landschulheim Caputh (1931–1938)* [A lost paradise; the Jewish home and agricultural school for children in Caputh, 1931–1938) Film, Havel-film, Babelsberg, 1995

NOTES

Chapter 5

1. A place where the dead are prepared for burial.
2. Benevolent Jewish society that carries out rituals prior to burial.

Chapter 8

1. The *Frankfurter Zeitung* appeared from 1856 to 1943. It was considered the only mass publication not controlled by the Nazi regime's Ministry for Propaganda. Not to be confused with the *Frankfurter Allgemeine Zeitung*, founded in 1949.

Chapter 18

1. Germany "annexed" Austria on 12 March 1938, to popular acclaim.

Chapter 31

1. The name given by the British to their notorious smog, particularly prevalent in London until the 1950s.

ACKNOWLEDGMENTS

Many people have supported me during the writing of this book. I want to express my gratitude to my teachers at the Whitireia writing course: Renée, my very first teacher, and Hinemoa Baker, for their encouragement at the beginning of what was to be a lengthy journey. Ngā mihi mahana ki a kōrua!

The New Zealand Society for Authors Te Puni Kaituhi o Aotearoa (PEN NZ) granted me a year's free mentoring, an honour which gave me a tremendous boost. I particularly thank James Norcliffe who read the manuscript at an early stage.

I wish to acknowledge the generous support of Gerhard Jochem of Nuremberg's City Archive who gave me access to information I would not have obtained otherwise. This led to the translation and publication of Bernhard Kolb's memoir *The Jews of Nuremberg,* which provided some of the background for this book.

I am deeply grateful to my dear friends Lynn Jenner, Helen McNeish and the late Sir James McNeish, the late Jane Schaverien, who encouraged me when difficulties arose; to Shayna Levick and Emily Friedlander, who reviewed the manuscript for me, and to Eve and Richard McKechnie, Denise and Doug Norris, and my dear sisters Gila Gerzon-Nieuwenhuizen and Noemi Mizrachi, who read the manuscript willingly. I also would like to thank my lovely community at Temple Sinai, and particularly Sue and David Esterman for their warm interest and encouragement.

I thank Maurice Clark for kindly providing advice and expertise regarding the probable method used by sappers to demolish Nuremberg's great synagogue. Also Dr Suzanne Kill from Deutsche Bahn AG, for sending me a 1936 map of Berlin's suburban train lines. Closer to home, I thank Dr. Julia Sardelic from Wellington's Victoria University Te Herenga Waka, for her willingness to discuss the legal implications of statelessness when there were other urgent calls on her time.

I thank Liesbeth Heenk from Amsterdam Publishers for her faith in this book and her patience, and Heather J Rothman for her most helpful editorial suggestions. Also Gila, for suggesting I get in touch with Amsterdam Publishers.

Above all, I am grateful to my family, who supported this venture with trust and confidence in its completion. My son Rowan for explaining grammar and discussing writing styles with me, and my daughter Tamsyn for coming to the rescue when I encountered technical challenges. More than anyone, I thank my husband Peter Clemerson, who was always patient, interested and helpful. I have been very fortunate.

I have endeavoured to remain faithful to the historical facts. Any errors are all my own.

AMSTERDAM PUBLISHERS
HOLOCAUST LIBRARY

The series **Holocaust Survivor Memoirs World War II** consists of the following autobiographies of survivors:

Outcry. Holocaust Memoirs, by Manny Steinberg

Hank Brodt Holocaust Memoirs. A Candle and a Promise, by Deborah Donnelly

The Dead Years. Holocaust Memoirs, by Joseph Schupack

Rescued from the Ashes. The Diary of Leokadia Schmidt, Survivor of the Warsaw Ghetto, by Leokadia Schmidt

My Lvov. Holocaust Memoir of a twelve-year-old Girl, by Janina Hescheles

Remembering Ravensbrück. From Holocaust to Healing, by Natalie Hess

Wolf. A Story of Hate, by Zeev Scheinwald with Ella Scheinwald

Save my Children. An Astonishing Tale of Survival and its Unlikely Hero, by Leon Kleiner with Edwin Stepp

Holocaust Memoirs of a Bergen-Belsen Survivor & Classmate of Anne Frank, by Nanette Blitz Konig

Defiant German - Defiant Jew. A Holocaust Memoir from inside the Third Reich, by Walter Leopold with Les Leopold

In a Land of Forest and Darkness. The Holocaust Story of two Jewish Partisans, by Sara Lustigman Omelinski

Holocaust Memories. Annihilation and Survival in Slovakia, by Paul Davidovits

From Auschwitz with Love. The Inspiring Memoir of Two Sisters' Survival, Devotion and Triumph Told by Manci Grunberger Beran & Ruth Grunberger Mermelstein, by Daniel Seymour

Remetz. Resistance Fighter and Survivor of the Warsaw Ghetto, by Jan Yohay Remetz

My March Through Hell. A Young Girl's Terrifying Journey to Survival, by Halina Kleiner with Edwin Stepp

Roman's Journey, by Roman Halter

Beyond Borders. Escaping the Holocaust and Fighting the Nazis. 1938-1948, by Rudi Haymann

The Engineers, by Henry Reiss

Memoirs by Elmar Rivosh, Sculptor (1906-1967). Riga Ghetto and Beyond, by Elmar Rivosh

The series **Holocaust Survivor True Stories** consists of the following biographies:

Among the Reeds. The true story of how a family survived the Holocaust, by Tammy Bottner

A Holocaust Memoir of Love & Resilience. Mama's Survival from Lithuania to America, by Ettie Zilber

Living among the Dead. My Grandmother's Holocaust Survival Story of Love and Strength, by Adena Bernstein Astrowsky

Heart Songs. A Holocaust Memoir, by Barbara Gilford

Shoes of the Shoah. The Tomorrow of Yesterday, by Dorothy Pierce

Hidden in Berlin. A Holocaust Memoir, by Evelyn Joseph Grossman

Separated Together. The Incredible True WWII Story of Soulmates Stranded an Ocean Apart, by Kenneth P. Price, Ph.D.

The Man Across the River. The incredible story of one man's will to survive the Holocaust, by Zvi Wiesenfeld

If Anyone Calls, Tell Them I Died. A Memoir, by Emanuel (Manu) Rosen

The House on Thrömerstrasse. A Story of Rebirth and Renewal in the Wake of the Holocaust, by Ron Vincent

Dancing with my Father. His hidden past. Her quest for truth. How Nazi Vienna shaped a family's identity, by Jo Sorochinsky

The Story Keeper. Weaving the Threads of Time and Memory - A Memoir, by Fred Feldman

Krisia's Silence. The Girl who was not on Schindler's List, by Ronny Hein

Defying Death on the Danube. A Holocaust Survival Story, by Debbie J. Callahan with Henry Stern

A Doorway to Heroism. A decorated German-Jewish Soldier who became an American Hero, by Rabbi W. Jack Romberg

The Shoemaker's Son. The Life of a Holocaust Resister, by Laura Beth Bakst

The Redhead of Auschwitz. A True Story, by Nechama Birnbaum

Land of Many Bridges. My Father's Story, by Bela Ruth Samuel Tenenholtz

Creating Beauty from the Abyss. The Amazing Story of Sam Herciger, Auschwitz Survivor and Artist, by Lesley Ann Richardson

On Sunny Days We Sang. A Holocaust Story of Survival and Resilience, by Jeannette Grunhaus de Gelman

Painful Joy. A Holocaust Family Memoir, by Max J. Friedman

I Give You My Heart. A True Story of Courage and Survival, by Wendy Holden

In the Time of Madmen, by Mark A. Prelas

Monsters and Miracles. Horror, Heroes and the Holocaust, by Ira Wesley Kitmacher

Flower of Vlora. Growing up Jewish in Communist Albania, by Anna Kohen

Aftermath: Coming of Age on Three Continents. A Memoir, by Annette Libeskind Berkovits

Not a real Enemy. The True Story of a Hungarian Jewish Man's Fight for Freedom, by Robert Wolf

Zaidy's War. Four Armies, Three Continents, Two Brothers. One Man's Impossible Story of Endurance, by Martin Bodek

The Glassmaker's Son. Looking for the World my Father left behind in Nazi Germany, by Peter Kupfer

The Apprentice of Buchenwald. The True Story of the Teenage Boy Who Sabotaged Hitler's War Machine, by Oren Schneider

Good for a Single Journey, by Helen Joyce

Burying the Ghosts. She escaped Nazi Germany only to have her life torn apart by the woman she saved from the camps: her mother, by Sonia Case

American Wolf. From Nazi Refugee to American Spy. A True Story, by Audrey Birnbaum

Bipolar Refugee. A Saga of Survival and Resilience, by Peter Wiesner

Before the Beginning and After the End, by Hymie Anisman

The series **Jewish Children in the Holocaust** consists of the following autobiographies of Jewish children hidden during WWII in the Netherlands:

Searching for Home. The Impact of WWII on a Hidden Child, by Joseph Gosler

See You Tonight and Promise to be a Good Boy! War memories, by Salo Muller

Sounds from Silence. Reflections of a Child Holocaust Survivor, Psychiatrist and Teacher, by Robert Krell

Sabine's Odyssey. A Hidden Child and her Dutch Rescuers, by Agnes Schipper

The Journey of a Hidden Child, by Harry Pila and Robin Black

The series **New Jewish Fiction** consists of the following novels, written by Jewish authors. All novels are set in the time during or after the Holocaust.

The Corset Maker. A Novel, by Annette Libeskind Berkovits

Escaping the Whale. The Holocaust is over. But is it ever over for the next generation? by Ruth Rotkowitz

When the Music Stopped. Willy Rosen's Holocaust, by Casey Hayes

Hands of Gold. One Man's Quest to Find the Silver Lining in Misfortune, by Roni Robbins

The Girl Who Counted Numbers. A Novel, by Roslyn Bernstein

There was a garden in Nuremberg. A Novel, by Navina Michal Clemerson

The Butterfly and the Axe, by Omer Bartov

To Live Another Day. A Novel, Elizabeth Rosenberg

A Worthy Life. Based on a True Story, by Dahlia Moore

The series **Holocaust Heritage** consists of the following memoirs by 2G:

The Cello Still Sings. A Generational Story of the Holocaust and of the Transformative Power of Music, by Janet Horvath

The Fire and the Bonfire. A Journey into Memory, by Ardyn Halter

The Silk Factory: Finding Threads of My Family's True Holocaust Story, by Michael Hickins

The series **Holocaust Books for Young Adults** consists of the following novels, based on true stories:

The Boy behind the Door. How Salomon Kool Escaped the Nazis. Inspired by a True Story, by David Tabatsky

Running for Shelter. A True Story, by Suzette Sheft

The Precious Few. An Inspirational Saga of Courage based on True Stories, by David Twain with Art Twain

---

The series **WWII Historical Fiction** consists of the following novels, some of which are based on true stories:

Mendelevski's Box. A Heartwarming and Heartbreaking Jewish Survivor's Story, by Roger Swindells

A Quiet Genocide. The Untold Holocaust of Disabled Children in WWII Germany, by Glenn Bryant

The Knife-Edge Path, by Patrick T. Leahy

Brave Face. The Inspiring WWII Memoir of a Dutch/German Child, by I. Caroline Crocker and Meta A. Evenbly

When We Had Wings. The Gripping Story of an Orphan in Janusz Korczak's Orphanage. A Historical Novel, by Tami Shem-Tov

Jacob's Courage. Romance and Survival amidst the Horrors of War, by Charles S. Weinblatt

Want to be an AP book reviewer?

Reviews are very important in a world dominated by the social media and social proof. Please drop us a line if you want to join the *AP review team* and show us at least one review already posted on Amazon for one of our books.

info@amsterdampublishers.com

Printed in the USA
CPSIA information can be obtained
at www.ICGtesting.com
CBHW030323050224
4029CB00033B/850/J